657

DISCARD

THE ACHIEVEMENT OF

WILLIAM DEAN HOWELLS

A REINTERPRETATION

THE ACHIEVEMENT OF

WILLIAM DEAN HOWELLS

A REINTERPRETATION BY

KERMIT VANDERBILT

PRINCETON, NEW JERSEY

PRINCETON UNIVERSITY PRESS

1968

FOR ELLA, CLIFFORD, AND GUDRUN

PREFACE

ANYONE who becomes interested in the life and achievement of William Dean Howells soon accumulates the materials for an outsized book. Because Howells was one of the most productive authors in our language, the literary scholar and biographer is forced to make major judgments in selection, proportion, focus, and interpretation. Understanding Howells has become a massive labor indeed. My own efforts began years ago in a graduate seminar taught by Professor Theodore Hornberger at the University of Minnesota. Several years later, I was working through the Charles Eliot Norton Papers at Harvard University. The correspondence between Norton and Howells began to indicate that Howells, like Norton, was waging a to-and-fro battle within himself, struggling to resolve many of the problems which characterized the late nineteenth century in America. These conflicts for Howells, as for Norton, touched on revolutionary changes in religious, social, economic, and esthetic life in America.

Ten years ago, I began to study closely all of Howells' fiction and criticism to discover in what ways these central issues of the period had become a part of his creative impulse and literary imagination. Predictably, a burgeoning accumulation of notes soon threatened to grow unmanageable. I was confronted with the embarrassment of riches so well known to Howells scholars. My solution appears in the angle of vision adopted in the present study. I have realized the need, expressed some years ago by Edwin Cady, that each of Howells' novels be given a full-scale rereading. To this end, I have selected for reinterpretation four novels which appeared in the 1880s: *The Undiscovered Country*; *A Modern Instance*; *The Rise of Silas Lapham*; and *A Hazard of New Fortunes*. The decade, however, has not been treated as a *cul de sac*. I have moved backward to trace the genesis of these novels in Howells' earlier life, as well as forward, from time to time, into his career after the eighties. At the same time, I have resisted the strong temptation to write biography for its own sake, and have related Howells' life to the range and complexity of his achievement as a novelist. (All of his novels and varied shorter pieces discussed or mentioned in the pages to follow are listed chronologically in the Index.) Above all, I have tried in these new readings to provide the encouragement and to suggest a method for scholars in the future who will undertake new assessments of Howells the man and his work.

Portions of several chapters have appeared in print elsewhere. A briefer version of Chapter One was published in *American Quarterly*, XVII (Winter 1965), 634-655. Several pages of Chapter Two appeared in "Marcia Gaylord's Electra Complex: A Footnote to Sex in Howells," *American Literature,* XXXIV (November 1962), 365-374. In Chapter Three, I have recast much of the evidence presented in two articles. These are "Howells Among the Brahmins: Why 'The Bottom Dropped Out' During *The Rise of Silas Lapham*," *New England Quarterly*, XXXV (September 1962), 291-317; and "Howells and Norton: Some Frustrations of the Biographer," *ibid.*, XXXVII (March 1964), 84-89. I thank the editors of these journals for permission to incorporate the articles here.

This book could not have been written without a grant-in-aid from the American Philosophical Society during the summer of 1964, enabling me to examine Howells materials in the libraries at Harvard, Yale, Columbia, Rutgers, Princeton, the American Academy of Arts and Letters, and the Huntington. My thanks go to the directors of these libraries for permitting me to examine and, where necessary, to quote from manuscript holdings. In this regard, I am chiefly grateful to Professor W. W. Howells and the

Harvard College Library for permission to quote from Howells' published and unpublished writing.

It is a pleasure, also, to acknowledge a grant from the San Diego State College Foundation which helped to pay the cost of typing the completed manuscript.

I could not begin to describe here the encouragement I have received from various Howells scholars. Several who disagree with some of my conclusions have been generous enough to welcome the stimulus of debate and even to suggest how I might strengthen my argument. Neither can I express fully my thanks to Robert and Nadine Skotheim for their critical sympathy in reading each of the chapters when they appeared in halting rough draft. I am grateful, too, for the efficient and sympathetic labors of Eve Hanle of Princeton University Press. And last, in ways too many to recount, I am indebted to my wife and daughter for their patience and support.

K. V.

San Diego, California
December 1967

CONTENTS

THE ACHIEVEMENT OF
WILLIAM DEAN HOWELLS

A REINTERPRETATION

INTRODUCTION

PREMISES AND METHOD

IN this book, I have reinterpreted a vital portion of William Dean Howells' life work in the hope that readers will gain a new sense of his achievement in our literature. I have tried to combine rather broad research with the activities of the explicator and critic. The work on this book began with a close reading of the Howells novel to discover his meaning through structure, setting, character, symbol, and so on. But in the close reading of a text, one uncovers a number of problems bearing on interpretation which cannot be solved by further inspecting the text itself. It is here that the explicator of a literary work must widen his enterprise and assume the labors of the literary scholar. He moves to extrinsic, but vital and relevant, materials—to the author's response to his time, to other work by the author, to other authors and works of the period. When he returns to the original work, he has gained a larger perspective and more precise knowledge to impart to an interpretation and criticism of the text. The intrinsic and extrinsic discovery of meaning, in other words, is a continuous, two-way process.

In his *Literary Biography*, Leon Edel has described a part of this process by suggesting the analogy to the sister art of painting. When we enter a gallery of paintings, Professor Edel reminds us, "however much we may isolate a picture on a wall and try to keep our eyes within its frame, we do not wholly lose our awareness of the wall or even of the adjacent pictures."[1] The literary scholar, in like manner, is drawn inevitably to questions of context. His

[1] Garden City, N. Y.: Doubleday and Co., 1959, p. xii.

3

main resource here is biography—the writer's intellectual and emotional response to the historical epoch into which he was born. From a deeper understanding of the writer's world, one tries to achieve a deeper understanding of the writer's work. This responsible, interdisciplinary approach to literary interpretation is no different, of course, from the one which has been urged by the American Studies program in a growing number of universities here and abroad during the past twenty years. For the literary scholar, moving to biography means, however, that he is entering the broad domain of history and philosophy, as well as the lesser, but equally treacherous, domain of modern psychology, or psychoanalysis, to mention only three related fields. "How are we to handle this difficult material while remaining true to our own disciplines—" Professor Edel asks, "and avoid making complete fools of ourselves?"[2]

The frustrations of a literary scholar who explores the act of literary creation in this larger context can be illustrated in the case of William Dean Howells. Whoever is willing to take Howells' fiction seriously soon runs into questions of interpretation which cannot be answered by even the most minute examination of the novel itself. One turns inevitably to biography. Indeed, Howells may be the ideal figure to illustrate in what ways biography can illuminate the meaning of a novel and how the novel, in turn, can cast a reciprocal light on hidden recesses of the author's life and his response to his time. First of all, Howells has been, in fact, the victim of the biographical approach to literature in its most irresponsible form. A little series of

2 *Ibid.*, p. 98. My comments on literary scholarship are derived in part from my paper on "Biography and the Literary Scholar," presented in a panel on American biography at the University of Southern California, May 13, 1967. Elsewhere in this study, I am indebted to fellow panelists Ray Allen Billington and Ernest Samuels for insights into the problems and pitfalls of biographical evidence.

clichés has accumulated over the years: here was a nice, kindly, quiet man, the self-proclaimed "reticent realist," a novelist of the "commonplace," who extolled the "smiling aspects of life" in America as the proper and exclusive subject of a native fiction. Wrenched out of context, these allegations have acquired the currency of literary folklore. Their appeal is quite obvious. One reflects on how many books one will never find the time to read in a lifetime, and gratefully accepts this tacit permission not to read extensively in the reportedly anemic fiction of gentle old Howells, one of our most prolific writers. More than one scholar of my own acquaintance, after reading Edwin Cady's excellent biography of a more complicated Howells, has returned with apparent relief to the simpler version of Howells, the placid gentleman who wrote far too much too easily.

The actual record of Howells' life and work uncovers a man who was one of the truly perturbed spirits of the late nineteenth century. As a writer, he left later generations a legacy in fiction that is the fullest and most distinguished account we possess of this turbulent period in American life. More than a few of these novels were written under extraordinary emotional stress. During *A Modern Instance*, in the early eighties, Howells was forced to bed for seven weeks with what he described as "some sort of a fever . . . the result of long worry and sleeplessness from overwork." During the writing of *The Rise of Silas Lapham*, in the mid-eighties, social and economic inequities in American life had become for him sufficiently painful that, as he later described it, "the bottom dropped out" of his life. And in the late eighties, after he had petitioned unsuccessfully for clemency for the Haymarket anarchists, and as he waged a somewhat lonely esthetic campaign each month in *Harper's* on behalf of the modern novel, Howells was also in the early stages of writing *A Hazard of New Fortunes*. In the midst of these pressures, he was struck an almost crippling blow: his daughter Winny died after a long, misdiagnosed illness.

The literary scholar can hardly resist the temptation to put on his alternate caps—those of historian, philosopher, sociologist, political theorist, or psychologist—and probe this suggestive biography for insights into literary creation. Exactly what were the tensions in Howells' life, and in what guise did they make their way into his work? In discovering these answers, perhaps one will relocate the central problem and meaning of the novel. And if one feels that Howells failed to resolve this primary conflict within the work, perhaps these biographical revelations may help to explain the failure.

To introduce this reconsideration of Howells, I had originally fashioned a routine biographical sketch— Howells' Ohio boyhood, his consular post in Venice under Lincoln, and his postwar editorship of the *Atlantic Monthly* up to the eve of *A Modern Instance*. Eventually, I chose to write a more difficult, and I hope for the reader a more rewarding, first chapter by reinterpreting *The Undiscovered Country* (1880). It seemed to me that in the mode and materials of this work Howells discovered his American novel. He focused here his private agonies over "reconstruction" in the postwar decade at the same time that he created a pioneering version of pastoral for the modern American novel.

The Undiscovered Country serves not only as prelude to the eighties. It also casts valuable light on the genesis and final conception of Howells' first fictional masterpiece, *A Modern Instance* (1881-1882). One can hardly appreciate the range and depth of *A Modern Instance* without an awareness of the pastoral motifs which Howells had dramatized in the previous novel. Among these configurations in *The Undiscovered Country* was a vital analogy to Latin myth, a correlative which allowed Howells to probe the undercurrents of moral and religious confusion in America, including the revival of spiritualism and its central question of immortality. In *A Modern Instance*, he turned again to a classical analogy for the central religious dilemma of the story. His subject in *A Modern Instance* was scientific determinism and moral individualism in America. This time, the correlative was Greek drama. Unlike *The Undiscovered Country*, however, Howells' "New Medea" would end not in happy pastoral resolution but in the darker mood of Euripidean tragedy.

In *The Rise of Silas Lapham* (1884-1885), Howells shifted the center of his inquiry into American life from the religious and philosophical concerns of the two previous works to confront the moral and political issues of social status in a rapidly changing American civilization. In my third chapter, I have leaned quite heavily on Howells biography, including his ambivalent attitudes toward wealth, labor, race, and Boston high culture, to provide a new reading of Howells' most popular novel.

Howells completed these ten years of achievement as one of the architects of the modern American novel by writing *A Hazard of New Fortunes* (1889, pub. 1890), the subject of Chapter Four. He later judged this final effort of the decade "the most vital of my fictions." It also marked another shift in his consciousness and his art. To be sure, *A Hazard of New Fortunes* resembles the three other novels in revealing the social and moral chaos of the American city. The unity of this novel, however, lies in another direction. Howells fully expressed here, for the first time, his esthetic of critical "realism." The novel was conceived and written just after, or concurrently with, some of his most important critical essays in the "Editor's Study" of *Harper's*. I have brought this vital esthetic controversy to bear on a reinterpretation of *A Hazard of New Fortunes*. Ethical and social themes explored in the previous novels reappear this time within a crystallized theory of art and its relation to humanity in the American metropolis, which is to say, in the modern world.

In reinterpreting these four novels, then, I began also to discover more clearly than before the major shifts in Howells' response to the "Gilded Age" of America. While it has not been my purpose to write an interior history of the time, it is always gratifying to the literary scholar, if he be also a historian *manqué*, whenever some of his insights into an author and a period attract the attention of the literary historian and the intellectual historian who can explore the hints in a larger configuration. My own debts to historical scholars of the past and present are extensive, too much so, in fact, to acknowledge properly here or in my "Bibliographical Comment." I should be happy indeed to have repaid a part of these obligations by granting, in return, some new perspective on Howells the novelist (for the literary historian) or Howells the contemporary observer (for the intellectual historian) as he tried to express the changing mood of his time in America. But having said this, I am more sensitive than ever that my debt incurred to historians heavily outweighs any repayment to them.[3]

The reader will notice that I have considered parallel themes from Howells' other fiction from time to time, but quite sparingly. A brief explanation is necessary. The problem was the nature of "evidence," and touches, once again, on the relation between the specialized concerns of the literary scholar and the wider investigations of the intellectual and the literary historian. In rereading Howells' other novels, even those which are frequently judged to be "minor," I soon realized that the texture of each work, for the most part, was too closely woven to permit my tamper-

[3] Even to write this paragraph, I am indebted to historiographer Robert Skotheim who has succinctly discussed the lines separating American literary and intellectual history. See *American Intellectual Histories and Historians* (Princeton: Princeton University Press, 1966), pp. 38-39, 145-146, and 304-305.

ing with it casually and at random to extract supporting
quotations and similar themes. The literary scholar does
no favor to the intellectual historian by citing virtually
identical passages on labor unrest in *Their Wedding Journey* (1872) and *The Rise of Silas Lapham* (1885) to
suggest that Howells felt an identical and unabated concern over class revolution during these years. Though one
can hardly resist touching on such parallels, the earlier
passage cannot serve prominently as evidence until it has
been placed in context through a painstaking analysis of
Their Wedding Journey and of relevant Howells biography bearing on his reactions to the American labor
movement. Nor is it a favor to the literary historian when
the specialist in Howells links a passage from one novel to
a passage from another and fails to consider fully the
impact of either passage as an esthetic experience. Howells'
best writing is charged with irony and multiplied nuances
which preclude this facile lifting of evidence from one
work to the next. If the extended readings in the present
study persuade in no other way, perhaps they will stand as
tacit argument for the difficulty of establishing the implications of a given dramatic moment in the Howells novel,
and by extension, the achieved meaning of the total work.

Parts of this study, as some readers will be aware, are
based on articles and reviews in which I have expressed
direct and at times spirited disagreement with co-workers
in the field of Howells studies. I welcome the ampler space
allowed by this book to indicate more adequately than in
the past my considerable debts to these scholars. These
obligations appear chiefly in the "Bibliographical Comment" at the end, where I have described the critical
controversy bearing on these four novels during recent
years. Within each of the chapters, I have injected this
debate briefly, that the reader may more easily follow the
new direction I have given to this reinterpretation of
Howells.

Finally, I shall admit at the outset that this will be, on the whole, a sympathetic study of Howells the man and artist. While sketching the outlines of this book, I have taught and occasionally written on various figures—James, Hawthorne, Poe, Stephen Crane, Fitzgerald, and others. Returning each time to Howells, I have gained a clearer sense that he stands prominently, in our literary history, between these earlier and later practitioners of fiction in America. One discovers in Howells the dark interiors of Poe, Hawthorne, and Melville merging with a vision of "reality" as tentative as that of James, Twain, Crane, or Fitzgerald. Howells' techniques for expressing this modernism after the Civil War were remarkable when one realizes that he had but few contemporary literary models at hand. Nor is this praise my immediate retreat, so familiar in later assessments of Howells, to say that we can admire his art largely by assuming a historical, and condescending, perspective on his pioneering labors to create a new American fiction. The four novels here can withstand the critical scrutiny of analysis and comparison. I consider them major achievements in our literature, ample in complexity, variety, and scope so that, as I hope the reader will be persuaded, one is able to unfold around and through these novels a valid account of the larger ordeal and achievement of William Dean Howells.

CHAPTER ONE

THE UNDISCOVERED COUNTRY
(1880)

HOWELLS' VERSION
OF AMERICAN PASTORAL

"My notion was not to explain anything in my story," Howells wrote when installments of *The Undiscovered Country* were appearing in *The Atlantic Monthly*.[1] He soon learned from friends and reviewers that the novel which had ushered in our American fiction of the 1880s was largely a study of spiritualism. Consistent with his lifelong habit, Howells let his readers and critics have their way. T. W. Higginson was left to puzzle why Howells should have tried to revive an interest in the dying fad of spiritualism, and W. C. Brownell to pronounce the task hopeless. Howells was pleased to learn, however, that his novel had sold eight thousand copies the first month.[2] Apparently it accorded with the temper of 1880 in America. But sales quickly slackened. *The Undiscovered Country* was soon buried under the creative outpouring of Howells' novels, farces, and travel sketches which followed in this most productive decade of his career. In later years, an occasional literary historian remarked in passing that among Howells' minor works lay the novel about spiritual-

[1] Letter to W. H. Bishop, March 21, 1880, in *Life in Letters of William Dean Howells*, ed. Mildred Howells (Garden City, N. Y.: Doubleday, Doran and Co., 1928), I, 282. Hereafter shortened to *Letters*.

[2] Howells noted the sales in a letter to E. C. Stedman, Aug. 1, 1880, in Butler Library, Columbia University. Higginson's review appeared in *Scribner's*, XX (Sept. 1880), 793-795, and Brownell's in *Nation*, XXXI (July 1880), 49-51.

ism. By 1956, Edwin H. Cady called for a reinterpretation of this neglected novel. Two revealing studies have since appeared. One demonstrates the important psychological and technical debts Howells owed Turgenev. The other describes the story as an obsessive spiritual quest defeated by the stronger demands of the knowable, the earthly, and the human heart.[3]

This recent attention paid *The Undiscovered Country* has not been misspent nor the claims overstated. This was to be Howells' first "big" novel. When read closely for its interior revelations, and understood also in the light of Howells' private conflicts during the reconstruction era, *The Undiscovered Country* becomes a considerable novel indeed. Howells labored four years with his growing conception of a New England story which could serve as an incisive portrait of an age. In late summer of 1875, he had written to Charles Dudley Warner concerning the nearby Shakers at Shirley, Massachusetts: "They present great temptations to the fictionist, and as Mrs. Howells has charged me not to think of writing a story with them in it, I don't see how I can help it."[4] In November, he began to serialize "Private Theatricals," drawing on his rural observations of the summer of 1874. Clearly he had begun to move away from the international situation of his third novel, *A Foregone Conclusion* (1875) or the convenient travel-narrative that linked incident, character, and scene in *Their Wedding Journey* (1872) and *A Chance Acquaintance* (1873). But he had not yet discovered a form which would illuminate and unify a larger treatment of moral and social disorder in America. The following spring, he

---

[3] See Cady, *The Road to Realism: The Early Years of William Dean Howells* (Syracuse: Syracuse University Press, 1956), p. 197; Olov W. Fryckstedt, *In Quest of America: A Study of Howells' Early Development as a Novelist* (Cambridge: Harvard University Press, 1958), pp. 183-191; and George N. Bennett, *William Dean Howells: The Development of a Novelist* (Norman, Oklahoma: University of Oklahoma Press, 1959), pp. 97-105.

[4] Sept. 4, 1875, in *Letters*, I, 209-210.

told Thomas Bailey Aldrich, "I am not writing one [story]," and added, in mock despair, that he planned to forfeit his *Atlantic* salary "if a plot doesn't come to me pretty soon. . . ."[5] But he did write a non-fictional record of his previous summer for the June 1876 *Atlantic*.[6] Shortly thereafter, the idea for the story which was to become *A Modern Instance* began to germinate. Howells wrote to Charles Eliot Norton that he had "begun that New Medea I once told you of."[7] What appears to have happened next was a significant cross-fertilization in the conception of two novels. Howells soon put aside the modern Greek tragedy in favor of the story of Egeria Boynton, the Shakers, and spiritualism. By early 1878, he had completed a draft of *The Undiscovered Country* and sent it to T. S. Perry for criticism. After Perry's reading, Howells revised extensively, but did not complete the rewriting until after *The Lady of the Aroostook*, during the summer of 1879.[8] In January 1880, the first installment of *The Undiscovered Country* appeared in the *Atlantic;* and in 1881, he was at last able to return to the long-delayed *A Modern Instance*.

In his original subject, Shakerism, Howells sensed the materials for a study of New England life in the 1870s which could mirror also the critical changes in American civilization at large. Spiritualism, skepticism, modern science, the uprooting and decline of the family, psychological disorders within the home, sexual repression (related to what James called America's salient "decline in the sentiment of sex") —all of these and other themes for a novel of postwar life appear to have grown out of the 1875 sum-

[5] March 3, 1876, letter in Houghton Library, Harvard. Hereafter shortened to (Harvard).

[6] "A Shaker Village," *Atlantic Monthly*, xxxvii, 699-710. The *Atlantic* is hereafter shortened to *At.Mo.*

[7] Sept. 24, 1876, *Letters*, I, 227.

[8] See Virginia Harlow, *Thomas Sergeant Perry: A Biography* (Durham, N. C.: Duke University Press, 1950), p. 51; letter to Norton, Aug. 12, 1879, *Letters*, I, 275.

mer experience among the Shakers and demanded artistic form and expression. Howells partly solved the problem of form by centering his novel on a father-daughter-lover struggle which developed simultaneously as religious conflict and as sexual contention.[9] Equally important, he discovered in the contending settings of city and country a unifying frame for the cultural dislocations of American life. From beginning to end, he achieved definitive expression of his themes by adopting the traditional mode of pastoral: civilized man's temporary reunion with nature whose powers restore him to physical, emotional, and spiritual well-being. *The Undiscovered Country* viewed as Howells' modern version of pastoral helps one to discover much of the design and texture of the fiction he would produce in the years just ahead.

I

Dr. Boynton, the frenzied convert to spiritualism, has dominated every important reading of *The Undiscovered Country*. This emphasis on Boynton as the all-important figure of the novel has necessarily raised serious questions about the unity of *The Undiscovered Country* and the focus of Howells' imaginative vision. One of Howells' best recent critics has charged that "we resent the shift of focus from Boynton to the rather pallid love affair of Ford and Egeria."[10] But Howells' main concerns carried him well beyond the characterization of Boynton. A larger dramatic pattern integrates Egeria and Ford in a broadly religious

[9] Howells may already have been developing this triangle in the abortive *A Modern Instance* in 1876, and realized that here was the breakthrough for the needed "plot" of the Shaker story. The incest motif in *A Modern Instance* is discussed in my "Marcia Gaylord's Electra Complex," *American Literature*, xxxiv (Nov. 1962), 365-374.

[10] Fryckstedt, *In Quest of America*, p. 187. Mr. Bennett also considers Boynton's spiritualist monomania to be the problem of the novel, but justifies the love affair and marriage of Ford and Egeria as an ironic counterpart to Boynton's dark obsession with the occult and unknowable (*William Dean Howells*, pp. 102-103).

theme from first to last. Our viewing the religious action in the novel from this new perspective will prepare the way to a complete reading of Howells' version of pastoral.

In the opening seven chapters of *The Undiscovered Country*, Howells introduces the religious conflict among the three main characters. The setting is not the rural village of the Shakers, but Boston and a spiritualist séance in an old prewar mansion. Dr. Boynton, ex-Calvinist and former practitioner of medicine in a Maine village, has turned spiritualist and come to Boston to practice his experiments in mesmerism and spirit-communication. His wife long since dead, he is accompanied by his nineteen-year-old daughter, Egeria, whom he has controlled and trained since childhood to serve as medium in his séances. Conflict develops at once in the opening chapter when the young Boston journalist Ford, an ex-villager become scientific skeptic, feels himself drawn to attend the Boynton séance. Amid the confusion of table-rappings and the apparent presence of spirit hands and voices, Egeria faints and Ford "reverently" carries the "pale phantom" maiden to her room, while Boynton, unconcerned over his daughter's health, remains behind to exult over this assumed contact with immortal spirits beyond the grave (p. 34).[11]

Several days later, Ford returns to challenge Boynton's methods of spirit solicitation. The conflict between the spiritualist and the scientist is now defined. Boynton and Ford, both deprived of the support of religious orthodoxy, have become seekers after tangible truth, verifiable in the present world. And Egeria, the "medium" or earthly avenue of revelation to knowable truth, has become a pawn in the conflict. Ford has already carried her off in symbolic rescue from her spiritualist father. Egeria soon confirms to her father that the young skeptic represents a force inimical to her powers as a spirit-medium. Alerted to the

11 All page references in my text to *The Undiscovered Country* are taken from the 1880 Boston edition.

danger, Boynton grows determined to preserve Egeria from Ford's "noxious influence" (pp. 72-73).

Boynton plans to dispose of Ford by arranging a public séance which will serve as a "contest" between himself and his young rival. A fellow townsman of Boynton's named Hatch intervenes to extract from Ford a chivalrous vow not to accept Boynton's challenge—for Egeria's sake. Hatch simultaneously persuades the Boyntons that Mrs. LeRoy, their landlady, falsely produced the "materializations" at the recent séance and that Boston at large is a hostile environment for the seeker after spiritual reality. The Boyntons depart from Boston intending to return to Maine. The first part of the novel closes as Egeria writes a farewell note to Ford. Uprooted once again, she is bewildered and upset by the ambiguous role she has been forced to play in the struggle between the two contentious men.

In this preliminary action in a new Boston, Boynton, Egeria, and Ford have responded to the far-reaching and unsettling impact of science in America during the decade after the Civil War. The effects on all three, while not identical, had been developing for many years within the psyche of Howells their creator. The immediate evidence lies in his postwar correspondence and, perhaps even more incisively, in the reviews he contributed anonymously to the *Atlantic*. For example, Howells had depicted the chilling touch of science on American religion—the effects evident on Ford—in the earliest reviews following his return from Venice after the war. When he reviewed the *Life of Benjamin Silliman* in 1866, Howells praised the famous chemist from Yale as a man who, though devoted to science, found time "to concern himself in religious affairs. . . ." The same issue carried Howells' review of a current book, *Fifteen Days*, which portrayed a scientist who warmed to the humanitarian imperatives of abolitionism:

Doctor Borrow, the botanist, is made to pass, by insensible changes, from a learned indifference concerning slavery, to eloquent and ardent argument against it, and thus to present the history of the process by which *even science, that coldest element in our civilization*, found itself at last unconsciously arrayed against a system long abhorrent to feeling.

Several months later, Howells reviewed what for him might seem an unlikely work, *The Open Polar Sea* by a Dr. I. I. Hayes. But the occasion allowed him to speak as an "unscientific reader" who "lacks perfect sympathy with the scientific purpose, and doubts if a geographical fact, as yet barren and without promise of fruitfulness, be worth the sacrifices made to ascertain it." He went on virtually to imply that the barren, passionless, and stark existence of the Esquimaux was the proper correlative to the world of science.[12]

In an extended review of travel and anthropological books, Howells again adopted the persona of the mere reader. Alfred R. Wallace's *The Malay Archipelago* contained data "which interest the mere human being uncontaminated by science," Howells wrote; and he added that "we cheerfully abandon to the learned or sophisticated man a vast amount of information relative to the animals and vegetation of the Archipelago, with the single remark that the author is a Darwinist, and meets everywhere abundant evidence to sustain the famous Theory." Howells was the plain reader again in a review of William H. Dall's *Alaska and its Resources*. The author, Howells wrote, had "handsomely fulfilled whatever duty he owed science by the methodical and straightforward statement of results and opinions." Now what was needed was "a smaller and lighter book" for the "unscientific reader."[13]

For all his modest protestations, Howells clearly was

12 See *At.Mo.*, XVIII (July 1866), 127; *ibid.*, p. 128, italics added; *ibid.*, XIX (April 1867), 511, 512.
13 "Recent Travels," *At.Mo.*, XXIV (Aug. 1869), 256-257; *ibid.*, XXVI (Aug. 1870), 245.

becoming an informed student of science in this new era. He wrote to James of the recent visits from John Fiske:

After living within a gunshot of Mr. John Fiske for several years, I am beginning to get somewhat acquainted with him, and take as kindly to him as anyone can I suppose who has no idea what positive philosophy is. He has almost a fashion of coming to see me lately, and I find him a very simple-hearted fellow.

After the turn of the century, Howells credited Fiske with providing, more than any other person in these years, a reconciliation between the new science and the older supernatural dispensation. He recalled that Fiske reaffirmed cosmic harmony and gave a benign aspect to Evolution. "He came to rescue the soul, and proclaimed that if a certain formation in an insect necessarily implied the existence of a plant or flower adapted to the insect's use, then the instinct for immortality in the human race implied as absolutely the existence of a life hereafter for its satisfaction."[14] But Howells' memory of this receding conflict may have been somewhat faulty. Time and again in the early seventies, he sounded the anguish over the impact of science as a severe blight on man's hopes for immortality. It was out of this anguish that Howells would depict the attraction which draws Ford to attend Boynton's séance in the initial action of *The Undiscovered Country*. More profoundly, Boynton in his wild obsession with spiritualism could be sketched with insight and to a degree with compassion, for his creator understood the agony of doubt.

Religious doubt in several forms had touched Howells before the war in the milder aspect of youth's questionings. He recalled, in *A Boy's Town* (1890) and again in *Years of my Youth* (1916), the prewar religious controversy in Ohio which prefigures the later crisis of his Dr. Boynton. The inherited orthodoxy of New England had succumbed

14 Letter to James, Jan. 2, 1870 (Harvard); "Editor's Easy Chair," *Harper's Monthly*, cviii (March 1904), 642.

in those early years to "the fires of spiritualism." In its wake, spiritualism left behind "a great deal of smoke and ashes." The organized church was weakened (Howells as a "new" Swedenborgian, however, did not attend a church) at the same time that man had no stronger faith in the immortality of the soul than before.[15] A highly sensitive youth in the sometimes harsh environment of Ohio in the 1840s and 1850s, Howells was given over to a strong preoccupation with death. On one occasion, at age nine or ten, he awoke to a premonition that he would die at sixteen, and he later recalled (writing in the third person) that "the perverse fear sank deep into his soul, and became an increasing torture till he passed his sixteenth birthday and entered upon the year in which he had appointed himself to die."[16] Taken together with other fears and insecurities, presently to be touched on also in the portrait of Egeria Boynton, Howells' reaction to death clearly underlies the questions of immortality and the spiritual nature of man which he would explore in the complex portrait of Dr. Boynton.

In his anonymous reviews, Howells shared these spiritual concerns also with the readers of the *Atlantic*. One of the features of John Morley's *Rousseau* which irritated Howells was Morley's scientific belittling of the Deity by referring to Him in lower-case letters:

Science having exploded the Supreme Being, Mr. Morley will not print the name of the late imposture with a capital letter: throughout he prints God, "god"; even when he quotes from another writer, he will not allow *us poor believers* the meagre satisfaction of seeing our God shown the typographical respect which Mr. Morley would not deny to Jove, or Thor, or Vishnu, or even Jones or Smith.

He could not celebrate, as Morley had, "mortality and the worm at the expense of those fond hopes of eternal life

15 *Years of My Youth* (New York: Harper and Bros., 1916) , pp. 88, 106.
16 *A Boy's Town* (New York: Harper and Bros., 1890) , pp. 204, 243. See also *Years of My Youth*, p. 91.

which most of us cherish." Instead, he sympathized with Harriet W. Preston in her *Love in the Nineteenth Century*. There she had presented the "despair and doubt" of a young husband upon the death of his partner in a marriage characterized by "gentle, kindly, duteous, refined unfaith with only a vague hope of immortality." Howells commented,

The whole episode is given with a sort of resentful sorrow, as if in indignation that men should be scienced out of what can alone sustain and console them under supreme trial. . . .

The same indignation that man should be "scienced out" of the consolation of a life after death appears in Howells' comments on George Eliot's poem, "A Minor Prophet." He hoped that the author next would try her gift of irony on the doctrine of vegetarianism implied in the poem:

It is the idea that we are to realize our inborn longing for immortality in the blessed perpetuity of man on earth; the supreme effort of that craze which, having abolished God, asks a man to console himself when he shall be extinct with the reflection that somebody else is living on toward the annihilation which he has reached.[17]

Again, Howells allowed his review of John Forster's *The Life of Charles Dickens* to become also the occasion to regret the influence of Darwinian science on Dickens and on the world's "hope of heavenly peace somewhere":

It is a solemn lesson that the exercise of genius is in itself only a momentary escape from the *ennui* that torments all of us who have not provided ourselves with some secure retreat from the world within the world. Religion used to be highly recommended for this purpose; we suppose that nowadays Evolution is to console and support us—not with the hope of heavenly peace somewhere, but with the elevating consciousness of primordial jelly.

Virtually the same regret is heard a few months later in a

[17] See *At.Mo.*, XXXII (July 1873), 105, italics added; *ibid.* (Sept. 1873), 376; *ibid.*, XXXIV (July 1874), 103.

review of Holmes's *Songs of Many Seasons, 1862-1874.*
Howells opened the review, in fact, by remarking that
science with its irreducible fact had blighted the expecta-
tion of a spiritual life hereafter:

> In those fond dreams of a future life which some of us still
> furtively indulge, despite the hard skeptic air of our science-
> smitten age, nothing is more dismaying than the chaos which
> the conditions of eternal life seem to make of all our mortal
> relations. If heaven is not to unite us with those we have lost,
> it is, to our earthly conceit of bliss, hardly heaven at all; but
> how can it fulfill this fond desire?

He then discussed the poem which seemed to him the most
moving, "Homesick in Heaven," in which Holmes had
expressed the yearning felt by one who has passed into
immortality and knows the ache of a wished-for reunion
with his loved ones remaining behind on earth.[18]

In summer of this same year, Howells was more than
prepared to visit extensively with the Massachusetts Shakers. Spiritualism was enjoying a brief revival in Boston
during the early 1870s among some of Howells' most
sophisticated acquaintances, and originally it had been the
foundation of Shakerism. Though himself dubious of
spiritualism, Howells was far from unsympathetic with
devotees of the cult which held that the immortal soul
returned after death to communicate with the living. In
May of 1874, he had received a manuscript for the *Atlantic*
bearing on spiritualism. He rejected it due to "a shyness,
which I believe Mr. Houghton has" about that unconven-
tional religious cult, Howells wrote to W. P. Garrison.
But he considered the manuscript "very striking. . . . I'm
not ashamed to say that parts of it touched me almost to
tears." Later in the year, he did print communitarian
Robert Dale Owen's "How I Came to Study Spiritual
Phenomena," and ignored the "general vulgar clamor . . .
in the press" which later attended this act of editorial

18 *At.Mo.,* xxxiii (May 1874), 622; *ibid.,* xxxv (Jan. 1875), 105.

daring.[19] Several months later, Howells made his sojourn among the Shakers, in part, perhaps, to feed his curiosity about their spiritualist origins, as well as to observe their current pastoral way of life. All of this and more appears in the remaining action of *The Undiscovered Country*.

In the second part of the novel, chapters eight through eleven, Boynton talks with two Shakers at the railroad station while he prepares to embark for the trip back to the Maine village. In his excitement, he and Egeria subsequently board the wrong train, lose their baggage, and after a discouraging trek through the countryside, make their way to the Shaker village. And so, in the final segment of the novel, Howells arrived at what had been the germ of his story, an action set in the socialist, celibate Shaker community of rural Massachusetts. In this setting, he continues the religious argument, first between Boynton and the Shakers, and presently between Boynton and Ford. Egeria, again, is caught in the crossfire, though upon arriving at the Shaker village she has become bedridden with severe fever. Boynton's main concern, however, is not his daughter's health but the mysteries of spiritualism, which he pursues among the Shakers. To this end Egeria is necessary to him, and he anticipates her return to health and the renewal of her powers as a medium. When she convalesces in the May sunshine and in walks through the countryside, however, she also subverts the delicate nervous equipment which her father had formerly controlled.

On a climactic evening, Boynton rebukes the Shakers both for abandoning their spiritualist beginnings and for sublimely withdrawing from a life of social action and earthly achievement. Then he proudly stages an exhibition of the powers which he believes have thrust him into the vanguard of spiritual reawakening in America. But the

---

[19] To Garrison, May 21, 1874, and Dec. 28, 1874, in Princeton University Library. Owen's autobiographical sketch appeared in *At.Mo.*, xxxiv (Nov. 1874), 578-590.

rejuvenated Egeria now fails to respond to his powers. A deranged Boynton discovers, the next morning, that his old scientist rival, Ford, had arrived by chance the previous evening. Boynton angrily attacks Ford as the skeptical influence who caused Egeria's failure the night before. Boynton thereupon suffers an epileptic fit, grows mortally ill, but for the first time becomes lucid enough to recognize his monomania for what it has been. Before his death he admits in extended, impassioned monologues to Ford that the spiritualist's quest for tangible proof of immortality is both materialistic and amoral—a counterfeit of the religious ardor of the ages. Boynton does not abandon the question, however, for he is now within easy distance of the answer. He dies with "a desire, amounting almost to frenzy, to know whether we live again" (p. 390) .

No longer dominated by her father's mania, Egeria submits to Ford's earthly "spell" and reveals to the bachelor-and-skeptic the knowable truth of earthly love. As lovers, they are forced to leave the Shaker village. They marry and live in a Boston suburb, where Egeria presently becomes a convert to the Episcopalian Church.[20] Ford, meanwhile, plays the protective husband and also dabbles happily, if somewhat mindlessly, in his scientific experiments. Their marital happiness is also an oblique criticism of the benign Shakers for their cloistered, celibate life on earth. Regarding the progress of spiritualism, Egeria and Ford have received no table-rappings from the departed Dr. Boynton. "They wait, and we must all wait" for reports from the undiscovered country (p. 419) .

20 One cannot be certain that Howells intends irony in Egeria's choice of organized religion. Here and in years to come, Howells seems to have flirted with High Church Anglicanism, possibly viewing it as a decent compromise between hierarchical and theological rigidity, on one hand, and an altogether diffused liberalism on the other. Yet in *The Lady of the Aroostook* (1879) , Howells had recently permitted Staniford to twit his friend Dunham for possessing no definable religious creed. Dunham, that is, attends the Episcopal Church.

II

The Undiscovered Country, then, achieves unity through the religious conflict Howells posed among his three main characters. All three are exiles from a village America no longer sustained by religious orthodoxy. Cast into the alien city, they return to gain a semblance of rural and spiritual identity in the Shaker village. Howells suggests a workable resolution of the conflict in Boynton's death and the young lovers' return to Boston. Howells enclosed the religious conflict, in other words, within the frame of pastoral. But so far, the interrelationships of character and setting have revealed little more than the slim contours of pastoral. We move, next, to the interior sources of intensity in the novel, to its significance as psychological drama. This second aspect of Howells' pastoral has been missed, perhaps, because the cliché about his sexual timidity has largely gone unchallenged. He anticipated with remarkable insight, here and in other novels, the findings of modern psychology. What Howells understood, in particular, was the confusion of sexual emotions resulting from religious disinheritance in America. They underlie Boynton's wrongful invasion of his daughter's freedom and their mutual unease over the rival male suitor Ford. Howells' manuscript shows, in fact, that he carefully revised several important passages to make less explicit the original treatment of this father-daughter relationship—the background of abnormal repression leading to suggestions of incest. In short, rather than containing an uncoordinated love subplot, *The Undiscovered Country* became, on its psychological level, a modern search for fulfillment through human love in the disturbed and spiritually barren lives of three disinherited American villagers.

In the first seven chapters of *The Undiscovered Country*, Howells establishes in Boston the double motif of the novel, the coincidence of religious and sexual disorders within the house of Boynton, together with Ford's role as skeptical irritant and masculine intruder. At the outset, Ford and Phillips, his dilettantish friend, are waiting in the parlor of Mrs. LeRoy's house where Boynton and Egeria have been holding public séances. Presently Egeria appears, a tall, beautiful girl, ethereal except for a "rich abundance" of blonde hair. She feels an instant attraction, or repulsion, when she sees Ford: "At the sight of the taller of the two, she halted . . ." (p. 4). Her father comes forward and excitedly discusses his spiritualist activities. But Egeria has become uneasy, and Boynton withdraws from the room with her, presently to return with the report that "my daughter felt so deeply the dissenting, the perhaps incredulous mood—sphere—of one of you that she quite succumbed to it" (p. 15). But Boynton has exerted his will upon Egeria and has safely mesmerized her against existing danger to her emotions.

The séance which follows is a curious and disorderly meeting where spiritual ecstasy merges with the sexual. Hatch, the Boyntons' friend from Maine, charges the ladies to hold his hands but to refrain, please, from giving them a squeeze. For the "devotional" singing, he playfully suggests "Maiden's Prayer" (p. 21). When the ladies implore that a rascal ghost named Jim be made to appear, Mrs. LeRoy, the bogus medium, quickly obliges. The appearance of Jim's hand is greeted with a female "burst of ecstasy" (p. 27), and Hatch determines that Jim would like to wear the rings of the tittering ladies present. After "many caressing demands from the ladies" to hold the hand of their "favorite spectre" (p. 27), Hatch asks Egeria for her ring. Her refusal introduces a further complication in her emotional life: "The girl gave a start, involuntarily laying hold of the ring, and Dr. Boynton said instantly, 'He cannot have it. The ring was her mother's'" (p. 28). (The decisive influence on Boynton of his wife's death will later be revealed.) In the darkened portion of the séance, another erotic poltergeist, John, the kissing ghost, appears; and Jim reappears "slapping shoulders and knees in the absolute darkness with amazing precision" (p. 31). In the midst of this "saturnalia," as one disapproving gentleman later terms the meeting, Egeria shrieks and faints to the floor. Someone (soon admitted to be Ford) had challenged Boynton's methods by seizing Egeria's hand, whereupon the sharp point of her mother's ring had pierced Egeria's finger. Nevertheless, Boynton is jubilant and does not notice that Ford has carried Egeria upstairs. From this brief action, Howells brilliantly suggests, in the mutilating ring of the dead mother, the main conflict out of the past; and he points to the action ahead—the lover's challenge to the abnormal father, and the ultimate rescue of the daughter.

In this opening chapter, the longest in the novel, Howells deftly interweaves the religious and psychological issues of the novel. Dr. Boynton is an honest but easily duped enthusiast of spiritualism, and Howells hints in the opening séance that this obsession to commune with the spirit world carries overtones of sexual repression, not only among the customers of Mrs. LeRoy but also in Boynton. The reader is told that Boynton lost his wife shortly after Egeria's birth. Boynton thereupon began to practice mesmerism upon his daughter and has imposed his will upon her ever since. Ford represents the first serious challenge in Boston to this closeness of the father and daughter. Egeria senses Ford's influence at once, but Boynton is, as yet, not aware of the threat posed by the tall, young male rival.

Nor is Boynton conscious of his motives in saving his wife's ring for his daughter to wear. But Howells supplies the necessary information for the reader, some of it strategically inserted later in the story. Boynton, after a youthful, and one assumes a repressed, experience within "the strictest sect of the Calvinists" (p. 178), had become a defiant infidel, an utter materialist, a doctor of medicine and a dabbler in mesmerism. His heart was apparently touched by an earthly love, but his marriage ended abruptly with the death of his wife in childbirth. The event had profound consequences for Boynton:

". . . her death was attended by occurrences of a nature so intangible, so mysterious, so sacred, that I do not know how to shape them in words. . . . In the moment of her passing I was aware of something, as of an incorporeal presence, a disembodied life, and in that moment I believed! I accepted the heritage which she had bequeathed me with her breath, and I dedicated the child to the study of truth under the new light I had received" (p. 179) .

Like Bartley Hubbard, Silas Lapham, and Basil March in the next three novels to be discussed, Boynton becomes the American whose wife, rather than the church, must provide moral strength or the husband deteriorates into moral confusion. One should not miss the strong irony that Howells attaches to this confidence in the spiritual force of Victorian womanhood; the American wife is perhaps more delicately structured psychologically than her dependent husband, and in his hour of crisis she can give no help. Boynton continues to look to this only source of moral strength by seeking a continuity with his wife's spirit through her living daughter Egeria. He describes the infant Egeria as " 'naturally a child of gay and sunny temperament, loving the sports of children, and fond of simple, earthly pleasures' " (p. 179) , but his passion for " 'spirit intercourse' " (p. 55) had led him to perform psychological experiments on his responsive young daughter.

"I argued that if spirit was truly immortal it was immutable, and that a nature like hers, warm, happy, and loving, would have the same attraction for persons in one world as in another" (p. 179) .

Inadvertently, he makes the object of this "attraction" specific when he later reminds his rebellious daughter that, as a medium, she can be brought " 'face to face with your mother' " (p. 218). Giving his wife's ring to Egeria signals the confused incest motives in Boynton's quest for his wife's departed spirit. He innocently boasts that, despite Egeria's periodic resistance to him, " 'in the end my influence always triumphed, for she loved me with the tender affection which her mother seemed to impart to her with the gift of her own life' " (p. 180).

Howells confirmed the pattern of Boynton's daughter-wife aberration by drawing from classic myth, an early literary passion which he had refreshed in the early 1870s before his Shaker visits.[21] Egeria (a prophetic "Pythoness," as Phillips terms her) bears the name of the prophetic water nymph of Roman legend. That Howells intended more than a chance allusion to the classical Egeria is clear from certain plot parallels to the ancient myth. The Roman king Numa, like Boynton, consorted spiritually with Egeria after his own wife's death. The Egeria of legend was a free spirit, sacred to Diana; one of the Shakeresses who makes it her sacred trust to tend Egeria in her rebirth into womanhood is named "Diantha" (p. 168), pointedly revised in the manuscript from "Octavia" (ms. p. 526). The water nymph Egeria possessed, beyond the gift of prophecy, the power of healing—as does Howells' Egeria in her "motherly" attentions to her distraught father. And in a later scene, she kneels at a brook, the image of her mythical counterpart, and wets the bandage for Ford's wounded hand. By adapting the Numa-Egeria legend, in brief, Howells was able to give a short-hand treatment—necessarily a cryptic one for his Victorian audience—of the emotional sickness of the wifeless Boyn-

---

[21] See *My Literary Passions* (New York: Harper and Bros., 1895), pp. 10-11. John Fiske dedicated his *Myths and Myth-Makers* (1872) to Howells "In Remembrance of Pleasant Autumn Evenings Spent Among Werewolves and Trolls and Nixies." Howells had accepted portions of the book as articles for the *Atlantic* in 1871 and 1872, and wrote the unsigned *Atlantic* review when the book appeared.

ton, and the essential pathos of his unnatural relation to Egeria.[22]

To return to the opening action of the novel. Ford comes to the Boynton's lodging several days after the séance to impugn Boynton's integrity as a spirit hunter, and even threatens to expose him. When Boynton returns to Egeria, she senses his perturbation. He is fascinated to know how she has sensed it:

"Oh, I suppose I knew it because I love you so, father. . . ." He had drawn his chair, in his excitement, close to her couch, and sat leaning intently over her. She put her arm round his neck, and gently pulled his face down on her pillow for a moment. "Poor father! What was it vexed you?" (p. 60).[23]

Buoyed by this sympathy, Boynton replies in a rage at Ford's insulting threats of exposure. When Egeria urges that they go back home rather than challenge Ford's opposition, Boynton fears the first weakening of his hold on his daughter: " 'Egeria! This to your father? Do you join that scoundrel in his insult to me?' " (pp. 61-62). Egeria submits to her father's will, whereupon he presses her to analyze her strange feelings of concern about Ford. She cannot, except to admit that no other rival of Boynton's has ever affected her so. Boynton next proposes a contest over Egeria in which he and Ford shall " 'enter the lists against each other in a fair struggle for supremacy' "

22 Poe may also have influenced Howells' handling of Boynton and Egeria. One recalls that Poe was Howells' first literary passion in fiction, and Howells wrote his first boyish stories in imitation of the *Tales of the Grotesque and Arabesque* (*My Literary Passions*, pp. 8, 18). In Poe's "Morella," the mother dies in childbirth and her spirit passes into the infant daughter. The name and classical antecedents of Poe's heroine Ligeia also point to a possible source for Howells' Egeria. Poe's treatment in "Ligeia" of spiritualism, vampirism, the hero's derangement through grief over his dead wife, and his morbid obsession to be reunited with her spirit through the body of a living woman—all suggest the interior world of Howells' Boynton.

23 Deleted immediately after in the manuscript: "she pleaded with that sacred caressing motherliness which is in every woman's heart somewhere for some one" (ms. p. 242). One need not belabor the point that Egeria as a "mother" is equivalent to Egeria as wife.

(p. 65). He is suggesting, unawares, the traditional encounter between two romantic knights over their lady fair. He hopefully attributes Ford's influence on Egeria to " 'the antagonism of opposites' " (p. 89) which will create progress in spiritualism, presumably in some Hegelian fashion; he fails to admit that the same law governs sexual interest and may threaten his paternal mastery. More accurately, Boynton may be seen to avoid looking closely at earthly passion, here and throughout the novel, for fear that he may discover his own forbidden feelings. His spiritualist ardor acts as a censor; it gives him a respectable excuse for controlling Egeria and rebuffing Ford, all in the name of spiritual progress for the race. What becomes poignant through it all is the more deeply buried motive—Boynton's desired reunion with the wife he had loved.

While Boynton is sublimely self-deceiving in matters of the heart, Egeria's behavior reveals that her father's stifling control over her emotional life has not been absolute. She is still the namesake of the nymph of classic legend, with the latent emotions of a passionate "Medea" (pp. 45, 379) or an "Ashtaroth" fertility goddess (p. 379). She senses her powers as a woman. Anticipating Ford's arrival, she plans to ask him to forgo Boynton's proposed rivalry in the public lists:

. . . all fear had left her. She hastily smoothed her hair and arranged her dress, and ran downstairs into the parlor to encounter *her enemy* with such eagerness as a girl might show in hastening to greet *her lover* (p. 76, italics mine).

When Ford gallantly declines the contest, Egeria writes (and rewrites) a secret note of gratitude to him. Before he can see her again, she has dutifully left Boston with her father. The Boston action closes as Phillips suggests to Ford the innocent, victimized and " 'deliciously abnormal' " young lady they have met: " 'It is girlhood at odds with itself' " (p. 109).

The four chapters which separate the Boston episode

from the Shaker action do little to illuminate the strictly religious theme of *The Undiscovered Country*. On the psychological plane, however, they unify and advance the interior drama of the novel. Howells brilliantly conveys the derangement of the uprooted Boyntons—the father's precarious hold on reality and Egeria's dangerously repressed feminine emotions. At the railroad station, Boynton sees the air bubbles from a submerged diver in the water. In a passage which anticipates Faulkner's Quentin Compson, who would preserve his sister forever from violation by other men, Howells has Egeria's father speculate

"if it were possible to isolate a medium thus absolutely from all adverse influences, [what] great results might be expected. A speaking-tube of rubber, running from the mouth of the submerged medium—" (p. 112).

Egeria refuses the role of water nymph in this regressive fantasy with " 'I shouldn't have the courage to go under the water,' " and adds significantly, " 'I should be afraid of the fish' " (p. 112).

The two Shakers at the depot, after speculating whether Boynton and Egeria are man and wife, are presently talking with an excited Boynton over the spiritualist origins of Shakerism, after which the Boyntons take the wrong train and are thrown penniless into a hostile countryside of suspicious rural folk. At a crossroads tavern, they are held captive under the fearful eye of a large bulldog (Egeria is believed to be a truant from a rural reform school). Egeria falls asleep during a spectacular thunderstorm which shakes the tavern and awakens her from a nightmare of being trapped at a drunken orgy from which her father could not save her. " 'Come! I can't breathe here!' " she pleads with Boynton (p. 157).

All of this action borders on surrealism. Yet Howells has handled the events firmly, and the motivation seems unmistakably right. For in portraying his sensitive and up-

31

rooted heroine, Howells could draw on his own history of insecurity: his feelings of inadequacy to cope with changing and unfamiliar environments, his fear of personal destruction, and, less definably, his own religious upbringing awash in the abstruse and sometimes fearful mysticism of Swedenborg. When he recalled his Ohio boyhood, Howells frequently returned to the insecurity created by his printer-father's somewhat precarious livelihood. The Dayton years especially were "a long failure." The older children sensed the family "adversity" and the "mother's unhappiness from it." Small for his age, Howells would still manage to forge a place among the boys of a new town, only to have his family move away. During this uprootedness, his mother sometimes grew homesick in the extreme and departed up river to visit her childhood home. To be sure, Howells also recalled, in long retrospect, many happy moments in the family's "widespread, never-ending struggle for life" in Ohio. Even during the happiest home at his boy's town of Hamilton, however, Howells had "peopled all its nooks and corners with shapes of doom and horror," while ghosts "shivered in the autumnal evenings." This was the "very morbid boyhood" which would haunt his adult life into the 1880s and after. Not only menacing ghosts entered his childhood nightmares and fantasies, but also fears of field and water snakes whose strike was lethal or who would climb the legs and encoil the ribs of their victims. And after a community case of hydrophobia, Howells conceived an obsessive fear of dogs. As late as his Columbus years, in the late 1850s, he was "still sometimes haunted by the hypochondria which had once blackened my waking hours with despair." His specific terror was an "abominable cur" who sensed Howells' fear of hydrophobia and plagued him in the streets of Columbus. In June 1880, in "The Contributor's Club" of the *Atlantic* he indicated more source material for this private history of neurosis. In addition to his recurring dreams of menacing ghosts, he also had experienced night-mares of suffocation, and of frantic mix-ups on illogically conducted trains. To all this experience, Howells the novelist was now able to turn and also to impart, many years before Freud, a surprising knowledge of the psycho-logical basis of dreams, including the symbols fashioned by the repressed unconscious. (Especially significant among his deletions in the rough-draft rendering of Egeria's night-mare orgy is the phrase, "and the walls were dripping with snakes," which recalls the phallic suggestion of her earlier fear of fish.) In the flight of the Boyntons from Boston into the countryside, Howells developed a pattern of traumatic experience which he could sketch with the certainty of personal knowledge.[24]

Within this cataclysmic action in the novel, Egeria is violently wrenched from her nightmare and begins slowly to be liberated also from the diseased association with her father. Nature has induced the liberating nightmare. Com-ing out from the tavern into the cold rain, Boynton dis-covers sanctuary in a graveyard equipment shed, but Egeria refuses to join him: " 'No!' she shouted back to him, 'I would rather die!' " (p. 158). (On a later walk with Ford, Egeria thinks they are back at this spot: " 'The fever must have begun. I thought—I must have thought you—were there! I oughtn't'—" [p. 329].) Her separation from her father increases while he grows wilder and more grotesque:

The rain dripped from him everywhere,—from his elbows, from the rim of his silk hat, and from the point of his nose; he looked at once weird and grotesque (p. 159).

A friendly Shaker rescues them and drives them to his settlement, where Egeria, now in a fever, will pass through a purgatory of illness to be reborn into physical health and earthly love. Boynton will experience during his mortal

[24] See *A Boy's Town*, pp. 18, 69, 242; *Years of My Youth*, pp. 22, 29, 36, 40, 41, 80, 91, 230; "Contributor's Club," *At.Mo.*, XLV (June 1880), 859; "The Undiscovered Country," ms. p. 509 (Harvard).

illness partial recognition of his submerged incest motives as a father. And Ford, also suffering emotional illness, will arrive to receive the balm of nature and the love of her healing goddess Egeria.

In his account of his summer visit of 1875 at the Shaker village at Shirley, Howells weighed the values of celibacy and heavenly striving. While he hinted that the rapture of the Shaker service was a sublimation of passions held in check by the celibate discipline, he did not explicitly link fleshly ecstasy to spiritual rapture. But he did suggest in two anecdotes that earthly love was perhaps man's proper sphere and passion, to be enjoyed as a certainty in this world rather than denied for the less certain promise of heavenly bliss. First was the case of Father Abraham, a nonagenerian who had left his betrothed sixty years before to rise above his "natural propensities" at the Shirley village. Was the decision right? The Shakers thought so. Howells questioned it:

... perhaps in an affair like that, a girl's heart had supreme claims. Perhaps there are some things that one ought not to do even with the hope of winning heaven.[25]

Howells ended the *Atlantic* article with a dramatic contrast between the celibate Shakers and a pretty young mother who had stopped to spend the night with her Shakeress sister. The married sister had brought her small child; she watched complacently as the self-denying Shakeresses "flocked round in worship of that deplorable heir of the Adamic order of life." The scene crystallized for Howells the contending claims of the seen and the unseen worlds, of earthly love and celibate striving for divine bliss: "Somehow the sight was pathetic. If she were right and they wrong, how much of heaven they had lost in renouncing the supreme good of earth."[26]

---

[25] *At.Mo.*, XXXVII (June 1876), 705.

[26] *Ibid.*, pp. 705, 710. Celibacy at Shirley was partly the reason for the depleted numbers of the village, a cause of concern among the elders.

The primacy of the natural world and human love, which Egeria and Ford learn to enjoy directly and reverently, defines the pastoral motif in the culminating action among the Shakers. Measured against this earthly standard of human aspiration, the spiritualism of Boynton fails. So does the bleak skepticism of Ford. And the Shakers, who quietly and sincerely pursue the perfect life on earth while denying "the supreme good of earth" in their celibate Arcadia, become the objects of Howells' gentle, implicit satire. The Shakeresses, in particular, are living at cross-purposes with their natural feelings as women. First, they almost compete for the privilege of attending the sick Egeria, come to them from the Adamic order of life. One is a sister whose "tresses had been shorn away as for the grave thirty years before" (p. 168). She gazes down on the earthly beauty of the feverish visitor, and then in tribute "she stooped and kissed Egeria's hot cheek, and [blushed guiltily] then went down to the office sitting-room . . ." (p. 168, bracketed deletion in ms. p. 526). Boynton obtusely wishes to believe that women are especially suited to the self-denial of Shaker celibacy. But Sister Frances admits to Egeria the pang of seeing the man she had forsaken for celibacy come with his bride for a visit to Vardley.

Boynton is particularly concerned with this celibate life of the Shaker women. Indeed, Howells rewrote and expanded Boynton's conversation with Sister Rebecca about celibacy the first evening (pp. 166-168, ms. pp. 533 and inserts). Because of his buried desire for his wife, Boynton must prevent Egeria's possession by an earthly suitor. But

---

Ironically enough, the uncelibate Oneida settlement was currently facing a future even more uncertain. Five years later, when *The Undiscovered Country* was appearing, the Oneida's "complex marriage" had so irritated the public conscience that the communist settlement was being dissolved. This sad contrast in the struggle of American communitarianism may well have occurred to Howells, for John Humphrey Noyes, founder of Oneida, was Mrs. Howells' maternal uncle.

his plans are thwarted when she recuperates from her sickness and is reborn into the natural world. Her fever abates in late May, and the Shakeresses find her awake at dawn "her large eyes wide and her lips open" listening to the singing of birds outside her window.

"It's like the singin' of spirits, ain't it?" said one of the sisters. . . . "No!" cried the girl, almost fiercely. "It's like the singing of the birds at home" (p. 187).

Howells now describes Egeria as an awakened "Ceres" (p. 213) with a "passion" (p. 187) for the natural world ("passion" recurs four times in a dozen pages). In his rough draft of the novel, Howells had described her recovery in language even more sensuous. She had become a "priestess of the wood-deity" in nature's "mighty tabernacle," and a "nymph" or "pretty wilding boy" (ms. pp. 593, 594). And he deleted an entire sentence of lush paganism: "Her long heavy hair had been cut away during her sickness, and the [young] [first] new growth clustered round her forehead and neck in sunny rings" (ms. pp. 593-594).

Meanwhile images of procreation beset poor Boynton at every turn, though he tries to dignify them within his program of spiritual progress. Howells removed one portion of the visit Boynton and Egeria pay to a nearby farm (pp. 197-198). In the deleted segment (ms. pp. 613-616) Egeria had remained safely inside the house while the farmer showed his prize black bull to Boynton. The scene virtually became light comedy as Boynton steered the conversation away from animalistic matters to a lofty consideration of "progress" through good breeding in the world.[27] On one

---

[27] This deleted scene is anticipated in the earlier "A Shaker Village" (*ibid.*, p. 708). Howells noticed "a vigorous sketch in oil of a Durham bull" in the Shaker barn, drawn by a boy who "never became a Shaker." Eighteen years later this boy turns up, oddly enough, in *The World of Chance*. The altruistic inventor Ansel Denton was a Shaker youth who drew a picture of a bull, was rebuked by the elders, and decided to leave the community.

walk with her father, Egeria gathers laurel boughs "now coming richly into bloom" and is unaware that Boynton has directed her into the Shakers' graveyard. While Boynton's thoughts are on death and the next world, hers are defiantly on life " 'here in this world,—on the earth' " (p. 201). When he sounds out her feelings about conversion to Shakerism, Egeria praises Shaker goodness, but her specific objection to their unworldly life was deleted from Howells' manuscript: " 'Why don't they get married and live together naturally? I think that is the best way' " (ms. p. 626). Several pages afterward, when Egeria thinks of her father's concern over her, she links it to Ford and asks Sister Frances, " 'Did any letter come for me while I was sick? . . . No, there couldn't have been any answer' " (p. 209). She then blushes and lapses into deep reverie. Boynton senses her imminent rebellion, as well as the Shakers' disapproval of him, and proposes that they leave, perhaps removing themselves to Europe. " 'I don't like my environment here,' " he tells Egeria. " 'I am conscious of adverse influences' " (p. 213). Egeria pledges her loyalty to him, and Boynton defiantly goes ahead to prove his powers of spiritualism at the next Shaker meeting. But the demonstration becomes a debacle, for Egeria no longer possesses the delicate responses to her father's will.

Unknown to Boynton and Egeria, Ford has accidentally arrived at the Vardley community the same evening, and with his arrival the novel moves toward gradual resolution of the religious and sexual conflict. Boynton has wandered stormily about all the night and, in the morning, coming upon Ford, Boynton attributes Egeria's failure to Ford's neighboring presence. But in clutching at Ford's throat, Boynton suffers an epileptic seizure, reels, and strikes his head. This dramatic encounter turns out to be the moment of Boynton's return to sanity. He regains consciousness and, lying on his deathbed, realizes that his spiritualism has been aimed at reunion with his dead wife. After his own agnosticism, Boynton tells Ford, " 'in circumstances of great sorrow, I embraced the philosophy of spiritualism, because it promised immediate communion and reunion with the wife I had lost' " (p. 281).

Howells' complex portrait of Boynton is nowhere so subtle as here. Boynton gropes toward self-recognition without knowing that he is solving a painful cryptogram within his own mind. Having admitted his spiritualist absorption in his dead wife, the next revelation for Boynton has to be the horror of his involvement with his daughter. But Boynton's true feelings have been buried for years. His mind has learned to practice many disguises. Boynton does admit his sin as a father, but the admission is devious and cryptic. Since it entails his rivalry with Ford, Boynton senses that Ford is the logical audience at his bedside and the agent who can lift the curse from the Boynton household. But it would be too damning for Boynton openly to recognize Ford as a sexual adversary. " 'You have somehow been strangely involved in our destiny,' " he says to Ford (p. 286); and again, " 'I find a great similarity of mind and temperament in us' " (p. 288). How can Boynton in some way admit his guilt and release Egeria to her natural suitor? He suddenly wishes to be reconciled to Egeria's maternal grandfather in Maine, who had objected to Boynton's isolating Egeria after her mother's death. Boynton's gesture here reflects some sense that his paternal behavior has been wrong and that the father-in-law has been right. Moreover, Boynton's words " 'my adversary is the father of my child's mother' " (p. 282) seem to be a coded way of admitting that father and son-in-law have a way of contending against each other within a family. By seeking the blessing of his father-in-law, Boynton seems also to express a desire to resolve the more immediate triangle which includes his younger adversary Ford. This possibility is supported when Boynton asks Ford to send the message to Maine, a gesture of trust but perhaps also a subconscious way of saying, "Act for me: i.e., replace me." It may be taken to mean that Ford is thereby invited to replace Boynton also in the closer triangle—to become the sole and proper contender for the affections of Egeria. That the grandfather had recently died is not important here. Boynton has made his gesture to Ford, and it enables him to move even closer to a conscious recognition of the incest taboo he has violated. He confesses his paternal vampirism to Ford:

"I seized upon a simple, loving nature, good and sweet in its earthliness, and sacred in it, and alienated it from all its possible happiness to the uses of my ambition. I have played the vampire!" (pp. 318-319).

Boynton finally can face death without dread, his cryptic confession made, his earthly anxieties somewhat lifted by partial self-recognition, and his spiritualism reassessed. Indeed, he must die, for his fulfillment can logically occur only beyond the grave. He can discover reunion with his beloved wife now without violation of Egeria, and he passes to the grave with his accustomed enthusiasm.

Egeria gains final release into life and earthly love during Ford's Shaker residence. Her bruised emotions gradually heal as she makes excursions with Ford into the countryside. Typical of Howells' mastery in depicting Egeria's unresolved feelings toward her father and Ford is the late scene in which the two have been collecting autumn leaves for Boynton's bed-table. Ford happens to apologize for the earlier injury he caused to Egeria's hand in the opening séance: "He looked at the hand on which she wore her ring, and she hid the hand in the folds of her dress, and turned her head away" (pp. 296-297). She suddenly realizes that they have forgotten the leaves they had picked for her father. Egeria cries, " 'No, no, I can get them. You mustn't come. I don't wish you to come' " (p. 297). Slowly she becomes able to offer herself without conflict or fear to the man whose presence had disturbed her before. In the culminating love scene, they discover what Ford's earthly "influence" over Egeria has been:

> "Do you think it is a spell, now?"
> "I don't know."
> "And are you afraid of it?"
> "No—"
> "What is it, Egeria?" he cried, and in the beseeching look which she lifted to his, their eyes tenderly met. "Oh, my darling? Was this the spell"—
> The rapture choked him; he caught her hand and drew her towards him (p. 411).

An inspired comic touch by Howells is the presence of Sister Frances, who has been furtively watching this successful and un-Shakerly end to her labors as Egeria's nurse. "But at this bold action, Sister Frances, who had not ceased to watch them, threw her apron over her head" (p. 411).

Finally, Ford himself has been rescued out of the bleak world of rationalism into the warmth of earthly passion. With a cynical bachelor's reluctance to admit that his restlessness might have been partly induced by a woman, he had spent a Sunday at a spiritualist meeting at Walden, only to return to Boston with a headache, followed by dizziness and the advice of his doctor to "get a change of air" (p. 256). His chance encounter with the Boyntons again enables him to discover that Egeria is the medium who will reveal for him the reality which all religions pursue. He says to a Shaker elder, " 'You talk of your angelic life! Can you dream of anything nearer the bliss of heaven than union with such tenderness and mercy as hers?' " (p. 352). At the end, he marries neither a spiritual Beatrice nor a passionate Medea. His wife is supremely normal, and Ford "feels it a sacred charge to keep Egeria's life in the full sunshine of our common day" (p. 419).

III

The Undiscovered Country, then, may be properly described as a drama of passion and forbidden impulses within an American family unloosed from older religious and emotional moorings, searching for an anchorage in the present. Howells enlarged even further this commanding pattern of dislocation in postwar life. He created within the action a contrapuntal movement which embraced the oppositions between city and country, present and past, complexity and simplicity, intellection and feeling. The novel contains references to Emerson and Hawthorne, and to Thoreau's *Walden*; the Boyntons are emigrants to Boston from a disappearing Maine village; Ford is an urbanized country boy writing articles for a Boston paper on changes in rural New England life; Mrs. LeRoy has come to Boston from the West, as have summer tourists who annually invade New England. Indeed, the novel opens against the background of radical change in postwar America:

> Some years ago, at a time when the rapid growth of the city was changing the character of many localities, two young men were sitting, one afternoon in April, in the parlor of a house on one of those streets which, without having yet accomplished their destiny as business thoroughfares, were no longer the homes of the decorous ease that once inhabited them (p. 1).

Not only the religious and psychological conflicts previously described, but also countless details which seem merely incidental, become significant when one views the novel in its final, achieved form—as Howells' version of American pastoral.[28]

---

[28] For this final aspect of Howells' pastoral, I owe general debts to Leo Marx's *The Machine in the Garden: Technology and the Pastoral Ideal in America* (New York: Oxford University Press, 1964). Another recent work from which I have profited is Glen A. Love's "Sherwood Anderson's American Pastoral" (doctor's thesis, University of Washington, 1964).

During his 1875 summer visit among the Shakers, as I have remarked, Howells was discovering the complex variety of materials which later would give density and significance to *The Undiscovered Country*. The list grew to include other problems of New England and national life: the disappearance of the family-sized farm, rural despair, the lure of the West, urban migration, the growth of industrialism and unemployment, communist alternatives to free enterprise. All of these and other changes in our national life led Howells to brood over the course American civilization was taking. The Shakers' own "decay of numbers" was "but their share of the common blight, and how to arrest it their share of the common perplexity."[29] These tensions, soon to demand expression in Howells' fiction, were increased by his own awareness at this time that the Ohio village was not a satisfying alternative to life in commercial Boston. By 1875, he was no longer the youth who had written Ohio pastorals in imitation of Pope. He was now willing to admit that "our ordinary country life" in America is "hard and often sordid commonplace."[30] *The Undiscovered Country* was to become, however, not antipastoral but a sobering version of American pastoral; and reconciliation of the tensions between America's present and past and would be an important part of Howells' pastoral vision in 1880.

29 "A Shaker Village," *At.Mo.*, xxxvii (June 1876) , 706.

30 *Ibid.*, p. 699. On Howells' youthful pastorals, see *Years of My Youth*, pp. 75-77. By 1860, Howells recognized the difficulties of framing a pastoral vision in Ohio. Returned from his first visit to Boston, he wrote to Lowell from Columbus: "The conditions in the west are rather against poetry, I think. It is hardly possible to assimilate and poetize the crude, harsh life we live" (Dec. 14, 1860 [Harvard]) . Not until the turn of the century did he return to a poetic sense of Ohio village life. He planned to model his verses this time after the tales of George Crabbe. But Norton quickly extinguished the spark, calling attention to the barren conditions Howells had earlier felt to exist—"the thinness, the poverty of the American background." Howells promptly abandoned the poetic experiment. See his "Charles Eliot Norton: A Reminiscence," *North American Review*, cxcviii (Dec. 1913) , 842, and my biography, *Charles Eliot Norton* (Cambridge: Harvard University Press, 1959) , p. 163.

Howells created these further dimensions of pastoralism at the same time that he kept his dramatic focus on the lives of Boynton, Egeria, and Ford. Boynton was Howells' distillation of New England's historical search for spiritual reality. He moved out of a brooding Calvinism through a stolid scientific rationalism. He opened an intercourse with the world through his marriage to an earthly woman, and upon her death he tried to discover the world of spirit by etherealizing his daughter's free and natural instincts. Unfortunately, Boynton is a grotesque from the past who is cut off from the present; his thoughts are on decay, autumn, and death. Though he considers Emerson " 'a very receptive mind' " (p. 141), he is more the villain of Hawthorne (pp. 109-110) whose desperate quest for truth has violated nature and the sanctity of the human heart. He has separated himself from the passional lives of men and women. He is properly described by Ford's friend Phillips to be " 'as curious an outcome of this bubble-and-squeak that we call our civilization as anything I know of ' " (p. 108).

Ford is Boynton's next-generation antagonist, similar to Boynton in his loss of traditional belief and also in being a refugee from a village America no longer self-sustaining. But Ford lacks Boynton's neurotic enthusiasm to extract from the natural world the spiritual secrets which Emerson had discovered there. Both Ford and Boynton, finally, are attracted to Egeria, in whom the properties of nature and "spirit" appear to dwell in precarious imbalance.

In the opening action in Boston, Howells rapidly unfolds the several layers of his pastoral theme. Ford's barren spiritual existence in the city is apparent in his curiosity and need to attend Boynton's séance. The melancholy old house, a "material token of a social decay" (p. 2), belongs to the devious Mrs. LeRoy. Her recent arrival from the West makes sufficient comment on the spiritual resources of the American Garden. In the tawdry parlor of this old Boston residence, Boynton tries to conjure up the departed spirits of the past. He attributes his and Egeria's failure to the hostile materialism of the present—Ford's religious doubt and the "mercenary" impulses of the age. He decides to leave Boston and to rediscover in the New England village a setting congenial to his pursuit of voices out of the past.

The remaining twenty-one chapters of the novel develop the theme of rural New England as a pastoral restorative for the malaise of postwar America. The Boyntons' first glimpse of the Massachusetts countryside is less than encouraging. They are met with suspicion and hostility. They are taken to be either displaced tramps or escapees from the law. They wander in the shadows of Massachusetts forests "where the farmer has ceased to coax his wizened crops from the sterile soil and has abandoned it in despair to the wilderness from which his ancestors conquered it" (p. 134). A schoolteacher who befriends them for the night teaches only sixteen pupils in a school that once held fifty. They see not country maidens, but instead, at the crossroads tavern, a painted woman. Elsewhere they come upon wandering "free" Negroes, unpainted dwellings of poor whites, and the ruined masonry of former homes rising amid the "brutal grotesquery" of a lost Arcadia cynically dubbed "Skunk's Misery" (p. 197).

Through Ford's eyes, Howells amplifies this theme of pastoral blight. On the country journey which will take him, unawares, back into the company of the Boyntons, Ford observes

the sparse farmhouses and the lonesome villages [which] afflicted him with the remembrance of his own youth; whatever his life had been since, it had not been embittered with the sense of hopeless endeavor, with the galled pride, with the angry ambition, which had once made it a torment in such places (p. 262).

More significant is the experience, already mentioned,

which impelled Ford to seek the New England hills—a
disheartening excursion to Thoreau's Walden Pond on a
Sunday. Howells inserted the incident in revising his
original manuscript (five pages of inserts at ms. p. 748),
and the relevance is obvious. The country-folk on a Sunday
picnic recall to Ford his own boyhood:

but here was a profaner flavor: scraps of newspaper that had
wrapped lunches blew about the grounds; at one place a man
had swung a hammock, and lay in it reading, in his shirt-
sleeves; on the pond was a fleet of gay rowboats, which, however, the railroad company would not allow to be hired on
Sunday. . . . [One] of the people in charge complained of the
dullness of the place. "What you want is a band. You want a
dance-hall in the middle of the pond, here; and you want a
band" (pp. 254-255).

This profanation of Walden Pond (nicely anticipating the
modern Thames of T. S. Eliot), together with the vulgar
spectacle of a nearby post-Transcendental spiritualist meeting, sends Ford back to Boston with a headache and several
days of dizziness and indigestion. Like Egeria, Ford has
experienced not restoration and health, but instead a more
severe illness in his initial return to a blighted New England Arcadia. But their mutual sojourn in the Shaker
village will be another story.

A sickness of spirit infects all three characters upon
their arrival at the Shakers' idyllic communist village, and
the novel traces from that point the effects of this quasi-
pastoral setting on each character. Boynton receives the
least benefit, but his fate is nevertheless instructive. Living
with his Idea, he never rallies into a love for the natural
world or communication with its eternal movements. He
responds only to its violent moods and its nighttime and
autumnal periods. His death is prefigured, and when it
comes, Howells supplies the physician's report. It contains an obvious comment on Boynton's diseased affections:
" 'The heart had been affected a long time' " (p. 391).

Prospects for the newer generation in America are more hopeful. Egeria experiences a renewed tie with the rhythms of nature during her convalescence, and a rebirth of her feminine emotions. She becomes divorced from her father's desperate vampirism. She learns to appreciate the simplicity of the Shakers' communal life. At the same time, she senses that Shaker denial of earthly passion is incongruous with their other good and natural instincts. She accepts, as the Shakers do not, familiar love, marriage, and earthly fulfillment. Ford also is redeemed out of his sterile unbelief as the Shakers' Arcadian surroundings help awaken him to the natural imperatives of human love. Returned to a world of feeling, he loses his cynical edges and, with Egeria as his wife, no longer feels alien to life in the city.

The Undiscovered Country ends, without yearning or regret, as a modern version of pastoral, an updated *Blithedale Romance*.[31] The death of her grandfather has severed Egeria's last family ties to the village home in Maine. But Egeria and Ford discover a reconciliation between city and country. They live in suburban Boston. Ford conducts his scientific experiments in a laboratory adjacent to their garden. Thoroughly urbanized, newly wealthy and glad of it (Ford's science has brought forth a profitable convenience for the modern housewife), they have also learned, while living in the present, to entertain the Arcadian moment out of the past. They retreat from their busy round of parties, dinners, and theater engagements during one month of each summer and receive, instead, the balm of nature as they live a simple, unhurried, and

---

[31] Howells' debts to Hawthorne seem considerable, if one recalls "The Canterbury Pilgrims," "Rappaccini's Daughter," and especially *The Blithedale Romance*, Howells' favorite. Egeria is a spiritual Priscilla who blooms into a warm Zenobia and becomes a whole woman. Boynton is a grotesque Westervelt with some of the visionary zeal of Hollingsworth. Ford is a Coverdale with the added good fortune of overcoming skepticism and choosing his ideal lady in time.

tourist-free existence in the undiscovered country of the Shaker farmers in rural Massachusetts.

The Undiscovered Country was Howells' first broad treatment of American life, a regional story which enlarged, through its pastoral motifs, into a national study of religious, psychological, and social dislocation in the late nineteenth century. Here for the first time, Howells came into possession of his major gifts as a novelist— an imagination far livelier and more allusive than previous criticism has granted him, and serving these imaginative gifts a high intelligence, a crowded memory, and a thorough apprenticeship to the craft of fiction. The present chapter has suggested the art and intent of this rich and interesting novel. The long gestation period, together with the extensive revisions, shows that Howells could be as demanding an artist as Henry James in developing his *donnée* and conceiving its dramatic form.[32] Howells also depicted sexual repression and awakening with a subtlety to rival James at his best. Perhaps we can now put to sleep the charge that, because his love scenes were tame, Howells avoided the problems arising from man's animal instincts. One can only assume that Howells, who also created—and this is only a partial list—the sexually confused characters Don Ippolito (*A Foregone Conclusion*), Staniford (*The Lady of the Aroostook*), Owen Elmore (*A Fearful Responsibility*), Marcia Gay-

[32] One last manuscript revision, in fact, may reflect how alike in the 1870s Howells and James were growing as novelists. Ford was originally named "Gifford." Howard H. Kerr has reminded me that in James's "Professor Fargo" (1874), Colonel Gifford and his daughter give public demonstrations of mathematical wizardry, while the medium-mesmerist Professor Fargo tries to lure the trance-maiden away from her quixotic father. Since Howells' Gifford (Ford) is also a scientist, we may have here one more tantalizing glimpse into Howells' literary creation. He seems to have been playing an unconscious variation on James's apparent variation on Hawthorne's original triangle in *Blithedale*. Perhaps he later recognized the Jamesian influence through the verbal parallel and, for whatever reasons, decided it best to change his Gifford to Ford.

lord (*A Modern Instance*), the Lapham sisters (*The Rise of Silas Lapham*), Colville (*Indian Summer*), Christine Dryfoos (*A Hazard of New Fortunes*), Faulkner (*The Shadow of a Dream*) and Westover (*The Landlord at Lion's Head*), must have decided to keep his private joke when he permitted his critics to complain about the timid evasions in his treatment of man and woman. Not only did he treat sexual neurosis again and again in his novels, but he understood its direct relation to the external disorders of a changing civilization.

Finally, it may be that *The Undiscovered Country* is the pioneering version of American pastoral in the post-Civil War novel. Certainly it anticipates the themes of Mark Twain, Frank Norris, Sherwood Anderson, Faulkner, Hemingway, Fitzgerald, Salinger, and other novelists who have posed the dialectical tensions of pastoral in modern America. Both for its fictional art and as Howells' first major attempt to reconcile the American present with the past, *The Undiscovered Country* deserves continued study and interpretation. How it leads also to a deeper understanding of *A Modern Instance* I hope to reveal in the next chapter.

CHAPTER TWO

———

A MODERN INSTANCE
(1881–1882)

FREEDOM AND FATE IN
MODERN AMERICA

HOWELLS attended a Boston performance of *Medea* in the spring of 1875. That evening he was certain that he had found the classic model for an "Indiana divorce case."[1] Howells had envisioned an American domestic tragedy in the Greek mode, ending in divorce and perhaps Medean violence. And implicit in this tragedy would be the failure of the American West as a pastoral setting to forestall the fated end of his Jason and Medea. The next year, he could write to Charles Eliot Norton that the "New Medea" was begun.[2] It then faltered. Meanwhile, Howells wrote the rough draft of *The Undiscovered Country*, the plays *Out of the Question* and *A Counterfeit Presentment*, *The Lady of the Aroostook*, a careful revision of *The Undiscovered Country*, "A Fearful Responsibility," *Dr. Breen's Practice*, and countless pieces of literary miscellany as editor of the *Atlantic*. Through it all, *A Modern Instance* appears to have been awaiting its turn. Early in 1881, Howells resigned his position with the *Atlantic* and almost at once wrote to Mark Twain that he was preparing a novel to be completed by the end of the year. "I don't know exactly how hard this work will be," he said, "but

[1] William M. Gibson, ed., *A Modern Instance* (Boston: Houghton Mifflin Co., 1957), p. v. All page numbers from the novel refer to this edition.
[2] Sept. 24, 1876, *Letters*, I, 227.

it won't be very light." His foreboding was all too accurate. In November, after writing the most powerful chapters of *A Modern Instance*, Howells was moving into the final segment of the novel when he was forced to bed for seven weeks with what he described to his father as "some sort of a fever . . . the result of long worry and sleeplessness from overwork."[3]

In the first chapter, I have sketched much of the biographical and historical background out of which Howells would conceive *A Modern Instance*. Chiefly in the writing of *The Undiscovered Country*, he had shaped these materials artistically into the controlling motifs of an American pastoral. The pastoral themes would reappear with greater complexity in this new and more powerful study of American life. As in *The Undiscovered Country*, Howells dramatized the aimlessness and disorder permeating American life after the weakening of religious orthodoxy. This time, however, he could leave behind the human yearning for immortality in the undiscovered country. In *A Modern Instance*, Howells focused exclusively on the dilemma of man in the present world. Was he a free agent capable of shaping his destiny on earth and reconstructing a civilization in the initial stages of moral decline? For the classic correlative, Howells would move out of Roman myth and immortality back to Euripidean tragedy and fate in the later years of Athenian civilization. Again, as in *The Undiscovered Country*, Howells created a drama of family instability arising from the new "freedom" from religious orthodoxy in America. Boynton, Egeria, and Ford were supplanted by Squire Gaylord, his daughter Marcia, and suitor Bartley Hubbard in a psychological drama charged, once again, with incest and fated Oedipal (Electra) overtones. In addition, Howells ranged broadly over the social disruptions in the reconstruction

---

[3] See letter to Mark Twain, April 17, 1881, in *Mark Twain–Howells Letters*, ed. Henry Nash Smith and William H. Gibson (Cambridge: Harvard University Press, 1960), I, 361; and to William Cooper Howells, Nov. 15, 1881, *Letters*, I, 303.

era to make both contemporary and prophetic discoveries
about the American village, the countryside, the city, and
the new West. The search would become more profound
and at the same time more bleak than in *The Undiscovered Country.* Not the restorative of American pastoral in
the previous novel, but instead the inevitable doom of a
green America, would characterize the darker logic of *A
Modern Instance.*

I

In the pages of *A Modern Instance,* Howells reflected in
miniature the state of religion in America and related
it not only to marriage and divorce but to a widespread
crisis in national morality. For years he had been a close
student of sectarian religion in America. He followed the
decline of orthodoxy and the rising tide of liberalism in
the 1860s and 1870s. In *A Modern Instance,* the action,
setting, and character portraits would emerge convincingly
out of this religious climate. Because he understood its
origins, Howells could describe the present turbulence
with economy and assurance, and by implication could
predict some of its effects on our history.

Religion had been a shaping influence in his Ohio
childhood. In *A Boy's Town,* written some ten years after
A Modern Instance, Howells recalled that his father had
been a skeptic for many years before he embraced the
doctrines of Swedenborg. The family read from the Swed-
ish philosopher and mystic within a home that was "very
religious." But Howells apparently felt an attraction to the
established church, and made furtive visits to the interior
of the local Catholic Church. For the most part, his early
religious life was emotional and diffuse rather than stern
and prescriptive. Lacking the precision of creed and ceremony in his own religion, he learned toleration and gained
insight into the diverse forms of organized religion. When
he came to the *Atlantic Monthly* in 1866, Howells found
himself in the company of religious skeptics. Yet implanted

emotional yearnings made his an uneasy skepticism amid this dissidence of dissent in postwar Boston. To say that "during his Boston sojourn his faith was rather passive, only mildly disturbed by doubts and questions" is not quite to account for evidence to the contrary.[4] Throughout his tenure with the *Atlantic* to 1881, Howells felt drawn to comment on books and movements of the period which formed the battleground between the new liberalism and the established orthodoxy. The volume of his reviews alone argues that Howells may have been more than "mildly disturbed" in his religious life. By assigning himself this task of religious scholar and critic, moreover, Howells gained a knowledge of his subject which would impart a solidity to the pastoral framework of *A Modern Instance*. And the uncertainties of his religious commitment would provide many of the subliminal tensions in the novel. Preliminary to a close reading of *A Modern Instance*, one can discover a part of the genesis of the novel by turning briefly to consider a cross-section of Howells' *Atlantic* contributions to the debate between sectarian orthodoxy and postwar liberalism.

One of his earliest reviews for the *Atlantic*, in June 1866, treated Bayard Taylor's *The Story of Kennett*. Howells admired Taylor's recognition of the strengths of Quakerism present in his heroine, as well as the dangers of sectarian oppression embodied in the heroine's father. Howells judged the book

the best portraiture of the contrasts which Quakerism produces in human nature. In the sweet and unselfish spirit of Martha, the theories of individual action under special inspiration have created self-reliance, and calm, fearless humility, sustaining her in her struggle against the will of her father, and even against the sect to whose teaching she owes them.[5]

4 Hannah G. Belcher, "Howells's Opinions on the Religious Conflicts of His Age as Exhibited in Magazine Articles," *American Literature*, xv (Nov. 1943), 270. In *A Boy's Town*, see pp. 11, 112.

5 *At.Mo.*, xvii (June 1866), 777.

Reviewing James Parton's *Famous Americans of Recent Times* the next year, Howells more clearly advocated a liberalized Christianity for postwar democratic society. For this new "social" emphasis in religion, Henry Ward Beecher deserved special praise:

> Mr. Beecher represents no new ideas in religion. He is the leading thought and speech of the strong, earnest, self-reliant element—not refined to intellectual subtlety or morbid doubt —which is perhaps the most hopeful element in New York, and which is the beginning of a social rather than a religious regeneration.[6]

The year after, Howells returned to Quakerism and this time pronounced the "narrowness of creed and of thought" in their religion to be an unequivocal liability. The charge came in a review of *The Life of Nathanael Greene, Major-General in the Army of the Revolution*:

> He seems never to have looked on his Quaker origin as a natural advantage; and he particularly resented that narrowness of creed and of thought which had forbidden him a liberal education in his youth, and held polite learning as little better than profane swearing. In fact, he never quite recovered from the injury thus done him, and we cannot greatly blame him if he did not quite forgive it to his ancestral sect.[7]

In 1869, however, Howells could cite once more both the strengths and weaknesses of this sect. Reviewing Longfellow's *The New England Tragedies*, Howells saluted the best aspects of Quakerism—their religious dedication and moral courage in the face of Puritan oppression—but also cited the inevitable results of organized sectarian zeal. Quaker martyrdom in New England could also be explained as a sublime, masochistic blend of "attitudes and suffering . . . to whose madness, indeed, it was perhaps impossible to give any method."[8] Howells at this time had

---

[6] *Ibid.*, XIX (May 1867), 637. [7] *Ibid.*, XXI (April 1868), 507.
[8] *Ibid.*, XXIII (Jan. 1869), 133.

grown deeply immersed in the pros and cons of sectarian religion to the degree that, in the same issue, he presented an extended and authoritative essay on the Moravian sect in America. He had obviously devoted many weeks of careful research and thought to writing the history of this tragic migration into early Ohio. The significance of the article, for our purposes, is once again that Howells revealed his specific admiration not for organized religion and sectarianism but for the humane benefits of Christianity. In their civilizing efforts among the Indians, the Moravians gave eloquent expression and example of Christian humanitarianism:

Their efforts were addressed to the reason of the savages, and to humanity's inherent sense of goodness and justice. I confess that this alone interests me in the history of Gnadenhütten, and lifts its events out of the order of calamities into a tragedy of the saddest significance.[9]

Howells' interest in the German pietistic sects and, indeed, his authority in writing on them, reappears in a later review of Mrs. P. H. Gibbons' *"Pennsylvania Dutch" and Other Essays*. The title essay had appeared in the *Atlantic*, and one suspects that Howells himself accepted it for publication. On the various sects treated in the book—Amish, Swiss Anabaptist, Dunker, German Seventh-Day Baptist, Quakers—Howells confirmed that the author "covers all the familiar and many of the significant traits of the peculiarly varied little world of rural Pennsylvania," and he praised the admirable simplicity of customs and life among these sects. And when Constance Fenimore Woolson's *Castle Nowhere* appeared, Howells elected to write the review. Miss Woolson's subject was the Zoar Community, the band of northern Ohio Separatists whose conflict he described as the familiar blend of humane feelings struggling to survive within an intransigent sectarian creed and discipline,

9 "Gnadenhutten." *ibid.*, XXIII (Jan. 1869), 104.

with its manners and customs, and that quaint mingling of earthy good-feeling and mild, coarse kindliness with forms of austere religious and social discipline, which seems to characterize all the peculiar German sectarians. . . .[10]

After the mid-1870s, when Howells relaxed his heavy schedule of reading and reviewing, one has more difficulty in tracing his religious opinions. Even so, it appears safe, in the light of the earlier evidence, to agree with the following conclusion on his criticism of religious orthodoxy during the *Atlantic* years:

His hostile interpretation of revivalism was in line with a movement within the churches to humanize religion, to put the stress on the moral rather than the theological phase of religion. These were the views being popularized by some of the great contemporary liberals in the pulpit, Henry Ward Beecher, Washington Gladden, Phillips Brooks, George A. Gordon, and Joseph Cook.[11]

Yet Howells' responses cannot be defined so easily. Pulled in one direction by the latitudinarian spirit of post-Darwinian Christianity, he was yet urged in another by a yearning for the security of a formulated creed. Even when he considered the most intolerant and unyielding of all home-grown sects, the Puritans, Howells could not arrive easily at final judgment. Palfrey's *Compendious History of New England* reminded him of the fanaticism which issued in the Salem witch trials. But while he could not condone the harshness and intolerance of Puritan conformity, he respected the firmness with which the Puritans grappled with the questions of the invisible world and at

[10] *Ibid.*, xxx (Oct. 1872), 489; xxxv (June 1875), 737. For Howells' uncharitable treatment of the Mormons, see "The Next President," xxxi (May 1868), 632, and "Recent Travels," xxiv (Aug. 1869), 258. And for equally harsh indictments of Catholic orthodoxy, see his reviews of Motley's *History of the United Netherlands*, xxi (May 1868), 632-638; Victor Rydberg's *The Last Athenian*, xxiii (June 1869), 768; *The Private Life of Galileo*, xxvi (Sept. 1870), 375-377; and Tennyson's *Queen Mary*, xxxvi (Aug. 1875), 241.

[11] Belcher, "Howells's Opinions on the Religious Conflicts of His Age," pp. 272-273.

the same time envisioned their own religious destiny. Howells could even detect in the Puritan annals a genuine poetry which lay hidden

under an array of facts as little showy and romantic as the garb and visage under which each Puritan hid the tenderness and strength of his nature. It is the record of a God-fearing community abandoning home and country for the freedom of the wilderness, but carrying like malicious kobolds, among their household gear the errors of superstition, intolerance, and persecution from which they fled. Yet they were a people who could learn mercy as well as righteousness.

He could sympathize with the impulses which later produced the Great Awakening. "No doubt we degenerate people should not have found the religious temper or observances of the time lax," he wrote, and by implication one could forgo the prospect that a latter-day religious revival might disturb the modern temper of confirmed skepticism and diffused liberalism.[12] Again in 1873, he deplored the looseness of an intuitive morality, subjective spirituality, and a liberalism which shirks the issues of evil and disorder and thereby degenerates into no firm theology whatsoever. He reviewed *A Memorial of Alice and Phoebe Cary*, the gifted daughters of a southern Ohio farmer. Of their religious household, Howells wrote, "There was a religious strain in them which as to creed took the most generous and hopeful form," and he then added in mild criticism, "and on another side shaded into a sad spirituality." Or again the next year, he commented on Christoper Pearse Cranch's *Satan: A Libretto* with the same sympathy for an adherence to creed, and more, he paid his respect to an un-Emersonian interpretation of evil and disorder. "The tendency of modern liberalism to ignore the chief of the fallen angels," Howells wrote, "has been one of the

12 *At.Mo.*, XXXI (June 1873), 743-746. Howells' close interest and scholarship in the religious life of early Massachusetts are convincingly recorded in an untitled and apparently unpublished review of Charles Wentworth Upham's *Salem Witchcraft* (Boston, 1867) in Yale University Library.

most painful spectacles which conservative theologians have had to contemplate. . . ." And he added editorially, "Whether we call him Devil or call him Disorder, we still have the same old serpent among us for all practical purposes."[13]

The next summer, in his visits to the Shaker village in rural Massachusetts, he came into close relationship with "a sect simple, sincere, and fervently persuaded of the truth of their doctrine. . . ." The Shakers forced upon Howells a reassessment of the advantages of a religion which preaches a stern morality (promises of immortality aside) over against the socializing of the liberal church elsewhere in the nation. He attended the Shaker meetings regularly, in itself an index of more than just interested curiosity. Of the Shaker worship, he wrote, "They sang with a fervent rapture that the self-possessed worship of our world's congregations no longer knows." The Shakers' march was "thrilling" for Howells "and it never failed to tempt the nerves to so much Shakerism at least as lay in the march." And he could announce, after hearing a Shaker sermon, "It is pleasant, after the generalizing of the pulpits, to have the sins of one's fellowmen frankly named and fully rebuked."[14]

From the outset of *A Modern Instance*, Howells portrays the decline of religious orthodoxy in postwar America. The new atmosphere of "chaotic liberality" has invaded the sectarian Christianity of Equity, Maine, the home of the Gaylord family. The result on the village churches has been a "relaxation and uncertainty of their doctrinal aim." Marcia Gaylord's father, the town lawyer and village skeptic, has returned, in fact, to the sterner mood and discipline of Puritanism (p. 18). Emily Dickinson had written in 1872 that the new latitudinarian preacher in New England "preached upon 'Breadth' till it argued him

13 *At.Mo.*, xxxi (March 1873), 360; xxxiii (March 1874), 370-371.
14 "A Shaker Village," *ibid.*, xxxvii (June 1876), 699, 702, 704.

narrow." Squire Gaylord would heartily have concurred. The villagers believe that the old infidel, in his perversity, has even worked to keep in permanent residence "the last of the rigidly orthodox ministers" of Equity (p. 25). Gaylord has rejected the church; yet he will not embrace the foolishness of Darwinian science. He survives as a dour old rationalist in a no-man's land of "old-fashioned deistical opinions" (p. 25).

Marcia's mother has fared worse. Unable to convert her husband to the church, she has ceased to attend. Her religious and emotional needs thwarted, she has become an outwardly self-sacrificing but inwardly calculating wife:

> Thrown in upon herself in so vital a matter as her religion, Mrs. Gaylord had involuntarily come to live largely for herself, though her talk was always of her husband. She gave up for him, as she believed, her soul's salvation, but she held him to account for the uttermost farthing of the price (p. 71).

Not surprisingly, then, Marcia, their only surviving child, possesses no moral footing whatever on which to build. With Bartley Hubbard, the cynical and irreligious young newspaper editor in town, she has attended the Saturday night "church sociables" and on Sunday has shopped around the liberal Equity churches, where religion "had largely ceased to be a fact of spiritual experience." For his part, Bartley knows that his career will actually prosper if he does not take religion seriously. Certain of his readers, depending on their prejudice, might object to his holding "fixed theological opinions" (p. 18).

Bartley and Marcia are soon betrothed, but the engagement of this undisciplined pair quickly erupts. Bartley retreats to the New England woods where he visits with the backwoods philosopher Kinney, a cook in the nearby lumber camp. Their talk soon comes around to religion— in the woods, in Equity, and in the country at large. Kinney serves chowder on Friday for the Canadian-

Catholic lumberjacks, for he " 'don't believe in interferin' with any man's religion, it don't matter what it is.' " The comment provokes Bartley into the following exchange on orthodoxy and the new liberalism:

"You ought to be a deacon in the First Church at Equity," said Bartley.

"Is that so? Why?" asked Kinney.

"Oh, they don't believe in interfering with any man's religion, either."

"Well," said Kinney, thoughtfully, pausing with the rolling-pin in his hand, "there's such a thing as being *too* liberal, I suppose."

"The world's tried the other thing a good while," said Bartley, with cynical amusement at Kinney's arrest.

It seemed to chill the flow of the good fellow's optimism, so that he assented with but lukewarm satisfaction.

"Well, that's so, too," and he made up the rest of his pies in silence (p. 84).

Once more, Bartley finds himself in uncongenial surroundings and, following a quarrel with Kinney, plans to pack and take the train to Boston the next night. But Marcia rushes to the depot at Junction, and they suddenly contract a minister who "contrived to make them man and wife." After this charade of holy matrimony, the preacher adds, " 'It seems as if there were something else,' " and then "bade them serve God, and let them out into the snowy night . . ." (p. 107).

The next evening, they are hurled into the alien city where Marcia has no ties of friendship, and Bartley knows but one person, his college classmate Ben Halleck. Howells here explores the mood of religious anarchy in Boston in far more depth than in *The Undiscovered Country*. The golden age of a settled, older Boston clearly exists no more. The interior of Ben Halleck's home recalls "the worst style of that most tasteless period of household art, which prevailed from 1840 to 1870," and the forms and colors which "abounded in a rich and horrible discord" become the esthetic correlative of religious discord within the house. The elder Hallecks have retained the village orthodoxy of their youth, but their daughter Olive has adopted an abrasive Unitarianism, while her crippled brother Ben, by missing Harvard to attend a college Down East, has been deprived of even the Unitarian compromise between "'radicalism and amateur episcopacy'" (p. 170). Amid his restless searchings for some form of meaningful duty, Ben discusses his religious doubt with Atherton, a Boston lawyer who hardly carries the credentials of spiritual counselor. Then there is Clara Kingsbury, the fatuous socialite who becomes Mrs. Atherton. Here, Howells reserves lighter treatment. "She had not yet found a religion that exactly suited her" (p. 179). Meanwhile, she has sponsored the "Indigent Children's Surf-Bathing Society," though less for her soul's need than for "social distinction" (p. 147). Privately, she has admitted that "indigent children were personally unpleasant to her" (p. 171).

Alienated and "spiritually poverty-stricken" in this new postwar Boston, Marcia suffers more than Bartley. Like the classic Medea, having stolen forth from father and home, she now resides in homesick exile. When her father visits the newlyweds in Boston, she entreats him not to leave. Afterwards, she lives from one emotional outburst to the next, as she and Bartley try fitfully to discover purpose and order in their urban lives. After their baby arrives, Marcia slowly understands some part of the problem. She asks the Hallecks to recommend a church for the baby that will impart the discipline (though not necessarily any belief) which she and Bartley have never owned. Her pathetic confusion briefly clears, however, in the comment to Mrs. Halleck:

"One mustn't be left too free. I've never had any one to control me, and now I can't control myself at the very times when I need to do it most, with—with—When I'm in danger of vexing—When Bartley and I—" (p. 202).

Bartley, too, after he has struggled to survive in the jungle of commercial Boston, ponders, albeit briefly, the need to attend to his religious slackness and initiate "some little moral reforms."

He had meant some time or other to have a religious belief of some sort, he did not much care what; since Marcia had taken the Hallecks' church, he did not see why he should not go with her, though he had never yet done so (pp. 262-263).

Their lives in Boston remain "free" of religious control, while the marriage moves inevitably toward divorce.

In the aftermath of the Boston action, Howells expands his canvas to include the "Indiana divorce case" of his original conception. The West offers no spiritual health for either Bartley or Marcia. During his more than two years of desertion, Bartley has grown fatter and more cynical. More broadly, the Midwest has failed to revitalize the anemic religious spirit in America. The Indiana village where Marcia arrives for the divorce wears "a more careless and unscrupulous air than the true New England village" (p. 348). The town loafers regard the lively divorce trial as welcome relief from the daily boredom of their lives.

In an ironic coda to this song of the open road, Howells moves Bartley to the Far West where he meets his dismal end. Bartley begins to publish in Arizona a weekly gossip sheet which gains immediate success among the townspeople. But he is killed when he chances to expose the domestic life of one of the esteemed local citizens. Bartley closes out his aimless, unhappy life by giving the people of Whited Sepulchre, Arizona, the low gossip and scandal they craved each week in his newspaper—an edition, be it noted, which appeared only on Sunday.

For Marcia, her child, and her father, the end is similarly irrevocable and bleak. They return to the house at the end of the street in Equity. There the Squire lapses into senility while he indulges his granddaughter as he once had her mother. Marcia keeps herself "closely housed" (p. 358). And her secret suitor, the woebegone Ben Halleck, ends his uncharted religious odyssey by entering the ministry. He has drifted back to the orthodoxy of his boyhood, a return in its way almost as hopeless as the Squire's infantilism. At the close of the novel, the crippled Ben remains both voyager and voyeur, luxuriating in the futile "sweet shame" of his sexual desire for Marcia as he departs for the unlikely sanctuary of a Down East church in the backwoods.

II

Ben Halleck's sexual confusion and psychic crippling—the products of his religious agony—return us to the world of Dr. Boynton and *The Undiscovered Country*. Indeed, Howells was prepared now to charge his religious theme with an interior pattern of sexual neurosis which would lead to far more profound consequences. The drama of *A Modern Instance* reverberated with the domestic upheavals of Euripidean tragedy, particularly the violent passions generated in the *Medea*, though it would carry echoes also from the *Electra* and *Orestes*. In his new Medea, Howells traced the stages of pathological jealousy, and related them to a destructive syndrome of incest within the house of Gaylord. At the same time, he deepened the tragedy by allowing his doomed Jason and Medea the illusion that they are free moral agents capable of circumventing their fate. Put another way, Howells had discovered in his Greek sources an esthetic analogue to a second feature of postwar morality—the withering effects of scientific determinism on traditional religious sanctions in America, and especially on the vaunted freedom of the American individual. Howells was able to arrive within the ten final chapters of this complex parable of freedom and fate in modern America before the immense output of creative energy, together with whatever private torments, led to his breakdown in November 1881. For these larger meanings of the novel, and perhaps also for a discovery of some part of Howells' creative impasse, one turns to the inner psychological drama which pervades *A Modern Instance.*

His later, Freudian-oriented readers did not realize how deeply Howells had absorbed the spirit of Greek life and Greek tragedy. Had they known, they might have returned to *A Modern Instance* and other novels to discover what it was in Howells they had missed. And they might have paid him the respect he clearly deserves for opening rather than thwarting the way to a more complex psychological novel in America. Ludwig Lewisohn served as spokesman for the group when he assailed Howells, in 1932, for prudish and genteel pussy-footing around the crucial facts of life between the sexes, for "falling into a kind of negative frenzy at the slightest suggestion of man's mammalian nature. . . ." According to Lewisohn, Howells became "as obsessed by sex as a fighting prohibitionist is by alcohol." To his credit, however, Lewisohn noted with apparent surprise and guarded praise that once, in *A Modern Instance,* "Howells struck a deeper and more impassioned note . . . than in any work before or after." What Lewisohn responded to most heartily was the portrait of Marcia Gaylord, whom he described as "a predatory and possessive female of a peculiarly dangerous and noxious kind, drawn with the most vivid energy and impassioned skill—an energy and skill that could spring from nothing less than an experience, personal or intimately vicarious, of the type."[15]

Since Lewisohn, a number of critics have commented briefly, and more perceptively, on the strongly passionate

[15] *Expression in America* (New York: Harper and Bros., 1932), pp. 244-249.

nature—even sexuality—of the heroine of *A Modern Instance*. William Gibson, in particular, has understood the complex psychology of Howells' heroine:

Marcia's violent outbursts of anger and her jealous accusations of infidelity are partly to be understood in terms of her strong tie to her father, whom she clearly resembles in her aquiline profile and more subtly resembles in her feelings and actions. These outbursts are also due to a rich emotional nature and to a strong sexual drive which is matched neither in intensity or timing to the easier, less fixed and centered libido of Bartley.[16]

Though Mr. Gibson does not link Marcia's "strong tie to her father" with her "strong sexual drive," one is tempted to make just such a connection. More clearly than in the portrait of Egeria Boynton, Howells was developing in Marcia Gaylord a remarkably accurate portrayal of the sexual neurosis which Carl Jung later would term the "Electra Complex."[17] Lewisohn may rightly have guessed that Howells had a "personal or intimately vicarious" experience with a Marcia Gaylord. More important for Howells, however, must have been the pervading correlatives with Greek philosophy and psychology which inspired this study of American character.

In the opening episode of *A Modern Instance*, Howells

16 P. xvi. Excellent though brief remarks on the portrait of Marcia Gaylord appear in Everett Carter, *Howells and the Age of Realism*, p. 151, and in Edwin Cady, *The Road to Realism*, p. 214. See also Cady, *The Realist at War* (Syracuse: Syracuse University Press, 1958), pp. 121-128, for valuable comments on Howells and pre-Freudianism.

17 In his "Versuch einer Darstellung der psychoanalytischen Theorie," 1913. Freud objected to the term, asserting that it implied an equivalent sexual pattern in both sexes. Freud maintained that the early castration complex behaved differently in boys than in girls, and that this difference caused Oedipal (Electra) feelings to develop later in girls. Professional antipathy is probably involved here; having given this technical qualification of the girl's sexual attraction to the father, Freud could as well have adopted Jung's term. Certainly it avoids the momentary confusion of Freud's "feminine Oedipus complex." See *The Complete Psychological Works of Sigmund Freud*, transl. from the German under the general editorship of James Strachey (London: Hogarth Press, 1955), XVIII (1920-1922), 155n; (1961), XXI (1927-1931), 229-230.

sounds the unmistakable chords of Greek family tragedy. Bartley Hubbard has just delivered Marcia Gaylord to her living room after an evening at a church sociable in Equity. After acquitting himself of a few mildly flirtatious pleasantries, Bartley prepares to leave. Howells tells us that Bartley's subtle flatteries have "filled [Marcia's] brain like wine. She moved dizzily as she took up the lamp to light him to the door." Bartley then surprises Marcia with a kiss, apparently the first in her Victorian maidenhood. Howells describes her extreme response: ". . . she panted; and after the door had closed upon him, she stooped and kissed the knob on which his hand had rested." But as she turns, "she started to see her father coming down the stairs with a candle in his hand" (p. 10). Like an avenging angel, or Fury, he "looked sharply down into her uplifted face." Howells next defines the close physical resemblance between father and daughter. The scene ends with this confrontation:

"Marcia," he asked, grimly, "are you engaged to Bartley Hubbard?"
The blood flashed up from her heart into her face like fire, and then, as suddenly, fell back again, and left her white. She let her head droop and turn, till her eyes were wholly averted from him, and she did not speak. He closed the door behind him, and she went upstairs to her own room; in her shame, she seemed to herself to crawl thither, with her father's glance burning upon her (p. 11).

This first chapter of *A Modern Instance* duplicates the compression with which Howells introduced the psychological drama of *The Undiscovered Country*. It also foreshadows the sexual disorder which will accompany the logic of determinism throughout the story.

To appreciate fully the range and insight of Howells' determinism, one turns first to the human drama of the undisciplined young newlyweds, Bartley and Marcia, who act out their marital tragedy with only brief awareness that their fate is controlled by a complex of forces both within and around them. In his heroine, Howells portrayed a pervasive neurosis which his Freudian detractors may have missed because the technique was too subtle and indirect. Writing for an age when literary taboos prevented forthright description of sexual relationships, Howells devised two methods of circumvention. First, he allowed the reader to establish the psychological pattern through occasional flashes of revealing detail throughout the novel, momentary glimpses into the deeply private recesses of Marcia's emotional life. Second, he employed symbolic strategies to suggest both the origins and the later stages of his heroine's unhappy married life.

One first assembles the explicit details, scattered throughout the novel, into a virtual case history of neurotic jealousy. Marcia's background led her to form a close attachment to her father and to reject her mother: "Her mother left her training almost wholly to her father; . . . and she held aloof from them both in their mutual relations, with mildly critical reserves" (p. 72). The opening scene clearly points to a dangerous result of the relationship. Marcia has stored up a powerful craving for physical affection, inhibited because directed toward her father, who is an impossible source of fulfillment physically. Now for the first time, she has released it in the company of a rival male. Her guilty feelings in the presence of her father are explicit. Emotionally unprepared for marriage, she impulsively elopes with Bartley after a brief courtship based almost entirely on ambivalent sexual attraction. The ambivalence arises from the rival claims of her father. After he has brought her belongings to Boston, he is about to leave.

"Why father! Are you going to *leave* me?" she faltered.

He smiled in melancholy irony at the bewilderment, the childish forgetfulness of all the circumstances, which her words expressed. "Oh, no! I'm going to take you with me" (p. 133).

After the baby is born, Marcia is anxious to see her father. She asks Bartley to write a letter requesting that her mother come to Boston. He knows better: "I will ask your father to come with her" (p. 186). She then innocently reveals to Bartley her conflicting feelings toward her father:

"Father was the first one I thought of—after you, Bartley. It seems to me as if baby came half to show me how unfeeling I had been to him. Of course, I'm not sorry I ran away and asked you to take me back, for I couldn't have had you if I hadn't done it; but I never realized before how cruel it was to father. He always made such a pet of me; and I know that he thought he was acting for the best" (pp. 186-187).

Bartley counters, with emotions one must partly guess at, by suggesting that the baby should be named after Squire Gaylord. " 'Bartley Hubbard,' she cried, 'you're the best man in the world!' 'Oh, no! Only the second-best,' suggested Bartley" (p. 188). After the Squire's next visit, this time to see the new baby,

They both undeniably felt freer now that he was gone. Bartley stayed longer than he ought from his work, in tacit celebration of the Squire's departure, and they were very merry together; but when he left her, Marcia called for her baby, and gathering it close to her heart, sighed over it, "Poor father! poor father!" (p. 194).

Paralleling Marcia's strong attachment to her father in these selected passages (the interested reader will discover more) is her rejection of her mother. Again, Howells has given what frequently appear to be obvious and consistent hints that he was reinforcing the Medean myth with Electra (or Oedipal) psychology. Mrs. Gaylord is first described rather harmlessly, in terms reminiscent of the mother of Daisy Miller. She has an "awe of her daughter and her judgments which is one of the pathetic idiosyncrasies of a certain class of American mothers" (p. 29). But Howells soon goes beyond social history to indicate that, in a subtler form, far more is involved between this mother and daughter. In a scene before the marriage, Marcia enters the room.

Mrs. Gaylord shrank back, and then slipped round her daughter and vanished. The girl took no notice of her mother, but went and sat down on her father's knee, throwing her arms round his neck, and dropping her haggard face on his shoulder (p. 74).

After the elopement, Marcia has banished her mother almost entirely from memory, barely asking about her when her father comes to Boston alone. She refuses to go home when her mother becomes ill (Marcia at this time, of course, is also distracted by Bartley's desertion). She finally arrives just before her mother's death, accepts it with no apparent emotion, and brings her father back to live with her in Boston.

Howells gave solidity and depth to this characterization of Marcia, also, through the method of symbolic revelation. After their betrothal, for example, Bartley discovers a ring on Marcia's finger:

"Ah, ha!" he said, after a while. "Who gave you this ring, Miss Gaylord?"
"Father, Christmas before last," she promptly answered, without moving. "I'm glad you asked," she murmured, in a lower voice, full of pride in the maiden love she could give him. "There's never been any one but you, or the thought of any one." She suddenly started away (p. 36).

After Squire Gaylord leaves Boston without waiting to see Bartley, the couple has a first marital quarrel. Bartley taunts Marcia about his disapproving father-in-law: "Did he come to take you home with him? Why didn't you go?" Though he runs to her at once to forestall the hurt of these words, Bartley receives a frigid rejection. Marcia's literal reaction is accompanied by symbolic overtones:

She thrust him back with a stiffly extended arm. "Keep away! Don't touch me!" She walked by him up the stairs without looking round at him, and he heard her close their door and lock it (p. 134).

Marcia's unhealthy closeness to her father, together with her continuing dependence on him, interferes with her responding to her husband in yet other instances. Howells again enlists covert symbolism. First are Marcia's caprices over saving money; another is in her insisting that Bartley become a lawyer. As early as their secret wedding supper, Marcia complains that they cannot afford to eat such a feast, but then cheers herself by thinking of her father:

> "Well, I know father will help us."
> "We sha'n't count on him," said Bartley. "Now *drop it!*" He put his arm round her shoulders and pressed her against him, till she raised her face for his kiss.
> "Well, I *will!*" she said, and the shadow lifted itself from their wedding feast . . . (p. 110).

During the first months in Boston, she is understandably upset by Bartley's uncertain income; yet her "frugality" becomes "a mania" and "frantic child's play." And after she has embittered Bartley with her thrift, she then joins him "in some wanton excess" (p. 145). Even when their means have entitled them to domestic comforts, Marcia continues to nag Bartley with her feelings of insecurity as his wife. During the climactic quarrel of their marriage, after she has wrongly blamed him for the appearance of Equity's fallen Hannah Morrison in Boston, Bartley goes upstairs. In a brief and apparently symbolic detail, Howells links Marcia's thrift to her increased coldness toward Bartley. In the bedroom, he observes that "the gas was burning low, as if she had lighted it and then frugally turned it down as her wont was" (p. 276).

Marcia also nags Bartley to return to the study of law, her father's profession. She has gathered from her father, even before Bartley elects to study law with him in Equity, that journalism is below the dignity of law, and a precarious profession at best (p. 143) . Even when Bartley may gain a secure niche in Boston journalism, Marcia says, "But I should only want that to be temporary, if you get it. I want you should go on with the law, Bartley. I've been thinking about that. I don't want you should always be a journalist" (p. 145) . They next quarrel after she has insisted that Bartley again take up the law (pp. 151-152) . Afterward, she promises never again to worry Bartley about the law, but he seems to know that she holds his profession beneath her father's (p. 255) and that if he should "take up the study of law in her father's office again," he would "fulfil all her wishes" (p. 273) . Too much might be imputed to this link with her father if it were not part of the pervasive pattern already discovered.

And indeed, one can not help noticing by now the interesting resemblances between the case of Marcia Gaylord and Freud's celebrated, and far more bizarre, case of Dora, reported in his "Analysis of a Case of Hysteria" (1905) . Freud soon recognized in his analysis of Dora the obverse of what he had previously discovered in the male Oedipus Complex. He termed Dora's abnormal sexual attraction to her father a characteristic of "those children whose constitution marks them down for a neurosis, who develop prematurely and have a craving for love."[18] Dora's mother was, somewhat like Marcia's, a woman with " 'housewife's psychosis.' " "The daughter looked down on her mother and used to criticize her mercilessly, and she had withdrawn completely from her influence" (p. 20) . When Dora became attracted to another man, she retreated to her love for her father "in order to protect herself against the feelings of love which were constantly pressing forward into consciousness" (p. 58) . Howells seems to have hinted at Marcia's periodic frigidity in *A Modern Instance* and related it, at least in part, to the same cause. He

[18] *Ibid.* (1953) , VII (1901-1905) , 56. All page numbers in the text refer to this edition.

comments on the seeds of Marcia's passionate jealousy, that she was so fond of her father "that she could not endure any rivalry in his affection" (p. 72). The passage helps to explain her wild accusations of infidelity whenever Bartley indulges his harmless, ego-gratifying flirtations with other women. *Projected* jealousy, as Freud terms it, suggests itself here; in her suppressed guilt over her failure to give Bartley undivided love, Marcia has projected faithlessness onto him. Again, how can Marcia love the man whom her beloved father so roundly condemns both early and late in the novel? Freud's Dora presented a similar problem. Freud asserts that in such instances, "thoughts in the unconscious live very comfortably side by side, and even contraries get on together without disputes—a state of things which persists often enough even in the conscious" (p. 61). And he suggests elsewhere that daughters with sexual disturbances of a Dora or a Marcia Gaylord will be attracted to a man either very similar to her father or at the other extreme (as with Bartley) very dissimilar. On one hand, Marcia urges Bartley to become a lawyer. But her marrying a man so unlike her father also allows certain emotional "contraries to get on together without disputes" —at least for brief periods at a time.

Freud's "Case of Hysteria" also grants an instructive parallel to the final portion of *A Modern Instance* after Bartley's desertion. Freud concluded the case of Dora by remarking hopefully about two dreams which he had analyzed late in her treatment:

> Just as the first dream represented her turning away from the man she loved to her father—that is to say, her flight from life into disease—so the second dream announced that she was about to tear herself free from her father and had been reclaimed once more by the realities of life (p. 122).

When Marcia feels the full impact of Bartley's leaving her, she begins, quite surprisingly, to undergo a salient transformation. She refuses to go home to her father when he now comes to Boston, and she displays hopeful signs that she is gaining some insight into her neurosis:

> The old man had to endure talk of Bartley to which all her former praises were as refreshing shadows of defamation. She required him to agree with everything she said, and he could not refuse; she reproached him for being with herself the cause of all Bartley's errors, and he had to bear it without protest. At the end he could say nothing but "Better come home with me, Marcia," and he suffered in meekness the indignation with which she rebuked him: "I will stay in Bartley's house till he comes back to me. If he is dead, I will die here" (p. 313).

Her wild hope for Bartley's eventual return notwithstanding, one feels that finally, to borrow Freud's words, she may be "reclaimed once more by the realities of life." Then Bartley's divorce notice from Indiana arrives.[19]

To end the novel, Howells did not devise for the young couple a reconciliation and new start in the West—an ending pleasantly tinged with pastoral sentiment and American myth. Instead, and with brutal honesty, he completed the predestined tragedy. Marcia emerges from her bewilderment as Howells rings in, like a *leitmotif*, the prophetic opening scene. Her features are again compared to her father's. She goes West with her father to hear him prosecute the divorce trial and see him lay open the old wounds with a fury that closes all avenues of reunion. Father, daughter, and child (the father's namesake) return to the old home in Maine. Even more strongly than

---

19 Some readers of my "Marcia Gaylord's Electra Complex," previously cited, have asked me to explore the possible relation between Howells' daughter Winny and Marcia Gaylord. This much may be ventured. In late 1881, Winny was receiving special treatment from Dr. James Jackson Putnam, pioneering specialist in nervous disorders at Harvard Medical School and later an acquaintance of Freud. Howells wrote to Twain that Putnam's prescribed cure of total rest was, in Howells' view, misfiring and that "the privation has thrown her thoughts back upon her, and made her morbid and hypochondriacal" (Sept. 11, 1881, *Twain-Howells Letters*, I, 373). The comment on Winny points, though only in part, to the behavior Howells assigned to Marcia during Bartley's desertion. Larger parallels do not obtain here, and Marcia, as I suggest, strangely benefits from her privation.

Freud's Dora, who had at times "identified herself with her mother by means of slight symptoms and peculiarities of manner" (p. 75) , Marcia "kept herself closely housed, and saw no one whom she was not forced to see." She had regressed to the point where she had become "as queer as her mother" (p. 358) . In the life of his new Medea, Howells gave his readers a modern instance of the irreversible fate which the ancient oracle had foretold to her Greek counterparts many centuries before.[20]

Marcia had grown up in a house deprived of any anchorage of religious faith. A creature of passion, she channeled her emotions to her father, and her home had become the setting for a prolonged and unhealthy oedipal relationship. Something remains to be said, in the Greek sense, about the House of Gaylord. Howells continues to probe the emotional undercurrents within this modern American family to suggest that Squire Gaylord, like Dr. Boynton, has been drawn to his daughter beyond the margin reserved for the concerned and protective father.

Howells first submerges the roots of this incest in the marriage of the elder Gaylords. Mrs. Gaylord had openly submitted herself to her husband's religion—or lack of it—but in the subsequent "disintegration of the finer qualities of her nature" (p. 71) , she extracted her own form of revenge:

Marriage is, with all its disparities, a much more equal thing than appears, and the meek little wife, who has all the advantage of public sympathy, knows her power over her oppressor, and at some tender spot in his affections or his nerves can inflict an anguish that will avenge her for years of coarser aggression (p. 71) .

---

[20] Beyond the parallels to Medea, Egeria Boynton, and Winny Howells, I suggest a fourth, the possible hints drawn from James's recent portrait of a "free" Isabel Archer. James's American heroine also throttles her emotional life in a marriage to a passionless egotist. One reviewer of *A Modern Instance* for *Athenaeum* (II [Oct. 7, 1882], 461) noticed that Isabel Archer's sickly admirer Ralph Touchett prefigures the role of serviceable and guilt-ridden Ben Halleck.

Subconsciously, she had turned her religious deprivation into sexual resentment toward her husband: "It was not apathy that she had felt when their children died one after another, but an obscure and formless exultation that Mr. Gaylord would suffer enough for both" (pp. 71-72). Howells' psychology here closely resembles Medea's motive when she killed her sons to rend the heart of Jason. Finally, Mrs. Gaylord turned her last-born, Marcia, over to Squire Gaylord, in effect to say that she rejected the child of what was to be her last pregnancy. Only once in the novel does Howells depict any explicit affection between the parents. During the excitement of Marcia's engagement, the Squire gives way to "his repressed emotion" and kisses his wife; "but he spared her confusion by going out to his office at once, where he stayed the whole afternoon" (p. 42). Drawn closely to Marcia, and she to him, "it charmed and flattered her father to have her so fond of him that she could not endure any rivalry in his affection" (p. 72). He apparently meant to preserve her in the role of daddy's girl. He took her on his trips, lavished gifts upon her, and did not encourage her to gain independence by developing household talents or acquiring a systematic education.

Squire Gaylord also plays knowingly on Marcia's jealousy to alienate her from her suitor Bartley. In her presence, after Bartley's flight with Henry Bird, Squire Gaylord questions Bartley pointedly about any intimacies with Hannah Morrison. The strategy works. Marcia, "suppressing a passion which had turned her as rigid as stone," returns Bartley's ring. Meanwhile, her father, in strange camaraderie with Bartley, confides that " 'I drew you out a little on that Hannah Morrison business,' " and admits that for Marcia he knew " 'that's the one thing she couldn't bear . . .' " (p. 64). When she presently rejoins her father, sitting on his lap, he tells her " 'I'm glad to have you back again' " (p. 74). After she runs away with Bartley, he enjoins her to be a good wife, but he continues to enjoy her dependence on him. The neglected Mrs. Gaylord, we are told, resents this close relationship "with that curious jealousy a wife feels for her husband's indulgence of their daughter" (p. 232). Squire Gaylord also prefers to believe, or have his jealous Marcia believe, that Bartley has been consistently unfaithful. The reader knows better. When Bartley's divorce notice arrives from Indiana, Marcia has no vengeful feelings toward Bartley. So her father, who does have and who knows how to kindle them in Marcia, inflames her imagination by fashioning Bartley into an unfaithful Jason. Let your "'perjured bigamist'" go free, he taunts his daughter.

The languor was gone from Marcia's limbs. As she confronted her father, the wonderful likeness in the outline of their faces appeared. . . . One impulse animated those fierce profiles, and *the hoarded hate* in the old man's soul seemed to speak in Marcia's thick whisper, "I will go" (p. 329, italics mine).

At the divorce trial, Marcia is far less vindictive than her father and objects to the Orestes-like hatred with which he prosecutes his blood-feud against Bartley. So rebuked by Marcia, Squire Gaylord "fixed a ghastly, bewildered look upon his daughter, and fell forward across the table at which he stood" (p. 355). Palsy-stricken and senile, he returns to Equity to live out his final days under the motherly attentions of his daughter.[21]

The pattern of this modern marriage, doomed by the pervading religious and sexual confusion, enlarges further to reveal other reaches of Howells' tragic vision. Time and again, Marcia and Bartley heroically vow to alter, or reverse, the direction of their doomed existence and to shape their undisciplined lives. Despite her unpromising

21 Thomas F. Walsh observes the resemblance between Squire Gaylord and Hawthorne's sexually morbid and vengeful Chillingworth. Mr. Walsh speculates briefly on possible further links with *The Scarlet Letter*—Marcia with Hester Prynne and Flavia with Pearl. See *The Explicator*, XXIII (1965), item 59.

background for marriage and her uncontrollable jealousy, Marcia can still inform Bartley, at their betrothal, that she has made a " 'resolve never to do or say a thing that could lower your opinion of me' " (p. 35), and adds, " 'I shall always *try* to make you good and happy . . .' " (p. 36). They have scarcely settled in Boston when Marcia vents her jealousy of women Bartley has previously known or happens to meet. When he begins to write his account of Kinney's logging camp, Marcia recalls at once the flirtatious woman Bartley had once mentioned meeting there.

> "Look here, Marsh!" he said, "didn't you promise you'd stop that?"
> "Yes," she murmered, while the color flamed into her cheeks.
> "And will you?"
> "I *did* try—" (p. 125).

On their first night in Boston, they attend a performance of Boucicault's *The Colleen Bawn*. During the play, Marcia has a premonition. For her, the drama serves as an oracle, foretelling in the characters Eily and Hardress Cregan the failure of her own marriage. Bartley is hugely amused: "He went on making a mock and a burlesque of her tragical hallucination till she laughed with him at last" (p. 116). The "tragic hallucination" soon turns into accurate prophecy as their marriage begins to deteriorate. Even so, Marcia continues to resolve that she will change her character and behavior and defy the warning. When she returns from a separate vacation in Equity, having reassessed their marriage, she promises Bartley, " 'I'm going to do differently, after this. I shall believe that you've acted for the best,—that you've not meant to do wrong in anything,—and I shall never question you or doubt you any more' " (p. 269). Inevitably, a short while later she grows passionately jealous and accuses Bartley of staying in the city during the vacation because (though unknown to him) Equity's Hannah Morrison had recently drifted to Boston.

Marcia not only tries to alter her fated marriage, but also holds herself responsible in her failure. Both concerns, deeply rooted in Howells' troubled sense of moral responsibility, reflect as well the heroic stance of the classic Greek hero or heroine. When Ben Halleck delivers home a drunken Bartley, Marcia blames herself for the earlier fight, which had been, in fact, a mutual contest of sexual accusations. It had been followed by her locking the bedroom door again, and Bartley's spending a night on the town. " 'I did it,—yes, I did it!' " she tells Halleck. " 'It's my fault!' " (p. 218). When her jealous rage inspires the final quarrel, and Bartley deserts to go West, Marcia continues to rebuke herself rather than Bartley: " 'I said things to him that night that were enough to drive him crazy. I was always the one in fault . . .' " (p. 303). In the final glimpse of Marcia in the novel, upon the news that Bartley has been murdered in Arizona, Howells comments that "her sorrow was not unmixed with self-accusal as unavailing as it was passionate, and perhaps as unjust" (p. 360).

Bartley shares with Marcia this heroic confusion, as one can rightly term it, between the moral agency of the individual and the forces which intervene to shape and control him. During their initial evening together early in the story, Bartley proudly recounts to Marcia "the processes by which he had formed his own character" (p. 10). Howells presently sketches in the actual processes which shaped Bartley's early life and character. He had been a pampered orphan with innate "smartness" who received virtually no moral training. He has grown into a sarcastic and independent bachelor. But his self-reliance is very dubious. He does not decide to propose to Marcia; instead, he comes to her to be pampered after a night of bad dreams growing out of his undigested mince pie. "With his nerves unstrung, and his hunger for sympathy, he really believed that he had come to tell her [that he loved her]" (p. 30). Nor does he intend to strike his office helper Henry Bird, the act which precipitates his departure from Equity. "The demons, whatever they were, of anger, remorse, pride, shame, were at work in Bartley's heart . . . , and he returned the blow as instantly as if Bird's touch had set the mechanism of his arm in motion" (p. 56).

Though predetermined forces, accompanied by chance, are continuously present to undermine their marriage, Bartley, like Marcia, resolves to forestall or undo the fated course of events. " 'If ever I do anything to betray your trust in me—' " is his fragmented vow to her after their unplanned meeting and precipitate wedding at the railroad junction (p. 109). Though he has required from women only the mild flirtations of letter-writing and inoffensive "love-making" to flatter his ego, Bartley tries to accept the unwilled chores of a family provider. Just before the baby arrives, "he did his best to be patient with [Marcia's] caprices and fretfulness, and he was at least manfully comforting and helpful, and instant in atonement for every failure" (pp. 185-186). The baby drives one more wedge into the marriage, Marcia falls into more jealous rages, and the pressures of yellow journalism mount during the next year. But Bartley is able to gain a business foothold in Boston. Alone in the summer of 1876, he proposes "some little moral reforms," for, as Howells explains,

no man wholly escapes the contingencies in which he is confronted with himself, and sees certain habits, traits, tendencies, which he would like to change for the sake of his peace of mind hereafter (p. 262).

Unfortunately, Bartley alone can no more affect the destined conditions of their life in Boston than can Marcia, who is at the same time making her lonely resolves in Equity.

At other times, they pledge together that they will create order and harmony in their marriage. The evening when they arrive in Boston to begin their life together, Bartley assures Marcia, " 'No use being afraid of *anything*, so long as we're good to each other' " (p. 113). Howells adds, "They talked a long time together, and made each other loving promises of patience. They confessed their faults, and pledged each other that they would try hard to overcome them" (p. 114). After the early fight over Bartley's going into the law, he leaves and happens to receive his first secure job. Marital peace follows, and he says, " 'It doesn't seem as if we should ever quarrel again, does it?' " Marcia replies, " 'No, no! We never shall' " (p. 161). The morning after Bartley's drunken night on the town, both are full of remorse and new determination. " 'We were both to blame,' " Bartley allows, but Marcia insists that the blame is all her own, for she broke her promise not to mention Hannah Morrison—" 'but I couldn't seem to help it.' " Bartley assures her that " 'it shall never happen again,' " convinced that now " 'we've both had a lesson' " (p. 222). A futility both heroic and tragic marks these attempts to gather strength from each other. Bartley begs Marcia, in a circular bit of reasoning, to supply the moral "inspiration" in his life by having "faith" in him (p. 114). Having no resources of discipline or religious strength to draw on, they "confess" to each other, pledge "devout faith" in each other, beg for mutual "forgiveness," and so on. Late in the novel, during a poignant scene after Bartley has deserted, Marcia has "prophesied" his return and "consecrated" the expected moment. She folds the baby's hands, not her own, and makes "her pray God to take care of poor papa and send him home soon to mama. She was beginning to canonize him" (p. 312).

Howells imparts to the action and characterization of *A Modern Instance*, then, a pervasive climate of Greek tragedy. Despite his comment at the outset, that "youth commands its fate" in America (p. 4), he depicts the failure of every resolution his young American couple makes. Fate overturns resolve as if in ironic counterpoint throughout the novel. Marcia vows to Bartley that she will make him happy; he promptly happens onto a main source of their destined unhappiness by noticing that she is wearing a ring given by her father (p. 36). Bartley asserts that he will " 'try to be all you expect of me' " and never to do " 'anything unworthy of your ideal' " (p. 44); he then runs accidentally into the sleigh of Hannah Morrison and provokes a jealous reaction from Marcia together with a prophecy: " 'I know she'll make trouble for you, somehow' " (p. 47). Bartley promises himself that if Henry Bird survives their fight, "he would try to be a better man in every way" (p. 58); but Marcia and her father soon discover that Hannah Morrison was the subject of the fight, and Marcia angrily breaks their engagement. And climactically, after recovering his bets on Tilden, Bartley tearfully resolves to himself that he will quit his "life of temptation," will ask the pardon of men he has injured as a journalist, and will start over in the Maine village and study law with Squire Gaylord. Just then, Marcia bursts into the room, "her eyes . . . dilated, and her visage white with the transport that had whirled her far beyond the reach of reason." She has seen Hannah Morrison walking the street below. The effect on Bartley is to shatter permanently "the frail structure of his good resolutions . . ." (p. 274).

Edwin Cady has estimated that the 1,466 manuscript pages Howells had completed by November 1881, before his seven-week breakdown, would have carried him just through this last quarrel before Bartley heads West. While one can never hope to recount in specific detail the causes for the "long worry and sleeplessness from overwork" which led to Howells' collapse, surely it is revealing that in the scene describing Bartley's departure, Howells forcibly upends the fatal logic of Bartley's defection. He first describes Bartley's blind and unintentional movements after Marcia has taken their child and fled the house. "He could not think, he must act," and "He did not know what his purpose was, but it developed itself" (p. 276). Even when he has bought the ticket to Chicago, there is "as yet nothing definite in his purpose" (p. 277). On the train to Cleveland, Bartley is "insensibly" preparing, rather than choosing, to return to Marcia:

> . . . all the mute, obscure forces of habit, which are doubtless the strongest forces in human nature, were dragging him back to her. Because their lives had been united so long, it seemed impossible to sever them, though their union had been so full of misery and discord . . . (p. 277).

Confronted by these "forces," Bartley has to "own to himself that he was beaten," and at Cleveland he waits in line to buy a ticket to Boston. But chance has now dealt the final blow, for someone has stolen his wallet. Howells then startles the reader with the final sentence of the chapter: "Now he could not return; nothing remained for him but the ruin *he had chosen*" (p. 277, italics mine). Even the reader unacquainted with Howells' conflicts over moral freedom and scientific naturalism will bolt at this rupture in the tragic consistency of the action, and suspect that what lies here is some form of lacerating doubt over man's ability to choose and control the design of his life.

I am suggesting that the crisis in Howells' mental and physical health must have been closely linked to the contradiction between freedom and fate he had expressed in the baffling final pages of chapter thirty-one. He was unwilling to grant that complex environmental and psychological forces can obliterate the moral distinction imputed to human activity. Yet Howells by the early 1880s had developed an enlarging imagination of disaster, intensified by acute worry over the strange decline in the health of his daughter Winny. Through each work of the 1870s, as he came to possess the talent and insight of a novelist chiefly concerned with human character, he had suspected more and more that occult psychological pressures lay behind human behavior and physical well-being. It is a salient fact that, as early as 1871, Howells had singled out for special mention in the senior Holmes's *Mechanism in Thought and Morals* the "analogy between mental defects and peculiarities of other organs. . . ."[22] Ten years later, he now suspected that Winny's physical pain may have been traceable to unknown psychological origins. What he was discovering through the aid of Holmes, William James, and his own private interpretation of dreams would give dramatic impetus to *A Modern Instance*, but the conclusions had become too uncomfortable for Howells to accept. To a degree, perhaps, he thus overworked himself, as his troubled Bartley did to effect "that strange separation of the intellectual activity from the suffering of the soul, by which the mind toils on in a sort of ironical indifference to the pangs that wring the heart . . ." (p. 67).

Finally, one can enlist hindsight and remark that when Howells selected for his model the work of Euripides, the Greek master of abnormal psychology, he had chosen a tragic analogue to modern determinism which would inevitably lead him to disturbing and painful questions. Howells' study of Greek life and Greek tragedy betrays a divided response. Here is not the place to pursue in detail the Greek influence on Howells, but the central difficulty can be isolated. With other Boston Hellenists, notably Charles Eliot Norton, Howells could urge Athenian wisdom as an example for American democracy—the older moderation, order, simplicity, humanism, and social justice, all nurtured by a vigorous physical life in the open air. It was this Greece of adventure and order which helped to

22 *At.Mo.*, XXVII (May 1871), 654.

form Howells' imagination as a boy in Ohio reading Goldsmith's *History of Greece* and rereading Greek myths "twenty or thirty times."[23] And it was this same Greece which would reappear in the 1890s to grant the model for his Altrurian fables of democracy, simplicity, and justice for a capitalist society in America.

But Howells understood, as well, the interior world of the Greeks, the religion and psychology which formed the basis for the Greek view of human tragedy. However noble man might be, however heroically he asserted his proud will and resisted his preordained fall, man's life was nevertheless determined by the fated ordering of circumstance. Howells had begun to read Greek drama in earnest as early as 1862. But he felt the deeper relevance of Greek tragedy ten years later, when it began to intersect his concerns over religious controversy in America.

In his review of Hippolyte Taine's *Art in Greece*, in February 1872, Howells did not comment on Greek views of determinism, but did object to Taine's own deterministic theory of artistic creation. He noted that Taine tried to predict the art from the conditions of an era "just as Agassiz can sketch you off a portrait of our affectionate forefathers the ichthyosaurus or the pterodactyl, after glancing at their fossilized foot-tracks." Some months later Howells again rebuked Taine for his "distorted philosophy" of aesthetic determinism in the *Notes on England*. Howells' reading of the legacy of the Greeks and his considerations on the art theory of Taine may have been leading him into both the role of determinism in human life and the roots of culture in an epoch of civilization. The next month, he considered the career of Lincoln as it had been suggested in Ward H. Lamon's *The Life of Abraham Lincoln*. In a long passage, Howells used Lincoln as example to argue the primacy of race, self-determination, and Divine (rather than natural) se-

[23] *A Boy's Town*, pp. 172, 80. See also *My Literary Passions*, pp. 10-11.

lection. He played down the implications of environmental determinism and Darwinist adaptation in human life:

It will not do to say that in no other circumstances than those which attended his development was Lincoln possible, but it is certain that he was the product of a state of things that, according to all our theories of transmitted qualities, of civilization, of education, ought not to have produced the man he was, but a brutal, ignorant clown.

Lincoln gave Americans the example of the rough-hewn, self-made man, "an irrefutable witness that the virtue is in the race, and not in mere continuous culture." The case of Lincoln, Howells wrote, "may even intimate that Divine Providence still concerns itself with human affairs, and selects its instruments by tests which the sciences do not know."[24]

The stage was now set for Howells' genuine plunge into Greek drama. During the next year and a half, he appears to have read, or reread, a sizeable amount of Greek tragedy in translation. In the spring of 1875, he not only witnessed Francesca Janauschek's performance in *Medea* but also completed a long essay on the Italian classical dramatist Alfieri. The essay indicated months of preparation and an extensive knowledge of Greek tragedy. Howells translated long portions of Alfieri's *Orestes*, and accompanied the translation with highly significant commentary. His observations on the inexorable logic of Greek fate, and on the psychological world of Greek tragedy, read like a set of stage directions for the mood of his "Indiana divorce case."

When you read Orestes, you find yourself attendant upon an imminent calamity, which nothing can avert or delay. In a solitude like that of dreams, those hapless phantasms, dark types of remorse, or cruel ambition, of inexorable revenge, move swiftly on the fatal end. They do not grow or develop on the imagination; their character is stamped at once, and

[24] *At.Mo.*, XXIX (Feb. 1872), 241; XXX (Aug. 1872), 240; XXX (Sept. 1872), 366.

they have but to act it out. There is no lingering upon epi-
sodes, no digressions, no reliefs. They cannot stir from that
spot where they are doomed to expiate or consummate their
crimes; one little day is given them, and then all is over.[25]

Although Howells' "New Medea," which he told Norton
was under way in September of the next year, failed to
come forth, Howells was working and meditating in the
vein of Greek determinism and modern tragedy. Two
instances can be cited. He proudly told Lawrence Barrett,
the main actor in Howells' adaptation of Estébanez's
Yorick's Love, that the play had been recommended by a
Harvard instructor to his class "as the best illustration they
could have of what he had been saying to them about
Greek tragedy."[26] And he wrote a revealing, non-fictional
piece before *A Modern Instance* which underscored his
concern over scientific determinism as an explanation of
human depravity. "Police Report," begun in the summer
of 1880, was completed concurrently with Howells' initial
roughing out of *A Modern Instance*. He had visited a
police court on two occasions and, despite his uncertain
tone, in which satire alternates with compassion, Howells
was clearly trying to account for these fallen types in the
Boston of the early 1880s. He steered a nimble course
between scientific adaptation in the natural world, on the
one hand, and the claims of moral freedom and Divine
Providence on the other. In his pity for a prostitute, who
had been put on public display in the courtroom, Howells
wrote, "The divine life which is in these poor creatures,
as in the best and purest, seemed to be struggling back to
some relation and likeness to our average, sinful humanity. . . ." He explained these fallen members of a
callow society as moral agents in God's merciful hands:

Humanity adjusts itself to all conditions, and doubtless God
forsakes it in none, but still shapes it to some semblance of

[25] "Alfieri," *ibid.*, xxxv (May 1875), 547.
[26] Jan. 25, 1880, in Princeton University Library.

health in its sickness, of order in its disorder, of righteousness in its sin.[27]

Yet an unreconstructed Bartley Hubbard in these same months would be left abandoned to the "ruin he had chosen."

So Howells' religious conflict in the period before *A Modern Instance,* and during its composition, had embraced not only the moral slackness of sectarian liberalism but also the irreducible "factuality" of a new scientific determinism. Perhaps this moral indecision within Howells also helps to explain why, when he returned to the novel following his illness, he developed more fully the character of Atherton, his Boston lawyer. Atherton has been an easily maligned figure in later Howells criticism. He may be worth our closer attention. Granted that he comes through as a confused arbiter of the norms of modern morality. Was he introduced to be a spokesman for Howells? Or was the confused Atherton merely Howells' type of modern man? Or perhaps in certain ways even an ironic self-parody of Howells himself? Or a Medean Chorus figure? (Scholars of Greek drama have remarked that *Medea* is the Euripidean drama in which the Chorus, while providing a moral voice, participates least in the action.) In any event, what appears to have been painful indecision in the narrative voice just before could now be effectively relocated in Atherton, a dramatic characterization of moral uncertainty and physical inactivity.

Atherton consistently announces a moral principle derived either from sentimental fiction, a diluted Swedenborgianism, or a proper bachelor's meager experience with "realities." He then confounds himself when he probes the action directly. For example, he discusses with Ben Halleck the Hubbards' marriage and locates with certainty a "blame on both sides" (p. 228). But as the two bachelors

[27] *At.Mo.,* XLIX (Jan. 1882), 15.

talk, Atherton admits that "married life is as much a mystery to us outsiders as the life to come, almost. The ordinary motives don't seem to count; it's the realm of unreason" (p. 229). After Atherton marries the wealthy, fatuous Clara Kingsbury, he has a willing audience to his bland observations on Bartley and Marcia's shortcomings in family status and "the flower of implanted goodness." A certain paralysis of the intellect sets in during these remarks, however, for by now he has been Marcia's legal advisor and knows some of the facts about her life. As he considers more closely the conditions of her marriage, Atherton becomes lost in a comically incoherent lecture on cause-and-effect, blame, choice, discipline, will, heredity, and fate:

"But somehow the effects follow their causes. In some sort they chose misery for themselves,—we make our own hell in this life and the next,—or it was chosen for them by undisciplined wills that they inherited. In the long run their fate must be a just one" (p. 333).

By the end of the novel, Atherton has privately experienced a fair amount of this "realm of unreason" which is the domain of marriage. He wonders, by then, what marital advice he can offer the lovelorn Ben Halleck. Almost as bewildered as Marcia had been in a previous interview with him, he closes off the novel by echoing precisely, and with unwitting irony, her earlier moral confusion: " 'Ah, I don't know! I don't know!' " (pp. 302, 362).

Atherton is too complex a characterization, however, to allow our writing him off as an abject fool. True, he mouths his moral platitudes to Clara in their new Back Bay home while he lifts "with his slim, delicate hand, the cup of translucent china, and [drains] off the fragrant Souchong, sweetened, and tempered with Jersey cream to perfection" (p. 333). But one cannot dismiss completely one set of Atherton's smug observations, several times re-iterated by Howells, that divorce is a destructive element in a modern society already declining into selfishness and disorder. Atherton may be an overly facile combination of Greek and Yankee; yet he touches on the more profound elements of American civilization which, for Howells, paralleled the ideals of moderation and order in the age of Pericles. He passes judgment on the decline of Marcia and Bartley, together with the sad involvement of Marcia's silent, crippled suitor Ben Halleck:

"You know how I hate anything that sins against order, and this whole thing is disorderly. It's intolerable, as you say. But we must bear our share of it. We're all bound together. No one sins or suffers to himself in a civilized state,—or religious state . . ." (p. 334).

Though he is "playing with his teaspoon" at the time, Atherton the proper Bostonian senses here, beyond a priggish *noblesse oblige*, the link between religious decline in America and the attendant moral chaos of modern society, which he has briefly experienced in his limited involvement with the Hubbards. He has perceived the symptoms of the disease, though he does not understand the causes— the decline of religion and civilization in the Equity village, in the New England woods, in the unproper new Boston, and in the postwar Midwest and Far West. While this larger education does not become Atherton's, it is the fictional experience of the reader of *A Modern Instance*. Howells had staged the marriage and divorce of Marcia and Bartley as the particular symptom, as the "modern instance," of larger disruptions in American civilization that produce undisciplined marriages which, in turn, lead to divorce. *A Modern Instance*, it can now be seen, is not merely a darker version of pastoral than *The Undiscovered Country*. More accurately, it is a version of anti-pastoral.

III

Sanctuary and convalescence for shattered spirits like Bartley's and Marcia's might have rested in a pastoral re-

treat from civilized disorder, such as Ford and Egeria had
found in the Shaker countryside of *The Undiscovered
Country*. But Equity, nestled in the New England landscape, is a counterfeit of a village America. It is fast being
overrun by standardization. During her two winters at
school, Marcia could see small difference between Equity
girls and those from Augusta and Bangor. Unlike her Greek
counterpart, this new Medea is no barbarian. For the more
citified Bartley, Equity offers no change or relief. Rather,
he moulds the *Equity Free Press* to conform to the racy
urban newspapers. And the citizenry willingly approves.
Indeed, when he lauded the pastoral virtues of Equity in
thinly veiled burlesque by singling out "its advantages as a
summer resort, and had published a series of encomiums
upon the beauty of its scenery and the healthfulness of its
air and water," the perceptive townsmen of Equity had
applauded the cynical spirit of it all. "In all this, the color
of mockery let the wise perceive that Bartley saw the joke
and enjoyed it, and it deepened the popular impression of
his smartness" (p. 22). But the joke is serious, for Howells
clearly depicts the suffocating stinginess of life in "Equity"
—a misnomer as sadly ironic as the "Free Press" and "Gaylord." Howells re-enforces this pattern of decline in the
American village with the example of the Morrison family
—the drunken father, the wild daughter who will migrate
to the streets of Boston. Again, the Hallecks sent Ben to a
small college Down East to grant him the moral advantages
no longer issuing from Harvard. He returned unfit for
either the church, the law, or the family leather business.
Already a physical cripple, he had become a moral cripple
as well. Bartley had also attended the same college and
emerged, says Ben, " 'with no more moral nature than a
base-ball' " (p. 170). Small wonder, then, that Equity provides no summer haven for Bartley and Marcia during
their life in the city. On the occasion when they both
return, and then picnic in a "pretty glen" several miles

from the village, the flirtatious Mrs. Macallister enters the pastoral scene once again. (She had disrupted Bartley's earlier visit in Kinney's woods.) Ben Halleck then accompanies Marcia to a ridge of rocks called "Devil's Backbone," a site which appropriately suggests both the unholy fires of Marcia's jealousy and the rather precarious sanctuary of American nature. Marcia and Bartley experience not emotional health but, instead, increased tension in this return to the village landscape of Equity.

Nor does the New England woods become a temporary refuge from the pressures of civilization. After his fight with Henry Bird and rejection by Marcia and her father, Bartley visits his acquaintance Kinney, who cooks in the nearby logging camp and has made weekly treks into the village to admire Bartley's smartness. To Kinney's facile pronouncement that "any man engaged in intellectual pursuits wants to come out and commune with nature, every little while," Bartley replies with less optimism, ". . . if you're not in first-rate spiritual condition, you're apt to get floored, if you undertake to commune with nature" (p. 82) . Howells is echoing the warning Emerson had given in his essay *Nature* to the man "disunited with himself": "He cannot be a naturalist until he satisfies all the demands of the spirit." Even so, Bartley might have received certain restorative influences from life in the woods but for the arrival of guests from the city. The sylvan revel they hold in the woods is a foolish "cotillion" staged in Kinney's cabin, while incongruously, "in at the window, thrown open for air, came the wild cries of the forest . . ." (p. 94) .

Bartley receives no benefit from the New England woods thirty years after Thoreau went there for spiritual rebirth and forty years after Emerson became a transparent eyeball there. Nor does Kinney qualify as a latter-day Thoreau. An aimless drifter, he is a travesty of the self-reliant American backwoodsman. Originally a rural youth in Maine, he headed West carrying with him a "gross and ridiculous optimism" based on "the metaphysics of Horace Greeley," together with "a few wildly interpreted maxims of Emerson" (p. 80). When the Pacific railroad brought an end to the California frontier, he returned to his Maine woods as a cook for the logging interests. But he has kept his transcendental faith. Like Thoreau, he has read his classics in the woods—Virgil, Horace, Goethe (" 'old Gutty' ") — as well as Darwin and Agassiz. To his Emersonian illusions of free opportunity, these authors have enabled Kinney to compile, in unconscious opposition, a patchwork of theories on the deterministic effects on human behavior produced by coffee, tea, molasses, beans, and other " 'brain food' " (p. 85). Bartley later steals these and other bizarre ramblings and mockingly titles them "Confessions of an Average American" (p. 257) after Kinney arrives in Boston in his customary role of defeated pioneer. He has been ruined after experimenting with health foods from which he intended to produce a rejuvenation of the loggers: " 'I calculated to bring those fellows out in the spring physically vigorous and mentally enlightened' " (p. 248). Not surprisingly, the loggers did not share his zest for this strange pastoral restorative.

In Boston, the same spiritual enervation pervades urban life—in the home, church, society, and business, not to mention Clara Kingsbury's "Surf-Bathing Society" for the children of Boston's great unwashed. Like the Athens which Euripides watched in its moral decline after the Peloponnesian War, Boston, too, has grown vulgar and callous after America's own civil war. Spokesmen for an older morality and taste have been silenced. Given his thin moral training, Bartley easily adapts within months to the editorial practices of Witherby and the Boston *Events*. To rival editor Ricker, a lonely advocate of dignity and public service in journalism, Bartley drunkenly expounds on the emerging newspaper of his dreams. It would not be a crusading "religious" newspaper, but instead would faithfully reflect the vice, crime, and scandal in the community. It would describe the state of politics, religion, and business while making no attempt to reform or elevate society. For as Bartley has accurately sensed, a newspaper turned moral will lose the forthrightly " 'dirty fellows' " at the same time that it disappoints the whited-sepulchre portion of its readers (pp. 210-211). Meanwhile, Bartley decays in the tensely competitive world of business, which leads him to drink (" 'it takes my nerves down at the end of a hard week's work' ") and to grow fat. The moralistic Ricker translates Bartley's obesity into moral degeneracy. He views the "increasing bulk" not as "an increase of wholesome substance, but a corky, buoyant tissue, materially responsive to some sort of moral dry-rot" (p. 243).

Howells depicts Boston, then, as a modern urban instance of the decline of moral civilization in America, and the picture, in pastoral terms, is the more hopeless after the reader has experienced the lessened natural vigor yielded by the New England countryside. Perhaps renewed hope and reconciliation for Marcia and Bartley lie to the West. In the final divorce action, Howells might have reversed their unhappy lives and fashioned a new career for his young couple, as in *The Undiscovered Country*. The reader does not abandon hope for this romantic reversal of the fated flow of events even to the point where Squire Gaylord collapses and may remove his influence from the marriage. The hope is strengthened when one recalls that Whitman in his own postwar *Democratic Vistas* had also castigated urban corruption, but then had projected a revitalized America in the Western village.

But the ominous signs appear already on the route westward to Indiana. At the Indianapolis station, Marcia encounters old Kinney, still pursuing opportunity while expounding his deterministic theory of " 'brain-food' " (p. 345). When the train arrives at the destination of Tecumseh, Indiana, the town gives small evidence of the wholesome individuality which characterized the earlier West.

Nor does one recognize the healthy wildness of the Indian for whom the town has been named. The residential section bears touches of Southern, as well as New England, migration; moreover, it betrays "a more careless and unscrupulous air than the true New England village . . ." (p. 348).[28] Presently, Marcia and her daughter, with the Squire, Olive, and Ben Halleck, arrive in downtown Tecumseh,

a section of conventional American city, with flat-roofed brick blocks, showy hotel, stores, paved street, and stone sidewalks [all of which] expressed the readiness of Tecumseh to fulfil the destiny of every Western town, and become a metropolis at a day's notice (p. 348).

When Bartley appears in the courtroom, with a "tender pink" complexion and a physiognomy more obese than two or three years before in Boston, one realizes that Howells has made his comment on the failure of the West to re-invigorate the fallen hero. And in the unremitting aftermath, Bartley moves his journalistic ventures to a new frontier in the Far West, where he finds a ready-made market for his "spicy" weekly, the Sunday paper he begins to publish in Whited Sepulchre, Arizona. Howells goes even further in underscoring this dreary standardization of American life. A citizen whom Bartley has maligned "takes the war-path" presumably in the fashion of the American Indian whom his fellow townsmen have routed from Whited Sepulchre. After Bartley has been killed, a local reporter easily fills the vacuum of yellow journalism left by his predecessor. He reports the death of Bartley with the same "cynical lightness" which Bartley himself would have enjoyed.

[28] Though Howells had recently made a trip to Indiana to ensure the verisimilitude of this final setting, he may have been indebted also to insights gained from reading Edward Eggleston's *The Hoosier Schoolmaster* ten years before. "Some of the worst characteristics of the West have been inherited from the slave-holding South," he observed in his review of Eggleston's novel, "—from Virginia and North Carolina and Maryland,—out of which the poor whites emigrated with their vicious squalor to the new Territories. . . ." See *At.Mo.*, XXIX (March 1872), 364.

For all his minor uncertainties in narrative moralizing, then, Howells created a sustained drama of Euripidean proportions. In its anti-pastoral overtones, it becomes an American tragedy endowed with a depth and geographic sweep which few novels in our literature have equalled. The force of the novel seems to have issued from a basic tension within Howells the man and artist. He resisted at the same time that he created the dark necessity of his action. Privately to others, he could admit his compassion for Bartley and Marcia; but as an artist, he was unable to rescue his hero and heroine from the appointed ruin of their lives. Throughout *A Modern Instance*, he had formed a complex web of ironic foreshadowings and reversals which linked together and advanced the fated events in the novel. I have already suggested how deeply Howells appears to have been disturbed by the Greek logic he was unfolding. Irony was integral in the Greek view of man's fate; it also was an important, though not always a protective, element in Howells' mental defences. As we shall see again in *The Rise of Silas Lapham*, when Howells relied heavily on irony in his fiction, he was usually protecting himself from the agony of doubt and self-contradiction, from a conflict between what his mind told him to believe and what his heart preferred to hope. The biographical data I hazard to enter into this reading of the novel shows how precariously poised were Howells' mind and heart. But finally he allowed the tragedy, strongly tinged with irony, to have its way.

In an early passage, for example, Howells describes the youthful beauty of his doomed heroine to be "of the kind that coming years would only ripen and enrich; at thirty she would be even handsomer than at twenty . . ." (p. 3). Or Bartley announces blithely to Marcia, before their engagement, that in his own time he will go to Chicago, but " 'I'm not ready yet' " (p. 7). The restless Kinney has not regained even a semblance of pastoral tranquillity in the New England woods after the debacle of his pioneering in the West, but he can declare rather unctuously to Bartley that " 'if a man's got anything on his mind, a big railroad depot's the place for him' "; and Marcia at the end meets the uprooted Kinney, still wandering and opinionating aimlessly, this time in the crowded railroad depot at Indianapolis (pp. 82, 345).

More complex is Howells' narrative comment in praise of "brotherly love" in the American city (p. 140). No trace of irony accompanies the remark. Yet in his dramatic action, Howells did not fulfill this heartwarming announcement of mutual help and fraternity in Boston, and so the disparity yields the same design of ironic reversal. So, too, does Marcia's fruitless trip West in the spring of 1879, as all of nature was being reborn, and she "abandoned herself to Flavia's joy in the blossoms . . ." (p. 340). In this brief reawakening, she brings into focus her father's morbid case against Bartley:

"Father said he only wanted to get rid of me, so that he could marry some one else—Yes, yes; it was that that made me start! Father knew it would! Oh," she grieved, with a wild self-pity that tore Halleck's heart, "he knew it would!" (p. 343).

Her illumination here, as in Greek tragedy, arrives too late.

Finally, Howells had begun the novel as he ended it, by dispelling hope as quickly as he had held it forth. The opening paragraph dwells on the "rich luxuriance" and "tropical riot of vegetation" of an Equity summer (p. 1). Howells then added, "But winter was full half the year," and he evoked the chill, thin air and "arctic quiet" of Equity in February, with bored villagers living monotonous, spiritless lives amid "the smell of rats in the wainscot and of potatoes in the cellar" (p. 3). At the close of the novel, Marcia returns with her daughter and father to her village home "in the first flush of the young and jubilant summer"—but only sadly to open "the dim old house at the end of the village street, and resume their broken lives" (p. 358).

CHAPTER THREE

———

THE RISE OF SILAS LAPHAM
(1884–1885)

THE CRISIS OF WEALTH IN
THE GILDED AGE

DURING the autumn of 1884 and into the winter months of 1885, Howells was writing hard to keep ahead of the serialized chapters of *The Rise of Silas Lapham* appearing each month in *Century* magazine. Some time during this period he suffered a psychic impasse. In the next decade, after *A Traveler from Altruria* had appeared, Howells recalled that he had felt at the time as though "the bottom dropped out" of his world. He was talking with an acquaintance who shortly afterward reported the conversation in *Harper's Weekly*. *A Traveler from Altruria*, Howells had said, was an attempt to resolve some of his conflicts about American society.

They made their demand—these questions and problems—when Mr. Howells was writing *Silas Lapham*. His affairs prospering, his work marching as well as heart could wish, suddenly, and without apparent cause, the status seemed wholly wrong. His own expression, in speaking with me about that time, was, "The bottom dropped out!"[1]

Later commentators on Howells, though aware of a deepening in his concern with social questions in America after *A Modern Instance*, have not speculated at any length on what matters, public and private, may have profoundly

[1] Marrion Wilcox, "Works of William Dean Howells," *Harper's Weekly*, XL (July 4, 1896), 656.

upset him.[2] Critics of the 1920s and 1930s generally ignored the question, more bent as they were on making sport of Howells the timid, prissy novelist, the quiet man and captive dupe of the Boston literary giants before whom he bowed in constantly fawning acquiescence. More recently, a better informed and more sophisticated view has had it that Howells was, instead, a disengaged observer during his twenty-year apprenticeship in Boston. In this revised portrait, Howells appears a dispassionate satirist-with-scalpel, coolly dissecting Proper Boston society in the period before and during *Silas Lapham*. Neither of these diverging estimates of Howells as a social critic has lent itself to an inquiry into Howells' apparently anguished soul-searching over the problem of "status"—of social and economic inequality—during the writing of *Silas Lapham*. From both of these opposing critical camps, however, the novel itself has received proper attention and praise for the art with which Howells traced the moral fall and rise of a back-country paint millionaire in postwar Boston. And indeed, there is much here to praise.

Howells brought to *The Rise of Silas Lapham* a mastery of his craft which later generations have admired and continued to reassess in this most popular of his novels. The opening chapter, for example, stands as a model for practitioners of the novel. Bartley Hubbard reappears. And if one has not read *A Modern Instance*, he quickly comes to know Bartley as a cynical, smart-aleck journalist. Bartley serves briefly and effectively as a foil to Silas Lapham, who is to be the next subject of Bartley's "Solid Men of Boston" series. As Bartley interviews Silas and records irreverent notes for his profile in the *Events*, the reader soon knows Silas for a rough-hewn, ungrammatical

---

2 Edwin Cady believes that Howells experienced a "psychic event" which must remain "essentially unknowable." Even so, Mr. Cady summarizes in two pages some highly relevant biography for these months. The present chapter has grown directly out of the provocative hints supplied by Mr. Cady. See *The Road to Realism*, pp. 243-245.

businessman who is not ashamed of his humble origins and is not willing to joke about them. Though something of a braggart about his self-made fortune, Silas does submit a small doubt whether his first million would have arrived without a certain assist from accident and fate. We discover within the dramatic frame of Bartley's interview, also, that Silas has two daughters, one pretty and one plain; that he married a schoolteacher of persistent will and stern morality; that he is uneasy about a former partner; that he has a disturbingly attractive secretary; and that he is building a house in Back Bay which will be completed the following spring. Save for the Corey family, whom the reader will presently meet, all of the central characters and issues of the novel have been suggested in this opening chapter. And Howells has accomplished the miracle of fiction in which a sharply realized hero suddenly emerges from the page full born.

As he advanced from chapter to chapter, Howells created a fabric of symbol and myth which not only achieved tightness and economy in his rendering the action, but also helped to conceal the rather meager detail and undeveloped contours of Silas's commercial world. The myth of the seasons is here: we meet Silas in the autumn of his harvested fortune in paint, follow him through the winter of his discontent, and witness his moral rise in the spring. The house rising in Back Bay accompanies the mythic pattern to symbolize Silas's mounting pride and material wealth, as well as his social aspiration to establish in Proper Boston the House of Lapham. When he unintentionally sets the house on fire at the end of winter, he has consumed, at the same time, his "poison of ambition" (p. 28) .[3] In this purgatorial action, the burned-out shell of the Beacon Street house becomes the hole which fortuitously opens for Silas and he decides to creep out. He

[3] All page citations to the final version of the novel refer to Edwin Cady's edition (Boston: Houghton Mifflin Co., 1957) .

had been unable to fit his great hairy fists into the slender gloves of Corey Boston society: his gloved hands had only hung down "like canvased hams" (p. 154). Or to borrow Silas's own paint metaphor from the opening chapter, he could gloss over many surfaces but should be wary of his own; and he was especially determined that the paint should not coat over his moral sense. Success in business, nevertheless, had led him into temptation and moral compromise. But in spring, Silas wisely returns to Vermont and there is able to restore "the manhood which his prosperity had so nearly stolen from him" (p. 294). Because the characters and scenes are memorable, the symbolism effective, and Howells' touch with social comedy masterly, this novel has seemed to embody the very essence of his gifts. It is readable and pleasant, instructive without being didactic. Howells granted *The Rise of Silas Lapham* the happy, pastoral resolution he had denied *A Modern Instance*.

But why, then, should Howells while writing this enjoyable novel have felt that the bottom had dropped out of his world because of unresolved problems of American democracy? Perhaps something is present in the novel that has been missed. Perhaps even more, what is *not* present in the novel may be in some ways as important as what does appear. Precisely what were Howells' feelings, for example, toward the newly rich businessman in Boston? Or the older Brahmins? Or the new immigrant laboring classes? And if one finds in Howells' correspondence that he discussed these matters of status in a democracy, how can one determine the precise meanings? A Howells letter to Charles Eliot Norton may be harder to interpret than a letter to Mark Twain. What were his relations to each man—early and late? When was he being ironic, or wearing a mask, and why? "With whom is one really and truly intimate?" Howells once asked Norton. "I am pretty frank, and I seem to say myself out to more than one, now and

again, but only in this sort to one, and that sort to another."[4] When the literary scholar has refined and polished
the biographical detail, his labors have hardly begun. The
way that a writer's life issues in literary creation is, in
general, still a mystery; and the mystery is unique in the
career of each writer. And it might be added, the conversion of life into art is to some extent unique in each
work of an author. Just as his craft may grow and change,
moreover, so may his previous attitudes toward morality,
art, and society. That is, fifteen years before *Silas Lapham*,
Howells was writing about social snobbery in Boston, but
he suffered no grievous conflict over what he saw. In fact,
he had treated the Boston scene several times in the period
immediately preceding *Silas Lapham* without undue harm
to his social conscience.

The literary scholar, lost in this welter of contradictory
and sometimes intractable biographical data, may liken
his task to a version of the quest for the Grail, wherein the
knight can free the waters and restore the land if only he
ask the right question. Among the materials which may
point one to the fruitful question about an author's feelings and intentions is the record of his prior revisions of
the work. Here he can be studied in the very process of
literary creation. Fortunately, with *The Rise of Silas
Lapham*, one can trace a fairly satisfactory history of
Howells' conception and composition of the work in the
evidence of how he revised the novel. First, he submitted a
short prospectus; second, he wrote the serialized version
which appeared each month in *Century* magazine; and
finally, he revised certain passages for the final copy of
the novel as it now stands. The way the novel grew and
changed can next be related to certain biographical evidence of the urgency and conflict with which Howells
wrote and revised. Because these data are somewhat meager

4 April 15, 1907, *Letters*, II, 242.

and difficult to interpret does not necessarily mean that one is foolhardy to try to use them.

In considering three of the most important of these revisions, one receives intimations that Howells in Boston was casting worried glances upward on the social ladder (the Proper Bostonian of Back Bay), downward (the immigrant slum-dweller), and alongside (the rising Jew). A fourth matter of revision (an anachronism which Howells refused to change) suggests the conflict between his social aspiration and his defiance of the good people of Boston who were opponents of his literary modernism. Finally, in moving from the synopsis through the main revisions of the serial, one discovers that in the Corey-Lapham "subplot" resides a set of conflicts together with a final resolution which may have been more crucial for Howells than the more celebrated dilemma of his businessman-hero. Taken together, these revisions suggest that *The Rise of Silas Lapham* is a novel ultimately concerned with social eruption in a new Boston, leaderless and morally adrift in the Gilded Age.

I

In the first installment of *The Rise of Silas Lapham* in the *Century* (November 1884), Silas and Mrs. Lapham are discussing the projected new Back Bay residence which will presumably bring them into the orbit of respectable Boston society:

> [Mrs. Lapham]: "Where is your lot? In the Diphtheria District?"
> [Silas]: "No, it ain't in the Diphtheria District . . . and I guess there's more diphtheria in the name than anything else, anyway."[5]

Howells modified the passage to read in the novel the next year:

[5] *Century*, VII, 24.

[Mrs. Lapham]: "Where is your lot? They say it's un-healthy over there. . . ."

[Silas]: "It ain't unhealthy where I've bought . . . , and I guess it's about as healthy on the Back Bay as it is here, anyway" (pp. 26-27).

The revised passage obviously removed the sting of sarcasm from the serial version. Small though it is, why did Howells make the change? Had Back Bay readers of the *Century* been annoyed at Howells' repeating what appears to have become a well-worn gibe at the status issuing, or oozing, from an address on the "New Land" in the "Diphtheria District"? And if they had resented the passage, why should Howells have been concerned? Nothing approaching a complete explanation of Howells' motives for easing his thrust at Back Bay society can ever be set down, but speculation at least can begin.

We shall start with what is known—and it will be necessary to summarize a fair amount of familiar Howells biography from time to time to reinterpret Howells' state of mind. After *A Modern Instance*, he had removed his family to Europe for a year of travel, convalescence, and, for Howells himself, the hard work of a self-supporting writer. (Among other tasks, he completed *A Woman's Reason*, germinating since the late 1870s, and gathered the materials for *Tuscan Cities* which would serve as well his last international novel *Indian Summer*.) When he returned to Boston in late summer of 1883, Howells took up temporary residence in a rented house at 4 Louisburg Square. Then in August of 1884 he bought the house at 302 Beacon Street and became a resident of Back Bay. He wrote to Henry James soon after and described his proud view from the new house:

The sun goes down over Cambridge with as much apparent interest as if he were a Harvard graduate; possibly he is; and he spreads a glory over the Back Bay that is not to be equalled by the blush of a Boston Independent for such of us Republicans as are going to vote for Blaine. Sometimes I feel it an extraordinary thing that I should have been able to buy a house on Beacon str.[6]

The note of fulfillment here, the hint of a fond dream at last realized, can be partly explained by Howells' knowledge that his neighbor only two doors away was the venerable Oliver Wendell Holmes. Howells could virtually chart his progress—his own "rise" in Boston—through this relationship. The two had met in 1860 when Howells, the self-educated youth from Ohio, had made his first trip to Boston. In 1866, Holmes was an early visitor at the Bulfinch Street apartment to welcome Howells back to Boston after his consulship in Venice. They were together at the Dante evenings at Longfellow's, and Holmes followed young Howells' progress as editor of the *Atlantic*, meanwhile continuing to offer his own pieces to the magazine. He read Howells' early novels of the 1870s (and Howells assured Holmes that the snob, Miles Arbuton of *A Chance Acquaintance*, was "*a* Bostonian, not *the* Bostonian") .[7] They attended together the monthly meetings of the Saturday Club after Howells became a member in 1874. Three years later, Holmes reassured a desperately mortified Howells that Mark Twain's tall-story burlesque at the Whittier Dinner (in which Holmes was impersonated by a "monstrous" tramp "wobbling his double chins") was not at all a grievous social blunder. Younger by some twenty-eight years, Howells had been naturally deferential to Holmes, and continued to be so when they became neighbors. Holmes had his "fences," as Howells later called the formality in which Holmes's Irish maid was instructed to keep all visitors waiting in a downstairs reception room until Holmes was ready to see them. Howells

---

[6] Aug. 22, 1884, *Letters*, I, 366. I will return to Howells' allusion to political conflict with his Brahmin contemporaries.

[7] *Literary Friends and Acquaintance* (New York: Harper and Bros., 1911) , p. 219. This edition enlarged the 1900 printing to include *My Mark Twain*.

would even write letters to his neighbor to avoid "boring" him with a personal call.[8] In short, Howells felt a continuing gratitude to Holmes and a somewhat awed respect for him. Conceivably, then, he might have deleted the "diphtheria" reference to Back Bay as a bit of satire which Holmes could have judged to be in bad taste. The embarrassment over Mark Twain's humor had been painful enough to avoid repeating. Or at least, if the respected Doctor had enjoyed the added medical interest which the phrase gave to his residential district, and had so informed Howells, one doubts that Howells would readily have removed it and revised the passage.

A far more significant and deeply personal motive may have caused Howells to play down his sarcasm about Back Bay. His daughter Winny, during this crucial time, figured in Howells' anxiety on more counts than her mysteriously failing health. Some years earlier, he had written Charles Eliot Norton that he hoped the play *A Counterfeit Presentment* would bring forth enough proceeds to allow Winny to attend a private school in Boston—a well-known preliminary step necessary to establish a young lady in the proper circles of the Boston social world. Again, when the Howellses made their new home on the water side of Beacon Street, they hoped the prestige address would help their ailing daughter to make her debut in Boston society. The ambition was entertained especially by Mrs. Howells. But the Back Bay investment took a fearful toll from the outset. "I have had a frightful year of work," Howells wrote in March 1885. "I must give my daughter her chance in this despicable world . . . ," he explained. In addition to making his payments on a $21,000 home, he was also paying to get his son through school and then to college.[9] To cover these mounting expenses, Howells

---

8 To Holmes, Feb. 5, 1885, *Letters*, I, 368.

9 See Cady, *The Road to Realism*, p. 223. The letter to Norton is dated Aug. 13, 1877 (Harvard). The letter of March 27, 1885 (Harvard) is addressed to a "Dear, dear friend," identified on the ms. folder to be James Parton.

had to rely chiefly on his earnings as a professional writer. Here, then, may have been the strongest reason of all to question, on second thought, the wisdom of belittling the exclusive district from which the Laphams, like the Howellses, were planning to launch their daughters into the company of the sons and daughters of Proper Boston.

II

A second revision further illuminates Howells' attitude toward Boston in the Gilded Age and also helps to make the reasons for his personal crisis somewhat more knowable. A passage which never reached the pages of the *Century* involved Howells' surprisingly bold allusion to current anarchist violence on the American scene. In February 1885, the editor of the *Century*, Richard Watson Gilder, was reading the proofs of the Corey-Lapham dinner episode. To Gilder's horror, Howells had allowed the Brahmin host, Bromfield Corey, to raise the terrifying spectre of anarchist revolution on Beacon Street. What restraint, Corey wryly asks, has kept the poor laborers of Boston from coming out of their stifling slums in summer with dynamite to blow up the spacious mansions standing empty on Beacon Street while their owners are away for the season at their Newports and Saratogas? Howells was here plagiarizing from two passages he had previously written in concern over this threat to the safety of well-to-do Americans. Isabel and Basil March, wandering through the oppressive heat of New York in *Their Wedding Journey*,

morbidly wondered what that day's murder would be, and in what swarming tenement-house, or den of the assassin streets by the river-sides,—if indeed it did not befall in some such high, close-shuttered, handsome dwelling as those they passed, in whose twilight it would be so easy to strike down the master and leave him, undiscovered and unmourned by the family ignorantly absent at the mountains or the seaside.

This possibility of burglary and murder became far more

real to Howells shortly after he had moved into Back Bay. "There are miles of empty houses all round me," he wrote to his father in late summer of 1884. "And how unequally things are divided in this world. While these beautiful, airy, wholesome houses are uninhabited, thousands upon thousands of poor creatures are stifling in wretched barracks in the city here, whole families in one room. I wonder that men are so patient with society as they are."[10]

But Howells had added something new this third time— the reminder that American laborers had grown less patient in recent years. The dread word was "dynamite." Gilder and publisher Roswell Smith panicked. Both men wrote letters to Howells imploring him to revise the passage.[11] Howells complied, whether with some reluctance or not we do not know. The conversation that appears in serial and novel versions goes like this (Bromfield Corey is speaking) :

"If I were a poor man, with a sick child pining in some garret or cellar at the North End, I should break into one of [those close-shuttered, handsome, brutally insensible houses], and camp out on the grand piano."

"Surely, Bromfield," said his wife, "you don't consider what havoc such people would make with the furniture of a nice house."

"That is true," answered Corey, with meek conviction. "I never thought of that" (p. 159) .

This second instance of a bold first writing again changing to rather insipid tameness leads us further toward a definition of Howells' private ordeal during these months. How deeply was Howells troubled by this second aspect of status in the literally explosive period before and during *Silas Lapham*, when labor strikes were already numbering into the hundreds each year?

Howells' attitudes toward the status of the workingman

10 *Their Wedding Journey* (Boston: James R. Osgood and Co., 1872), p. 48; to his father, Aug. 10, 1884, *Letters*, I, 363.
11 Both letters dated Feb. 18, 1885 (Harvard) .

in America, which involve also his opinions about race, can be traced from his early years in Ohio, a generally unhappy boyhood, as Professor Cady has ably shown in his biography. The grandfather, Joseph Howells, had engendered in his family a sense of their Welsh superiority to other mill hands in Steubenville. Howells later made sport of his Welsh "pedigree," inherited from the "royal blood" of the ninth-century Hywel Dha, but the fact was important enough for him to repeat with undisguised pleasure.[12] The father, William Cooper Howells, was a socially respectable printer and a Whig, a member of the "employing class."[13] True, for a brief period at Eureka Mills he was a utopian—to the despair of his comfort- and status-conscious wife—but a utopian of a rather exclusive brand. What he mainly passed on to his son William Dean was not a practical commitment to an egalitarian society. "My convictions were all democratic," Howells recalled many years later, "but at heart I am afraid I was a snob. . . ."[14] Olov W. Fryckstedt notes that Howells, arriving in Europe as Lincoln's consul to Venice, was first alarmed at the poverty that resulted from a caste-ridden aristocracy, but presently discovered it to be "picturesque."[15] Nor did the abolitionist idealism of his youth dispose Howells, after the war, to welcome the new influx of urban laborers. His early *Atlantic* sketches and reviews, for all their irony, do not disguise his concern over the numbers of Chinese, Irish, and free Negroes on the national scene. He was wait-

[12] Two instances, one early and one late, appear in a letter to his father, Jan. 3, 1875, *Letters*, I, 200; and to Dr. Rice, Sept. 12, 1912, Rutgers University Library.

[13] *A Boy's Town*, p. 20.

[14] *My Literary Passions*, p. 128.

[15] *In Quest of America*, pp. 34-59. Mr. Fryckstedt discusses chiefly Howells' "A Little German Capital," *Nation*, II (Jan. 4, 1866), 11-13; "Letters from Venice," which ran periodically in the *Boston Advertiser* during 1863-1864; and *Venetian Life* (1866).
The "picturesque dilapidation" amid otherwise disheartening squalor in Venice reappears in the response of Ferris, artist and American consul in *A Foregone Conclusion* (Boston: James R. Osgood and Co., 1874), p. 102.

ing "with an anxious curiosity the encounter of the Irish and the Chinese, now rapidly approaching each other from opposite shores of the continent. Shall we be crushed in the collision of these superior races?" He praised Thomas Wentworth Higginson's *Black Regiment* in part because it was not "a celebration of the negro in any of his familiar aspects of martyr, or hero, or his present 'transition state' of bore. . . ." In another sketch of Boston, he questioned whether the current horse-car era would hold any of its present charm for the mongrel "oblique-eyed, swarthy American" of the next century.[16] His alleged Western "democratic idealism" seems largely to have been an *idealized* utopian view of the Ohio village which he occasionally fancied as a psychological refuge from the urban-industrial complexities of the new Boston, and later of New York. Even his voting with the Western Populists for Bryan in 1896 can be interpreted as a protest vote against the chaos wrought by the new industrial democracy, on one hand, and the newly rich captains of industry and finance on the other. Through the years, he had yearned periodically for a simpler prewar Western democracy which, in fact, he had never really experienced in his fibre and bones. Indeed, what his father did pass on to young Howells was the important lesson of rising in the world through intensive self-education. Howells in Ohio seems to have been, above all, a rather alienated youth who admired the culture of Europe and aspired to be published in Lowell's *Atlantic Monthly*. His future wife, the daughter of Squire Mead of Brattleboro, Vermont, during her Western visit to Columbus in the winter of 1860, quickly recognized this refinement and intelligence in young Howells.

---

[16] "A Pedestrian Tour," *At.Mo.*, XXIV (Nov. 1869), 596; review of Higginson, *ibid.*, 644; "By Horse-Car to Boston," XXV (Jan. 1870), 122. See also "A Day's Pleasure," XXVI (July 1870), 108; and "Doorstep Acquaintance," XXIII (April 1869), 492. For a complex portrait of the Negro after emancipation, see Howells' "Mrs. Johnson," XXI (Jan. 1868), 97-106.

So one has his work cut out in trying to make Howells into a democratic champion of the village commoner and a satirical "observer" of cultivated Boston society. Indeed, a stronger case can perhaps be made for Howells' disengagement from Western "democracy" than from Boston aristocracy. When he came to Boston to live after the Civil War, Howells was, in spirit, virtually an insider, with four years of marriage to a daughter of New England as practical apprenticeship. Up to then, he had never been closely identified for an extended period, intellectually or socially, with any group. The Boston and Cambridge community, not Ohio, was the logical home for the maturing Howells. He was received with civility by the most revered of the elder Brahmins, and greeted with affectionate cordiality and invaluable help by Lowell, Norton, and Fields. For the first time in his life, Howells could enjoy a stimulating intellectual and social milieu. In his earliest months there, he admitted to "an undercurrent of homesickness" after a three-day holiday by the sea. He was homesick not for the Western village but for his new home in Cambridge. "I don't believe that when I am rich as I one day intend to be," he wrote Norton, "I shall ever leave Cambridge at all."[17] In the early seventies, he expressed, with Aldrich and Norton, the native feelings of "exile" brought on by the "progress" being wrought in the new community.[18] Later in the decade when he moved just beyond Cambridge to Belmont, he urged Norton, Lowell, and Longfellow to believe that he had in no way meant to separate himself from their valued company.[19] If these Brahmin associations may never have developed into the warmth of his friendship with a fellow Westerner, Mark Twain, one can be

[17] Aug. 13, 1866 (Harvard).

[18] Howells to Aldrich, Jan. 20, 1874 (Harvard); Norton to Lowell, May 30, 1873, in *Letters of Charles Eliot Norton* (Boston: Houghton Mifflin Company, 1913), II, 12.

[19] To Norton, April 16, 1878, *Letters*, II, 254; to Lowell, June 22, 1879, *ibid.*, 270; to Longfellow, Jan. 15, 1879 (Harvard).

reminded that Howells' natural reticence kept him from seeking many close relationships. (Recall also that in his *My Mark Twain* he praised his friend for "never putting his hands on you.") He could satirize the Boston of the 1870s with authority and even a proprietary interest because he had fast become a knowledgeable citizen of that city. Almost incredibly, he had, in only a few years, gained a personal influence which brought the Brahmins to him for favors (Norton in search of an editorship, Lowell an ambassadorship), and in the editor's seat of the *Atlantic* he had become one of the arbiters of literary taste in the East. His editorial correspondence reveals that Howells rejected offerings from Aldrich, Horace Scudder, E. C. Stedman, James Parton, Sarah Orne Jewett, and even Emerson, who had recommended to Howells a poem by Emma Lazarus. Though he knew Lowell to be hypersensitive to the very smallest criticism, Howells judged one of Lowell's offerings unsuitable and returned it. Paul Hayne, whom Lowell had published in the *Atlantic* half a dozen times, complained to Bayard Taylor that Howells had rejected a recent piece. Taylor consoled Hayne by admitting to similar treatment. Taylor then explained Howells the editor as an "enigma, which I no longer try to solve." In extenuation, he allowed that Howells was "living under influences which are probably more potent than either you or I suspect. . . ."[20] One notices also, in the manuscript correspondence, that as Howells moved from his assistant editor's desk into the editor's chair, his handwriting grew larger and bolder.

During his rise to a position among the leading citizens of Boston and Cambridge, Howells was quite aware, however, that the peerage had come through hard work rather than inheritance. The feelings of a natural aristocrat were

[20] Taylor to Hayne, March 13, 1878, in *The Unpublished Letters of Bayard Taylor*, ed. John R. Schultz (San Marino, Calif.: The Huntington Library, 1937), pp. 206-207.

not identical to those of the hereditary aristocrat. Lowell prodded Howells for appearing to be constantly on the alert for a snub from the first families. Howells' sensitive awareness that he had not been permitted by birth to feel a secure identity inside the closed circle of Boston "cousinships" stands revealed in a passage of *Silas Lapham*. He described the Corey ladies pondering their selection of dinner guests from among "one of the most comprehensive of those cousinships which form the admiration and terror of the adventurer in Boston society" (p. 141). Even while he lightly satirized an undemocratic exclusiveness based on the accident of birth, Howells would not have destroyed these distinctions which characterize a stable, stratified society. For although a fluid society is necessary to allow a family to rise, some semblance of a stratified division of classes must be maintained to make the rise meaningful—and the debut of one's own daughter possible.

The leveling power of dynamite could not have been comfortably entertained by Howells. Indeed, one can see in the Lapham-Corey dinner conversation an extremely revealing attitude toward social revolution. Silas the rising man in America, in his concern over the safety of his hard-won property holdings, has become even more conservative than the aristocratic Corey, who has taken his own inheritance for granted. During the dinner-table talk about labor discontent, Howells gives us Silas's reassuring thoughts about the essential conservatism of the laboring classes, apparently without heavy irony.

Lapham wanted to speak up and say that he had been there himself, and knew how such a man felt. He wanted to tell them that generally a poor man was satisfied if he could make both ends meet; that he didn't envy anyone his good luck, if he had earned it, so long as he wasn't running under himself (pp. 159-160).

Reassurance was needed because the fear of social revolution existed. In fact, Howells recalled at the end of the century his "mean and cruel" reactions to the swelling population of immigrants in the postwar slums. On a walk with Lowell, during Howells' early years of residence in Cambridge, "in one of those squalid Irish neighborhoods I confessed a grudge (a mean and cruel grudge, I now think it) for the increasing presence of that race among us. . . ." Lowell rebuked Howells not for harboring these nativist sentiments, but for expressing them so forcefully: "he did not wish you to be more of his mind than he was himself."[21]

Howells reacted publicly, also, to the new radicalism in American life. In his essays, sketches, and reviews, he warned his *Atlantic* readers that the stability of American life, and Jeffersonian democracy, was being jeopardized by the growing numbers of an ignorant, lower-class electorate. In 1869, he remarked on "the well-known ambition of Dubliners to rule the land," and predicted that their population might "one day make an end of us poor Yankees as a dominant plurality." During the 1872 political campaign he wrote: "The Irish vote—the intelligent, the logical, the delightful Irish vote—will be cast, as it has always been, for the choice of the Democratic Convention, whoever or whatever that may be." The "sable despotism" in South Carolina politics, Howells wrote in 1874, "would present a prospect too alarming and shocking, if it were not relieved by the amusing fact that the present legislators of South Carolina cannot for the most part read or write the laws they make." To ensure that he did not lose the reader through this light sarcasm, Howells soberly continued, "Though, upon reflection, we do not see why this fact should be amusing to any one." Again in 1874, he wrote, "Universal suffrage now seems our evil, not because suffrage has not been limited by a property qualification, or some other aristocratic device, but because it is not limited by the only democratic device, that of education."

---

[21] *Literary Friends and Acquaintance*, p. 219.

Three years later, he was reviewing the poetry of Lowell: "As for the magnificent passage beginning 'I, Freedom, dwell with Knowledge,' it might fitly be the *vade mecum* of every American who would think as coolly as he feels warmly about America; it seems to us a final expression of common sense and political wisdom. . . ."[22]

In 1878, Howells lessened his indictment of the average voter and denounced, instead, the corruption of machine politics in the new metropolis:

. . . a New Yorker of the reign of Mr. Tweed, if he survived in spirit five hundred years hence, could rightfully reject the historical inference that a million New Yorkers, his contemporaries, were mostly thieves and ruffians, or shameless slaves, the culpable prey of municipal plunderers.

Two years later, he assailed once again the new power of the political demagogue who, said Howells, is able to "stupefy" though not actually "corrupt" the voter. Even so, Howells was depressed by "how low the capacity of the masses—the public-schooled masses—still is for right thinking." And in 1882, after a visit to a Boston police court: "I came to wonder if the thick-headedness of average uneducated people was not much greater than I had hitherto suspected, in my easy optimism." During the interim vacation in Europe, before he returned to write *Silas Lapham*, Howells praised the Swiss for holding their political election in a church, and regretted that Americans could not adopt the practice. He wrote, this time privately to his father, "What a damper it would be on repeating and shoulder-hitting if the Irish performer had to do his work in the presence of his saints!"[23] Howells' fears of postwar

[22] "A Pedestrian Tour," *At.Mo.*, XXIV (Nov. 1869) , 594; "Politics," XXX (July 1872) , 127; review, J. L. Pike, *The Prostrate State: South Carolina under Negro Government*, XXXIII (Feb. 1874) , 234; review, James Parton, *Life of Thomas Jefferson*, XXXIV (July 1874) , 111; review, J. R. Lowell, *Three Memorial Poems*, XXXIX (March 1877) , 374.

[23] "A French Poet of the Old Régime [Marmontel]," XLI (March 1878) , 332; "A New Observer," review of J. B. Harrison's *Dangerous Tendencies*

immigration were fully confirmed by 1884. When he was beginning to write *The Rise of Silas Lapham*, this new electorate had helped to accomplish what he and proper Boston for more than fifteen years had dreaded. Boston in this fateful year had just installed its first Irish Catholic mayor, Hugh O'Brien, in city hall. The event must have struck Howells as the symbolic beginning of the end for the old order. (Four years earlier, as he probably knew, New York City had also elected its first Irish Catholic mayor, William R. Grace.) How much longer could one now expect the poor man in the North End to be satisfied if only he could make both ends meet?

Not that Howells had become deadened to the humanitarian sympathies of his Swedenborgian and Quaker heritage. The unhappy plight of the lower classes was occasionally included in the pages of the *Atlantic*, and memorably by Howells himself in one issue during the early 1880s. Earlier, in his Ohio apprenticeship to journalism, he had avoided the human drama present in the streets and police-stations of the Ohio city: "it might have been the necessity of my morbid nerves to save themselves from abhorrent contacts."[24] Remarkable in several respects, then, are the visits Howells paid to a Boston police court early in the eighties and reported in the *Atlantic*. His tone was uncertain, and even embarrassed. Perhaps to protect his nerves during these difficult months before *A Modern Instance*, he fashioned the parade of human misery— prostitutes, drunks, and thieves—into a lively performance "at a variety theatre, without any disagreeable waits or the drop of a curtain." But later he took a sober and compassionate glance at the performers (chiefly Negroes and Irish "adoptive citizens") as well as the spectators in this human comedy:

---

in *American Life*, XLV (June 1880), 849; "Police Report," XLIX (Jan. 1882), 6; letter to his father, Nov. 12, 1882, *Letters*, I, 326.

24 *Years of My Youth*, p. 141.

I have tried to treat my material lightly and entertainingly, as a true reporter should, but I would not have my reader suppose that I did not feel the essential cruelty of an exhibition that tore its poor rags from all that squalid shame, and its mask from all that lying, cowering guilt, or did not suspect how it must harden and deprave those whom it daily entertained.[25]

The next year, he returned to Venice and recognized, in slight shock, that daughter Winny responded, as he once had, to the "romantic" picturesqueness of the old city. "She thinks it is *all* beauty and gayety," he wrote to Mark Twain; "but for my part, the poor old place is forlorner and shabbier than ever. I don't think I began to see the misery of it when I lived here. The rags and dirt I witnessed in a walk this morning sickened me."[26] When he returned from Europe and lived in Back Bay, Howells admitted twinges of social conscience once when he gazed out his window onto a scene of the less fortunate of his townsmen clambering onto his fence to watch the rowing on the Charles River. The feelings of guilt, however, occurred *after* he had thanked a policeman for driving the spectators off. Another brief moment of illumination, described in *My Mark Twain*, came during a visit from Twain when the two men rushed out to save a desperate woman preparing to commit suicide in the Charles.[27] The short glimpse into the slum environment of Zerilla Dewey in *Silas Lapham* is symptomatic of Howells' widening social awareness in 1884 and 1885. So, too, is the satirical treatment of Clara Kingsbury's charity activities on behalf of Boston's indigent Italians, the society lady's self-satisfied *noblesse oblige*. The original scare of dynamite in the serialized *Silas Lapham* may have been Howells' attempt to force some of his readers to begin—as he was now be-

[25] "Police Report," *At.Mo.*, XLIX (Jan. 1882), 4, 13.

[26] April 22, 1883, *Letters*, I, 340.

[27] See Owen Wister, "William Dean Howells," *At.Mo.*, CLX (Dec. 1937), 712; and *Literary Friends and Acquaintance*, enlarged edn. (1911), pp. 368-369.

ginning—to confront some of the vital problems of social revolution in post-Civil War Boston. The implications of the problem for Howells were, however, apparently too immense and too threatening. The dinner-table discussion of social unrest that we are given finally in the novel is so "safe" as to be almost meaningless.

III

Howells' developing conflict over the problem of status in an increasingly fluid and complex American society took still a third direction. The serialized version includes references to newly rich Jews rising in Boston society. In the second chapter published in the *Century*, Mrs. Lapham has heard at the summer resort that wealthy Jewish outsiders are invading the fashionable residential districts of Boston, including Nankeen Square where the Laphams live. Is it true that the property of the established owners is worth less than they paid? Silas the businessman can answer with authority, "It's worth a good deal less. You see, they *have* got in—and pretty thick, too—it's no use denying it. And when they get in, they send down the price of property." Though he claims to deplore the housing discrimination against Jews, Silas still feels moved to reaffirm that "prices begin to shade when the first one gets in." Several pages later, Mrs. Lapham returns to the same topic, and says "thoughtfully" that a prosperous "Mr. Liliengarten has bought the Gordon house across the square." She then "sighs" as she announces, "They've all got money."[28] To assess fully what Howells is suggesting here, we need to recall, first, who is the original source of Mrs. Lapham's information about the Jewish menace. It is Tom Corey, the young Boston aristocrat. (The extent of Brahmin apprehensions about Jews will deserve a hard look in just a moment.) Further, Howells apparently was trying to present the Laphams' rural-parvenu attitudes toward the

28 *Century*, VII (Nov. 1884), 22-23, 25.

Jews. Mrs. Lapham, forgetting that they are as yet really outsiders from Vermont trying to rise in Boston society, has rapidly adopted the attitude of an established Bostonian toward the aspiring Jew. Silas does offer his religious objections to anti-Semitism. The Savior, after all, was a Jew, and Silas believes that Adam must have been one, too. But for all this comic confusion, Silas clearly has his own strain of racial bigotry. Howells, in fact, allows Silas to repeat his forceful misgivings over the economic and social disorder created by the newly rich Jew in Boston. In short, Howells was again tapping one of the vital nerve centers of Boston society in the Gilded Age. It may have been also, in a quite painful and ambivalent way, a nerve center of Howells himself.

Anti-Semitism in this period was an attitude which Howells had many chances to experience at first hand. Virtually every old-guard Bostonian of his acquaintance harbored suspicions and fears of the rising Jew in America. In the early 1880s, the professional Anglo-Saxon was beginning to take arms against a sea of immigrants. Among them were Fiske, Parkman, Shaler, Hart, and Barrett Wendell. In 1881, the British historian Freeman lectured to a Boston audience on the appalling decline of the Anglo-Saxon, and in private conversations could be heard to advocate elimination of the Irishman, Negro, and Jew from the entire English-speaking world. In his visit in 1881, Herbert Spencer warned Americans that the immigrant races were undermining the pure Anglo-Saxon development of America.[29]

Among his closer acquaintances, Howells knew the personal anti-Semitic fears of Henry Adams, Charles Eliot Norton, and, most paranoiacally, James Russell Lowell.

[29] For a full-scale study of the immigrant threat to nineteenth-century Boston, and the eventual founding of the Immigration Restriction League of Boston, see Barbara Solomon, *Ancestors and Immigrants* (Cambridge: Harvard University Press, 1956). On Norton and the Jews, see my *Charles Eliot Norton*, pp. 219-220.

Adams abhorred the Jews *en masse* as early as 1858 in Berlin, where he had gone to study law. It seemed to him that the streets and the University were virtually glutted with Jews. Not until the Gilded Age, however, did he fully sense the crumbling social structure in America which threatened to bury the Adams dynasty and fortune. The *nouveau riche* entrepreneur was, for him, the Jew. Adams' anti-Semitism was nourished by visits with Lowell in Europe during the 1880s, and by the time of the Panic of 1893, Adams was certain that he had located the single cause of his family's devastated fortunes—the capitalist Jew who had been the villain in the world ever since he had corroded medieval idealism with destructive greed.

Howells' acquaintance with these attitudes and the men who expressed them was not remote. Norton, who was one of Howells' earliest patrons and most enduring friends, shared some of the same fears with Adams. When Norton returned from Europe in 1873, he looked to Howells for a favor—to find out the conditions of tenure in his old editorial office of the *North American Review*, then occupied by Adams and T. S. Perry. Though Norton would presently begin to make a far more significant contribution as Professor of Fine Arts at Harvard, Adams in a few years regretted that Norton was not available to take up once more the reins of the *Review* and ensure an editorial outlook purely native. "My terror is lest it should die on my hands or go to some Jew," Adams wrote to Henry Cabot Lodge, who fully shared his mentor's fears and would, as a senator in the years to come, lead the forces opposing further immigration in America.[30] And Norton, for all his humanity and (vacillating) liberal democratic sympathies, was soon advocating a quota to restrict Jews at Harvard and periodically bemoaning the decline of the pure American type in the wake of the new immigration

[30] May 26, 1875, *Letters of Henry Adams*, ed. W. C. Ford (Boston: Houghton Mifflin Co., 1930), I, 267.

at the bottom and the new gold at the top. In a letter whose contents probably infuriated Lowell as much as they amused him, Norton described the rise of the prominent, and to Norton semi-literate, Jewish Leiter family into Eastern cosmopolitan and summer-resort society in the 1880s:

They live now in Washington and Newport, and have bought their place in fashionable society. They give great and costly parties, and Mrs. L declares that society in Washington has become so overgrown that she is "really obliged to confine her invitations to the *demi-monde.*" She wanted her daughter's portrait painted as she said not with any splendid ornaments and dress "but entirely *au naturel.*" She was speaking one day of Baillie Loring's daughter, who is marvellously stout,—"a charming girl, full of talent, but what a pity that she's so obscene"![31]

It is finally Lowell in whom one senses the bewildered panic of anti-Semitism in the 1880s at its most extreme. Again, the personal ties for Howells were strong. Lowell, with Holmes, was Howells' oldest Boston acquaintance. In 1860, the young Ohio contributor to the *Atlantic* met its famed editor at the dinner arranged by publisher Fields. Howells considered Lowell's accepting the "Recent Italian Comedy" for the *North American Review* in 1864 to be the turning point of his life. After the war, when Howells made his home in Boston, the two frequently went on long walks and had dinner together each week, as Lowell helped to advance Howells' career as a writer, editor, and even, briefly, as college professor at Cornell in 1870. But in the later 1870s, it was to Howells that Lowell turned for favors, as did Norton also. Howells was responsible for Lowell's receiving the ambassadorship to Spain in 1877— Howells was campaign biographer of Hayes, a cousin of Mrs. Howells—and again helped Lowell receive the appointment to England in 1880. In this continuing friend-

31 Sept. 8, 1889 (Harvard).

ship, made close by mutual interests and mutual favors, Howells came to know Brahmin anti-Semitism from its leading exponent. By 1882 and 1883, when the two men were frequently together in London, the subject of the Jew had taken on for Lowell the proportions of a nightmarish paranoia. A visitor of his at this time wrote later in the *Atlantic Monthly* (anonymously!) : "He detected a Jew in every hiding place and under every disguise." In the fields of finance, real estate, publishing, politics, diplomacy, "this insidious race had penetrated and permeated the human family more universally than any other influence except original sin." When the Jews gained complete control of the earth, what would they do with the world and the gentiles in it? Lowell was asked. " 'That,' he answered, turning towards me, and in a whisper audible to the whole table, 'that is the question which will eventually drive me mad.' "[32]

Exaggerated as Lowell's response may have been, and he was probably exaggerating even further to amuse his dinner-table listeners, his fear of the Jew grew out of a recognized fact of Gilded Age social history: the Jews were among the most spectacular rising men of the period. With understandable pride in rising from his former status of street vendor, the Jew often displayed his new wealth flamboyantly, and thereby encouraged the making of an ethnic symbol of financial power combined with the ostentatious crudity of the enterprising, status-seeking parvenu in America. By 1877, as Howells was himself vacationing at Newport, the quarter-million Jews in America had become a threat to fashionable summer resort society. The most celebrated case that year was banker Joseph Seligman's being denied a room at Saratoga's Grand Hotel. In the 1880s, with the foreigner-as-

[32] "Conversations with Mr. Lowell," *At.Mo.*, LXXIX (Jan. 1897) , 128-129. The *Atlantic Index* later identified the author to be Sarah Butler Wister, mother of Owen Wister.

labor-anarchist threatening social stability from one direction, and the foreigner-as-successful-newly-rich-businessman assaulting established social barriers from another, *Life* magazine could expect its readers to be sympathetic to its anti-immigration cartoons. Among its most severe caricatures of the Jew is one depicting a vulgarly overdecorated carriage loaded with overdressed Jews in which "Mr. Moses Lichtenstein" is aping the "Four Hundred."[33] Howells' friend Henry James noted the same change in the American scene when he returned shortly after the turn of the century and discovered at first hand what he had heard Lowell inveigh against in England during the period just before *Silas Lapham*. In New York, James grimly surveyed "the extent of the Hebrew conquest . . . a Jewry that had burst all bounds." He likened this inundation, in tones reminiscent of Adams and Lowell, to "the bottom of some vast shallow aquarium in which innumerable fish of over-developed proboscis, were to bump together, for ever, amid heaped spoils of the *sea*." In Boston, the new immigrant races whom James confronted face-to-face presented an even grimmer scene: "The people before me were gross aliens to a man, and they were in serene and triumphant possession."[34]

Howells, then, was hitting close to the heart of one of the most threatening aspects of the rising man in that age when he presented the Anglo-Saxon fear of the growing

[33] See John Higham, *Strangers in the Land* (New Brunswick, N.J.: Rutgers University Press, 1955) , p. 211. For a valuable treatment of anti-Semitism in the industrial decades after the Civil War see, in addition to Solomon cited previously, Mr. Higham's "Anti-Semitism in the Gilded Age: A Reinterpretation," *Mississippi Valley Historical Review*, XLIII (March 1957) , 559-578; and the same author's "Social Discrimination Against Jews in America, 1830-1930," *Publications of the American Jewish Historical Society*, XLVII (Sept. 1957) , 1-33.

Historian Oscar Handlin's earlier minimizing of anti-Semitic attitudes in the Gilded Age is strongly questioned by Mr. Higham in his recent scholarship of the period.

[34] *The American Scene* (New York: Harper and Bros., 1907) , pp. 131-132, 231.

status of the Jew in Boston. As could be expected, Jewish readers of the *Century* studied carefully the implications of Silas's and Mrs. Lapham's comments. Three of these readers wrote to Howells and accused him of actually encouraging a rise of anti-Semitism in America. To repeat, without dispelling it, the vicious rumor that Jewish neighbors lowered the value of property was, in fact, an indirect way of feeding the prejudice. Howells defended the ironic intention of the passages, but he deleted them forthwith. He explained in his reply to one of the readers, Cyrus L. Sulzberger, editor of the *American Hebrew*:

I supposed that I was writing in reprobation of the prejudice of which you justly complain, but my irony seems to have fallen short of the mark—so far short that you are not the first Hebrew to accuse me of "pandering" to the stupid and cruel feeling against your race and religion. . . . In that passage I merely recognized to rebuke it, the existence of a feeling which civilized men should be ashamed of. But perhaps it is better not to recognize all the facts.[35]

The final sentence surely moves us closer to the heart of Howells' conflict. Had he been able to recognize all the facts regarding this unlovely aspect of the Brahmin mentality, he might well have felt a strong disengagement from his Boston acquaintances, the tough-minded attitude

[35] July 17, 1885, quoted in George Arms and William M. Gibson, " 'Silas Lapham,' 'Daisy Miller,' and the Jews," *New England Quarterly*, xvi (March 1943) , 118-122. The authors here provide a brief interpretation that falls just short of the mark. They consider the Laphams' remarks to be admirably ironic and therefore wish that "Howells had considered more acutely the possibility of not yielding to a pressure group" (p. 122) . They miss, also, some of the intensity and confused ambivalence of anti-Semitism by imputing mere snobbery to Mr. Sulzberger's objection, "It is not alone upon the ignorant and uncultured of the Jews that you reflect" (p. 120) . The more established and educated German-American Jew was concerned that the new immigration of unschooled and foreign-speaking East European Jews in this period would rouse to even higher pitch the mounting anti-Semitism among American nationalists, whom Mr. Sulzberger refers to as "the number—unfortunately too large—of Jew-haters in America" (p. 122) . See, for example, Zosa Sjajkowski, "The Attitude of American Jews to East European Jewish Immigration (1881-1893) ," *Publications of American Jewish Historical Society*, xl (March 1951) , 221-235.

which has sometimes been attributed to him. Instead, what startles one here is the very frank self-irony with which Howells defined his own dilemma. Though he recognized the strain of racism in these eminent colleagues, and allegedly meant to satirize and rebuke it, he felt himself tied to Lowell, Norton, and the rest on too many other counts to allow him to "recognize all the facts" about these "civilized men."

But there is more. What of Howells' own private feelings about the Jews? Deleting these passages out of sympathy for Jewish feeling, since his irony had misfired, was one thing. But one strongly suspects that Howells may have been willing to avoid, thereby, an issue on which his own feelings were probably not clear to himself. Why, for example, did he not rewrite the passages to make the "stupid and cruel feeling" more apparent to the victims of it, the audience with whom he professed his sympathy? Anti-Semitism could easily have been made a bit less vague. Tom Corey as the indoctrinator of Irene and Mrs. Lapham had been identified only as a "young man" in the original passage. And if Silas's remarks actually were meant to portray him as unwittingly anti-Semitic, surely Howells' artistic subtlety would not have suffered greatly by a slight elaboration of the comic portrait. Irony has literary uses, to be sure, but it can also provide a convenient shield for hiding one's personal, ambivalent feelings. By recasting the passage, Howells could also have alleviated whatever residual guilt he may have felt for once writing in the *Atlantic* that the "dread advance of the Irish" was at that time lowering the value of homes. Or if an ironic Howells was then recognizing to rebuke anti-Irish prejudice and panic selling, still he had written to Norton in the same month:

Our Sacramento Street has lately become much less desirable than it was: Irish have moved in, and I think it would be the part of prudence to sell the house if I could find a good pur-chaser. I'm afraid it will depreciate on my hands.[36]

Howells' sympathetic letter to Mr. Sulzberger indicates that by 1885 these early sentiments about race had grown perhaps more complex and divided. No conclusive proof has come to light that Howells ever was able to resolve these feelings.

Indeed, to the extent that he retained his village re-flexes, why should we expect Howells to discover within himself, as he did not in his rural Silas Lapham, clearly pro-Semitic feelings? In *A Modern Instance*, Howells had posed Kinney, the vulnerable and faded pioneer of the West, in opposition to the unscrupulous new pioneer of business—the Jew. Not once but twice, Howells indicated that Kinney travelled into the city only to be victimized by the "cheap clothier" Jew.[37] In this period, the Jew rather widely called to mind, also, the financial tyranny of a fixed gold standard emanating from the House of Roth-schild in England. It may be worth speculating whether this fact helps to explain why it should be English money in search of Silas's Western property that threatens to corrupt him during his moral crisis in the book.[38] In the

[36] "A Pedestrian Tour," xxiv (Nov. 1869), 595; to Norton, Nov. 7, 1869 (Harvard).

[37] *A Modern Instance*, ed. Gibson (Boston, 1957), pp. 86, 245. The Jew as shyster-haberdasher appears elsewhere in Howells. Two instances are "A Romance of Real Life," *At.Mo.*, xxv (March 1870), 305; and *Their Wedding Journey*, pp. 67-68.

[38] In a rather cryptic note at the end of a letter from Europe in 1883, Howells had written, "The young Baron Rothschild has taken a fancy to Clarence King (as if that man had not luck enough already!) and wants to live with him" (letter to Warner, March 4, 1883, *Letters*, I, 337). In view of King's associations with the West, the implications of this mild corruption for *Silas Lapham* are at least tantalizing.

Norman Pollack's recent work effectively shows that, excepting Ignatius Donnelly's *Caesar's Column*, anti-Semitism cannot be documented in the Populist Movement in the West. Highly suggestive, however, is Howells' comment in 1890 as he was casting about for a third party which would aid the farmer: "I should like to see the government lending to any one on good security at interest so low that industry might live *and usury perish* (to his father, April 27, 1890, *Letters*, II, 3, italics added). The year after *Silas Lapham,* Susy Clemens wrote that one evening at Hartford Howells had alluded to the matter we have been discussing: "After he received letters from 'two or three Jews' objecting to 'a sentence about a Jew' " in the serialized novel, he had deleted it.[39] This is skimpy evidence, to be sure. But assuming that Susy, then in her early teens, was quoting Howells accurately, one cannot help noticing the casual under-playing of the actual passages and the intensity of feeling they had occasioned.

Indeed, one hears the same casual note in *My Mark Twain,* when Howells writes of Lowell's wholesale anti-Semitism: "He stopped as if with the long Semitic curve of Clemens' nose, which in the indulgence of his passion for finding every one more or less a Jew he pronounced unmistakably racial."[40] Professor Bennett here interprets Howells' unwillingness to rebuke this old-guard nativism of Lowell, Longfellow, and the others to be "a tribute to the balance of his intellect and the sweetness of his personality," a compliment which only "the professional humanitarian" would deny Howells.[41] I do not argue that Howells, in the letter mentioned previously, was insincere when he rejected anti-Jewish prejudice. But the difference in the sympathy and outrage of that statement and the rather offhand tone of his other comments may suggest unresolved conflict rather than intellectual balance. This uneasiness would have come from the need to ignore some of the facts about his friends—and perhaps also about himself. In the light of Howells' own rise in social status on Beacon Street, was he not agreeing to a conspiracy of

---

Jew as international usurer was one of the favorite stereotypes of later Gilded Age anti-Semitism, and his influence, Howells implies, has been felt in the West.

[39] Quoted in *Twain-Howells Letters,* II, 555. See also *Susy and Mark Twain: Family Dialogues,* arr. and ed. by Edith C. Salsbury (New York: Harper and Row, 1965), p. 223.

[40] *Literary Friends and Acquaintance,* p. 350.

[41] *William Dean Howells,* p. 141.

silence about the vicious aspects of racism because of his
own disturbed feelings about the advancing Jew? Humanitarian sympathy had certain limits when one recognized
that the Jew *was* threatening a time-honored Boston social
stratification that excluded Jews from respectability, the
social structure which had been the necessary gauge of
Howells' own rise. More fully than he sometimes may
have cared to admit to himself, Howells identified himself
with an older Boston of established Anglo-Saxon culture
and enterprise. Twice before, he had contrasted the dignity and integrity of the older entrepreneur with the new
men of business, high and low, who were vulgar, acquisi-
tive, and amoral. One recalls the encounter between
Ricker and Bartley Hubbard in *A Modern Instance*. The
same conflict pervaded the early chapters of *A Woman's
Reason* (1883) and charged the novel with momentary
vitality and interest. But Howells could not sustain the
theme after his elderly India merchant died and the focus
shifted to his job-seeking daughter. In *Silas Lapham*, however, Howells was prepared to shape an entire novel out
of this scramble for new wealth and status in America.
Crucial in the outcome of Silas Lapham's career would be
the oblique but unmistakable victory which Howells assigned to the old order. And in the years to come, he would
yearn for the purer Boston of the earlier part of the century and write about it in tones even more nostalgic than
his elder contemporaries who had actually lived in the
golden days of clearly marked social distinctions and unmixed good breeding.

IV

One more passage in the serial gives us a further glimpse
into Howells' troubled spirit in 1884. At this point we
begin to sense how his incipient social conflict over status
was being complicated and intensified by his literary conflict with Boston and Cambridge, including some of his

closest acquaintances. The revealing passage I have in mind occurs in chapter one during Bartley Hubbard's "Solid Men of Boston" interview with Silas Lapham. Silas is proudly recounting his self-made rise to riches, while Bartley amuses himself by jotting down sardonic phrases in his notebook. Silas reminds himself momentarily that brave Mrs. Lapham must share at least partial credit for the Laphams' first million. The tribute obviously tickles Bartley, and he describes Mrs. Lapham as "one of those women who, in whatever walk of life, seem born to honour the name of American Woman, and to redeem it from the national reproach of Daisy Millerism" (p. 18). Howells was probably not aware that he had just committed a four-year anachronism (the parallel action in *A Modern Instance*, chapter nineteen, dates roughly at August 1874; "Daisy Miller" first appeared in *Cornhill Magazine* in June-July 1878). Presumably he was embarrassed when an alert reader promptly informed him of his error. Yet Howells, with surprising stubbornness, maintained that the allusion to Daisy Miller was indispensable and could not be deleted. It suggested "the complexion of the period," he argued, and added even more cryptically that it gave "a characteristic tint in the portraiture."[42] What important revelation of the period and the characters was Howells claiming for the tiny anachronism in this reference to the fiction of Henry James?

Howells and James had met in 1866. The two seem to have dismissed all formality and engaged at once in long talks on the art of the novel. Howells launched his younger friend on a successful literary career in the seventies, publishing James as often as he could in the pages of the *Atlantic*. They reviewed each other's work, and drew mutual courage from a shared encounter against proponents of an older theory of fiction. The friendship continued fifty years to James's death in 1916. In an unfinished

[42] "'Anachronism,'" *Century* XXIX (Jan. 1885), 477.

essay four years later, Howells was still discussing, in the year of his own death, one of his favorite subjects—"The American James."

One important period in this relationship concerns us here—the years between "Daisy Miller" and *Silas Lapham*. During the months after James's novella appeared, Howells watched in dismay the popular misreading of his friend's ambiguous but essentially sympathetic study of the American girl. Howells summed up for Lowell in Spain the American reaction to James's heroine:

> Harry James waked up all the women with *Daisy Miller*, the intentions of which they misconceived, and there has been a vast discussion in which nobody felt very deeply, and everybody talked very loudly. The thing went so far that society almost divided itself in Daisy Millerites and anti-Daisy Millerites.[43]

In the same year, Howells gave implicit support to James's characterization of the American girl by presenting readers with Lydia Blood in *The Lady of the Aroostook* (1879). And he made more direct his campaign for lifelike heroines in fiction through explicit dialog in *A Modern Instance*. Ben Halleck remarks during one conversation with Atherton, " 'I wonder the novelists don't take a hint from [real life], and stop giving us those scaly heroines they've been running lately.' " And later, the two bachelors realize why they cannot understand or predict the behavior of a Marcia Gaylord. As he closes the novel he is reading, Atherton observes that " 'we bachelors get most of our doctrine about women from [the novelists]. We don't go to nature for our impressions; but neither do the novelists, for that matter.' "[44]

After he had completed *A Modern Instance*, and before sailing to Europe in the summer of 1882, Howells argued the case of Daisy Miller and her author in an essay for *Century* magazine. He was in no mood to mollify James's

---

[43] June 22, 1879, *Letters*, I, 271.
[44] *A Modern Instance*, ed. Gibson (Boston, 1957), pp. 171, 225-226.

detractors, and in return he was about to absorb some of
the strongest abuse of his life. During his defense of Daisy
Miller, Howells linked James to Continental fiction while
slighting his British contemporaries, Thackeray, Dickens,
Reade, and Trollope as "great men . . . of the past."[45] The
article landed among the English with bombshell effect,
and Howells was promptly vilified in both *Blackwood's*
and the *Quarterly Review*. But Howells defied his English
critics. Given a chance to rewrite the essay, he would
delete nothing he had written, he told Roswell Smith of
Century. In fact, he "should only wish to amplify and
intensify the opinions that they object to."[46] Writing to
Perry the next year, Howells confessed that, aside from
drawing James into the fracas, he was upset mainly over
the "stupid" reaction at home.[47] Disparagement of some
of the favorite English novelists of the American reading
public had not won friends for Howells in Boston and
elsewhere. The attack against him in the *Quarterly Review* was reprinted in *The Boston Transcript* and, despite
Curtis's defense of Howells in *Harper's* "Easy Chair,"
Howells found himself entering a new and decidedly less
tranquil phase of his writing career.[48] Having defended
James's sensitive study of an American girl's "indestruct-
ible innocence, her invulnerable new-worldliness," Howells himself was, in effect, being reproached for Daisy
Millerism. Hamlin Garland, in Boston during the year of
Silas Lapham, observed that

all literary Boston was divided into three parts, those who liked
[Howells] and read him; those who read him and hated him,
and those who just plain hated him. The most fiercely debated

45 "Henry James, Jr.," *Century*, xxv (Nov. 1882) , 28.
46 Nov. 19, 1882, *Letters*, I, 329.
47 March 13, 1883, *Letters*, I, 338.
48 The "Easy Chair," *Harper's*, LXVI (Jan. 1883) , 304, called attention to
the American misreading of Daisy, but made no reference to Howells. In
April, however, Curtis reviewed the entire affair, including the specific
charges of Anglophobia the *Quarterly Review* had levelled against Howells
(*ibid.*, 791-793) .

question in many clubs ran something like this: "Are Howells' heroines true to life or are they merely satiric types?" and most of his feminine critics were fiercely indignant over his "injustice to women." *"He never depicts a noble woman,"* they declared.[49]

His female critics could not have known that Howells, far from being a callow anti-feminist, had preferred the conversation of women to men since his youthful evenings in Columbus. And in later years, he would champion American women's suffrage in his pages of *Harper's*.

The misunderstanding of "Daisy Miller" and resentment over Howells' defense of James crystallized, as he well knew, the attitudes against the new postwar fiction shared by many of his Brahmin and other acquaintances— Hayne, Bayard Taylor, Stedman, W. C. Brownell, Warner, Lowell, and Norton.[50] One cannot help marvelling that Howells bore up under this knowledge so well as he did in his personal relationships with these men. The problem which has plagued Howells critics is implicit at this very point—the difficulty of explaining how he could possibly feel a strong identification with the social ideals of the Boston élite when their tastes in fiction often ran counter to his own. The logic has seemed to be that Howells, in developing as a modern novelist in Boston, *must* have admitted to himself that he was an outsider. He therefore developed a satirical perspective on these acquaintances. But the evidence up to now does not consistently support such a conclusion. That Howells maintained his friendships with these men despite certain differences on the theory of fiction argues instead that the mutual social interests and ideals already mentioned had to be closely shared. His theory of fiction demanded an outlet which would, at the same time, allow the friendships to remain

---

[49] "Meetings with Howells," *Bookman*, XLV (March 1917), 2.
[50] I have described some of the intensity of Howells' esthetic quarrel with one of these Brahmin idealists in *Charles Eliot Norton*, pp. 150-158.

intact. He found the needed release with a certain im-
punity at this time whenever he permitted the characters
in the novels to carry on the debate.

So in 1884, as his co-warrior James was bringing together
his defense of the new novel in "The Art of Fiction,"
Howells was preparing his in the pages of *Silas Lapham.*
Indeed, in his zeal to strike back at his opponents, Howells
seemed at times in the novel to be asking the reader to
side with the character who displayed the best taste in
literature. Irene Lapham reveals her shallowness by telling
a comically indulgent Tom Corey that the library in the
Lapham's new Back Bay home will need to have the right
books and the right bindings. Shakespeare aside, she is certain only of two names—Scott and Cooper. She has not read
their novels, however, and thereby is innocently admitting
that she has been influenced by what is obviously the popular "romantic" taste of the day. In the love triangle that develops, she loses out. Her more perceptive sister Penelope,
on the other hand, does read sentimental fiction, and complains of the currently popular novel, *Tears, Idle Tears,*
"Why can't they let people have a chance to behave reason-
ably in stories?" (p. 178). At the Corey dinner, however,
Clara Kingsbury describes the same novel as "perfectly
heartbreaking" (p. 161). At that point, the Reverend Mr.
Sewell intercedes to bring logical and perhaps, by implication, supernatural support to Howells' and James's
concept of the novel. He considers sentimental fiction
dangerous and "noxious" to a sane view of life, and adds,
"The novelists might be the greatest possible help to us if
they painted life as it is . . ." (p. 162). Again, when the
Reverend Mr. Sewell meets with the elder Laphams and
recommends the "economy of pain" as the solution to the
romantic triangle of Irene, Penelope, and Tom (the same
practical formula, incidentally, which will solve Silas's
own ethical dilemma with Rogers and the English financial agents), the minister suspects why so much moral

confusion prevails in the world: "It comes from the novels that befool and debauch almost every intelligence in some degree" (p. 198).

All of these passages (the novel contains more) help to explain why Howells refused to delete even the brief, ironic defense of Henry James. If both he and James were out of step with the literary spirit of Boston, they could at least enjoy their private laugh together. Moreover, in a relationship marked by a fair amount of mutual banter and gentle prodding, we have reason to believe that James responded to the joke. In his essay on Howells the following year, in fact, he specifically praised the "admirable, humorous image" of that "ineffectual sinner," Bartley Hubbard. And more pointedly regarding heroines of fiction, the Daisy Millers of Howells' novel, James added, "Everything in *Silas Lapham* is superior—nothing more so than the whole picture of casual female youth. . . ."[51]

Howells' growing warfare against the sentimental and improbable in fiction led him to the obtrusive literary polemics in *Silas Lapham*. And yet for all his jibes against the old-fashioned novel, Howells appears not to have greatly offended the romantic-idealists among his older friends. Indeed, some of them were highly pleased with this dramatic study of new Boston. What was the essential meaning they had discovered in the book?

V

In the original five-page synopsis, actually a prospectus, entitled "The Rise of Silas Needham," Howells devoted nearly the entire sketch to his intended portrayal of Silas. He buried in two short sentences the subject of a closely related subplot:

His family and its social status in Boston is depicted in a series of incidents all bearing on the main story. The romance

[51] "William Dean Howells," *Harper's Weekly*, xxx (June 19, 1886), 394.

of his daughter's love-story, and her marriage against his liking is told.[52]

One suspects, then, that crucial conflicts troubling Howells during the composition of the novel after he had submitted his synopsis to the *Century* can rightly be predicated from the enlarged subplot.

Keeping the synopsis in mind, one realizes how fully Howells shifted his conception of the novel from the central moral dilemma of a blustering and uncultivated new millionaire to a more general inquiry into the social structure of a new era in America. The problem was specifically a Boston changing from the Brahmin certainties of Bromfield Corey's youth to a more fluid social order in the Boston of the seventies and eighties. In the early serialized chapters Howells was prepared to go into some of the most critical problems confronting new Boston, including the anti-Semitism of Tom Corey (willingly adopted by Mrs. Lapham and echoed by Silas) and, augmenting the threat of the new immigrant plutocracy, the threat also of the impoverished radical workingman in Boston's slums. But if he had been forced to modify and delete some of this bold first writing, he could still project the *solution* to this complex problem of "status."

As the novel developed, Howells apparently meant to keep the families Lapham and Corey in balance. He was not going to satirize the Coreys to the advantage of the ambitious, newly status-conscious Laphams.[53] The elder

---

[52] "The Rise of Silas Needham," pp. 2-3, ms. in Huntington Library, San Marino, California.

[53] In addition to the Laphams' original comments about rich Jews was Silas's annoyed impatience with their furnace-tender: "I'll be the death of that nigger *yet*." See *Century*, VII (Nov. 1884) , 26. Howells retained the passage in the published novel, but revised Silas's word "nigger" to what Howells apparently intended the reader to feel was the more sympathetic term, "darky" (p. 30) .

For Howells' later role in the founding of the NAACP and his relationship with Paul Lawrence Dunbar, see Cady, *The Realist at War*, pp. 161-162. Thomas W. Ford, "Howells and the American Negro," *Texas Studies in Language and Literature*, V (Winter 1964) , 530-537, praises Howells' sophisticated handling of the "color line" in *An Imperative Duty* (1892) .

Coreys have, unarguably, the prior claim to Boston by virtue of birthright—and are rather haughtily aware of it—while the elder Laphams have earned a rightful place in the new Boston, albeit insecure as yet, through solid achievement. But we soon come to know that the elder Laphams are not being groomed for the leadership of new Boston. In the opening chapter, Bartley Hubbard, for all his cynical humor about the yokel-on-the-rise, provides us with some correct intuitions about the Laphams. Silas *is* a humorless bore about his not quite self-made millions. Mrs. Lapham, with her moral angularities and her ludicrous jealousy of Zerilla Dewey late in the novel, *is* rightly contrasted to James's Daisy Miller. Similarly, Howells can admire the civilized virtues of Bromfield Corey, while allowing that the suave Corey gentility and prim social correctness cannot give the city the new leadership it needs in a rugged era of industrial enterprise. The Bromfield Coreys have a theoretical sympathy for the poor, but their practical acquaintance with the masses of society, who must soon be reckoned with, is seen to be too slight. Bromfield Corey moves, an alien figure, through the commercial streets of new Boston, and transacts (in Italian) the business of buying an apple (only to hold it) from a "swarthy fruiterer" (p. 117). And we easily see through the self-congratulatory charity work of a Clara Kingsbury, who knows her Italian slum dwellers even less well. What, then, is Boston of the future to do for leadership? Howells answered the question by developing and interweaving the subplot.

The story of Silas's business rise and his conflict between moral integrity and the gospel of wealth is proportionally much shorter in the novel than the reader may at first realize. The Corey-Lapham "subplot" interweaves roughly eighty per cent of the novel and frequently dominates the first twenty of the novel's twenty-seven chapters. It is, in other words, a *co-plot*. In developing this social conflict,

Howells also struck on the happy notion of creating a love triangle for the "Penelope's romance" of the synopsis. The advantages were important. Howells was able to establish an effective contrast between the Lapham daughters. Irene is the predictable heroine of romantic fiction, slight and pretty. Everyone assumes from the beginning that Tom Corey must be in love with her. But he displays his responsible taste by choosing the less stunning sister, a William Dean Howells heroine with character and good sense. Penelope has a third quality that makes her the more suitable wife for Tom Corey. Through self-education she has become a cultivated, natural aristocrat. Here Howells was covertly making his heroine somewhat palatable to his reading audience in Boston. The romantic triangle, then, had enabled Howells to develop the full significance of his earlier notebook jotting, "the young trees growing out of the fallen logs in the forest—the new life out of the old. Apply to Lapham's fall" (p. xv).

The crucial issues begin to merge in chapters twelve to fifteen, the heart of the novel which brings the Laphams and Coreys together at the Corey dinner party. The episode turns out to be an elimination ceremony for the Laphams—save for Penelope, who is conveniently absent from the socially complex affair. On the other hand, it is no victory for the Corey's and their "sterile elegance" (p. 118). What happens during and immediately after the dinner chapters becomes highly significant, and one is tempted to locate the moment when the bottom dropped out at just that point. Themes of Proper Boston smugness, new immigration and lower-class discontent, parvenu crudity, and Daisy Miller "realism" converge here.[54] At

[54] The Corey dinner could well have opened an old lesion in Howells' mind—that suffered at the traumatic Whittier dinner in 1877 when his friend Twain, like Lapham, seemed to be talking endlessly and indecorously before an apparently unamused audience of entrenched Bostonians. The incident is well known. I want only to suggest the strong parallels between the Whittier and Corey dinners—the dramatic social

the very least, the dinner scene forced upon Howells a crucial moment of truth early in the novel. With what one suspects to have been strong personal feelings of self-identity, Howells had described the dissimilar backgrounds of the Boston Laphams and the Boston Coreys. Yet his integrity had forced Howells to delineate the shortcomings of social and moral vision in both families. What hope then remained for Boston in the mid-seventies? Who was to lead the city in the turbulent era just ahead? Even the casual student of political democracy in 1884 could observe one of the signs; an Irish mayor had just been installed in city hall by a mass electorate of nineteenth-century immigrants.

In *The Rise of Silas Lapham* Howells tried to restore hope after the Corey dinner fiasco by turning in the next five chapters to the love triangle. Esthetically, too, he was trying to restore tension to the novel after the near-climactic scene which foreshadows the elder Laphams' exodus from Boston. This dramatic tension now depended on his developing and bringing to a successful resolution what had begun to comprise the important underlying theme of the novel, the forces of new Boston in conflict with the old, and an implicit struggle for the power to guide the future destinies of the city. Neither the elder Coreys nor the elder Laphams can provide the leadership which combines the moral and intellectual values of the past with the energy and vision necessary to forge a con-

---

conflict of the two events and the similar attitudes of mortification, remorse, and apology of Twain and Lapham. Howells' psychic blackout (he could remember no more of the Whittier dinner even though he had introduced eight more speakers) was followed by earnest excuses for Twain's "hideous mistake," a task he considered proper at the same time that he may deeply have resented both his friends' misjudgment and the genteel reaction to Twain's Western humor. Howells' keen memory almost certainly must have fixed on this abysmal occasion and forced him to relive its horrors (as he did again long afterwards in *My Mark Twain*) during the writing of Lapham's nervous preparation for the dinner, his hideous social blunders at the Coreys, and the agonizing aftermath.

servative path into the future. This happy blend does exist, however, in mingling the best of the Laphams (Penelope—a mixture of new native vigor with the old respect for intellect and morality) with the best of the Coreys (Tom—a mixture of the old culture and the new enterprise). Be it noted also, we are given subtle assurance that sentimental-romantic fiction will find no place in this ideal marriage.

So at the end, Silas, with chastened moral vision, gives up his aspirations for a status Back Bay address and, it is to be hoped as well, his sinful love of fast horses. He has refused to allow the devilish mischief of his ex-partner Milton Rogers and English gold to corrupt him and his America. He returns to a village America and the agrarian virtues that have managed to survive the roadway advertising of "Lapham's Mineral Paint" in the Vermont hills. At the same time, Howells provides us with the wedding of a streamlined Brahminism and a de-provincialized agrarian America. In the marriage of Tom and Penelope, he projected a vision of an ideal Boston of the future that his closest friends could not help but feel was a comforting prospect. The novel gave Lowell and Norton, both advocates of romantic idealism in fiction, a high degree of satisfaction. Lowell liked *Silas Lapham* immensely, and Norton read and reread the novel. Aside from their undoubted pleasure in the moral allegory of Silas's fall and rise, their approval must have come from the heartening prospect that Boston society, through impeccable young gentlemen like Tom Corey, might remain essentially intact despite the Silas Laphams, Bartley Hubbards, and a mounting population of immigrants. But Howells' *dramatic* problem of setting the prospect into actuality was harder, and he avoided it. Instead, he sent the couple to Mexico, where Tom will complete his apprenticeship as a Boston businessman. The hopeful possibility for the future was unmistakable, current political and economic realities of the Gilded Age notwithstanding. In the fullness of time, Lowell and Norton could feel, the counterparts of Tom Corey and Penelope Lapham would reappear to provide traditional Anglo-Saxon leadership for a new Boston. Perhaps it was to keep this brave hope alive that in his next novel, *The Minister's Charge* (earlier set aside for the more urgent *Silas Lapham*), Howells would include that the Coreys had grown rich once again "due to a piece of luck, and . . . the young Mr. Corey, whom they expected in the summer, had brought it about."[55]

VI

Reading *The Rise of Silas Lapham* in the light of biographical evidence that Howells was less than encouraged by the progress of democracy in Boston and in America—this is clearly a difficult and even treacherous method of adding to the insights one has gained from a close internal reading of the text itself. Yet given Howells' own admission that he suddenly had awakened to the mounting dangers of social inequality at this time, how does one escape the biographical approach to Howells' meaning within the novel? The present reinterpretation of *The Rise of Silas Lapham* has indicated that Howells seems a more complicated and troubled man during his residence in Boston than his critics, old and new, have fully conceded. The profound impasse that caused the psychic crisis during this intensive study of Boston in the Gilded Age demands an explanation that moves beyond the premise that Howells was either a servile captive or a detached critic of the city that had become his first long-time home. Howells appears to have resisted, unsuccessfully, a number of painful questionings about the inequities of Boston, and American, society during the writing of *The Rise of Silas Lapham*. These questions brought him certain identifiable conflicts which he could not resolve. While he was opposed to the undemocratic snobbery

55 Boston: Ticknor and Co., 1887, p. 382.

of Bostonians—both the Proper New and the Proper Old —he was more than dimly aware at this time that he did not welcome a new Boston electorate, or leadership, dominated by Italians, Irish, and Jews. A theoretical friend of an increasingly restive laboring class, he also aspired to the safe comforts of a residence in aristocratic Back Bay. He was first a grateful disciple and then a devoted friend of the Brahmins, and he regretted that their older taste for romance created an inevitable opposition to his new school of fiction. When he wrote of these friends, in both early years and late, he emphasized the cordial and humble qualities which commanded his respect. In an early letter to Lowell, he wrote, "I [have] never forgotten—how could I—the cordial and flattering reception you [and Dr. Holmes] gave a certain raw youngster who visited you in Boston five years ago—you old ones who *might* have put me off with a chilly patronage." After Norton had sailed to Europe in 1868, Howells described him as "a man of almost ideal purity and goodness—one of those incomprehensible beings who are always looking about the world, and seeking occasion to be useful and comfortable to somebody." After leaving the frequent company of Longfellow in 1871, Howells told his father, "I feel that I've not only been in contact with a great man, but a very good and humble man." Later in *Literary Friends and Acquaintance*, he paid his public tribute to the generous and delicate nature of these men, and recalled that his occasional differences with "any one" (a neat ambiguity) gave him a "bad conscience":

At times, when I had experienced from those elect spirits with whom I was associated, some act of friendship, as signal as it was delicate, I used to ask myself, how I could ever do anything unhandsome or ungenerous towards any one again; and I had a bad conscience the next time I did it.[56]

56 All letters appear in Vol. I of *Letters*: to Lowell, Aug. 21, 1864, p. 84; to J. M. Comly, June 27, 1868, p. 130; to William Cooper Howells, April 23, 1871, p. 164. See *Literary Friends and Acquaintance*, p. 287.

One of these cases of conscience concerned the "blush of a Republican" during the 1884 political campaign briefly mentioned earlier. During the months when he was writing the opening chapters of *Silas Lapham*, Howells affirmed his loyalty to the Republican Party and supported Blaine against Cleveland. Most of the Brahmins, plus Mark Twain, believed that Blaine had proved himself politically corrupt. They had turned Mugwump and, despite growing Irish power in the party of alleged "Rum, Romanism, and Rebellion," were supporting Cleveland's reform candidacy. Twain, in fact, was even more severe, apparently, than Howells' Boston friends. He baited an already disturbed Howells by accusing him of lacking a sensitive conscience during the bitter campaign. In replying, Howells countered Twain's moral objections to Blaine's politics by making an *ad hominem* attack against Cleveland. He said that he would not support the Democratic bachelor candidate because Cleveland was the father of an illegitimate child, and was therefore riding toward the White House on the double standard of sexual immorality. One suspects that an equally urgent reason for opposing Cleveland and his party was being camouflaged here—namely, Howells' objection as a practical politician to the mounting numbers of Irish in Boston and national politics.[57] And a practical politician Howells assuredly was. Few writers have been more knowledgeable than he on political affairs in America. He had served as campaign biographer of Lincoln and Hayes, and was a warm social acquaintance of both the Hayes and Garfield families. In chapter forty-nine of *April Hopes* (1888), Howells depicts life in Washington, D.C., with the economy and assurance of a novelist who treated the experience he knew most thoroughly. Not ignorance but an uncomfortably keen awareness of political and social conflict led Howells to devise

[57] Twain to Howells, Aug. 31, and Sept. 17, 1884; Howells to Twain, Sept. 4, 1884, in *Twain-Howells Letters*, II, 501, 503, 508-509.

the ultimate theme, or tacit counter-argument—the return of the native—for *The Rise of Silas Lapham.*

So Howells had gravitated to his spiritual home in Boston during the years of some of the most radical changes in our national life. His reactions toward urbanism were Brahmin even to the degree to which they contained the perspective of Western agrarianism. His Boston friends may have quarreled with Howells' portraying a "commonplace" America in fiction. But in actuality they had long cherished the Jeffersonian dream of an agrarian and village America. The yearning was never felt more strongly than after mid-century, as they began to watch the dreaded rise of the city and the mongrelization of Cambridge and Boston. Norton moved his summer residence from Newport to rural Ashfield in western Massachusetts in 1864. There only one Irish family tainted the purity of the village. And in the year of *Silas Lapham* Norton informed an audience in England that "The Great West [is] peopled by the children of New England"—so that Western agrarian virtues were closely linked with the pure Anglo-Saxon.[58] As a transplanted Westerner in Norton's Boston, Howells could fully understand his friends' playing down the role of "foreigners" in the winning of the West. More openly than Norton, Howells had remarked to his own countrymen, in the *Atlantic Monthly,* that the descendants of the Puritans had moved to the West. Unfortunately, foreign races had then moved into the vacuum created in New England.[59] And while the context cannot be established here, a comment by the Reverend Mr. Waters in *Indian Summer,* written just before (but published after) *Silas Lapham,* repeats the

[58] Address at the Tercentenary Celebration at Emmanuel College, Cambridge, England, 1884, in Norton Papers (Harvard).
[59] See for examples, "A Pedestrian Tour," *At.Mo.,* XXIV (Nov. 1869), 595; and "A Shaker Village," *ibid.,* XXXVII (June 1876), 706. Both in "Private Theatricals" (1875-1876) and in *Out of the Question* (1877), Howells had portrayed unsavory Irish "tramps" in the New England countryside.

historical observation Norton also was expressing at the time. The pure New England, Howells' minister remarks, had migrated to " 'the great middle West and the Pacific Coast.' "[60]

Howells' sentiment toward the average man in America was perhaps most like Lowell's (as Howells himself was able to recognize it in his friend)—a democracy of the head but not profoundly of the heart. His life and career both before and after *Silas Lapham* reveal the continuing lack of resolution in the mind of a natural conservative with a humanitarian conscience who was trying, but ultimately was unable, to respond to the radical democracy of the new industrialism in the East. What Tolstoy's Christian brotherhood would do for Howells soon after *Silas Lapham* would be to provide him with a non-violent ideological formula for bridging the chasm between the haves and have-nots in America. He rebuked the capitalists for having failed to practice the Christian virtue of brotherly love toward the laboring classes. And he deplored in equal degree the violence which characterized the labor movement in its desperate early struggle for a share of the nation's wealth. Why could the laborers not quell the monster of industrial capitalism by just choking it to death quietly with votes?

After *The Rise of Silas Lapham*, Howells successfully negotiated with publishers from year to year for his own share of the nation's wealth, to become, with Mark Twain, one of our wealthiest authors. His net worth in 1890 had risen to $60,000; in 1892, to $68,000; and (despite the panic of 1893) to $84,000 in 1894.[61] In the midst of this plenty, he admitted privately to his father the difficulty of finding a creed of social and economic democracy to live by:

[60] Boston: Ticknor and Co., 1886, p. 176.
[61] Cady, *The Realist at War*, p. 192.

[Mark Twain] and his wife and Elinor and I are all of accord in our way of thinking: that is, we are theoretical socialists, and practical aristocrats. But it is a comfort to be right theoretically, and to be ashamed of one's self practically.[62]

So by 1890, neither Tolstoy nor the writing of *The Minister's Charge* (1887), *Annie Kilburn* (1889), and *A Hazard of New Fortunes* (1890) had brought for Howells a satisfying articulation of the problems of social brotherhood, status, and privilege in America. Nor had he discovered it by 1894, after *A Traveler from Altruria*. In Paris to see his son in June of that year, he told Jonathan Sturges (as James remembered Sturges' account):

"Live all you can: it's a mistake not to. . . . I see it now. I haven't done so—and now I'm old. It's too late. It has gone past me—I've lost it."[63]

The remark gave to James the germ of *The Ambassadors*; does it not also furnish us with one more glimpse into a life of unresolved definition? Howells' concern over the inequalities of American society, during and after *The Rise of Silas Lapham,* had enlarged to become at times both courageous and profound. It was also confused. The theoretical socialist in him continued to be ashamed of the practical aristocrat. These conflicting sympathies led to irresolution of spirit and, at least once, during the writing of *Silas Lapham,* to some form of psychic desolation. Out of this returning ordeal of indecision in the years to come, he would create the novels which might yet advance the good and the true in human life, a fictional world which embraced, but never would solve, Howells' "riddle of our painful earth."

---

[62] Feb. 2, 1890, *Letters,* II, 1.
[63] *The Notebooks of Henry James,* ed. F. O. Matthiessen and Kenneth B. Murdock (New York: Oxford University Press, 1947), p. 226.

CHAPTER FOUR

A HAZARD OF NEW FORTUNES
(1889–1890)

ART AND HUMANITY IN THE
AMERICAN METROPOLIS

LATE in 1885, as *The Rise of Silas Lapham* was taking its chances with a partly hostile public, Howells contracted to give all his work to Harper's. Included in the agreement was a clause which was to become decisive in his literary future. He would write three to five pages a month in the "Editor's Study" of *Harper's Monthly.* Howells could not have known at the moment that he was turning a corner to begin a third phase of his career in the 1880s. In *The Undiscovered Country* and *A Modern Instance*, he had created a modern version of pastoral to encompass and unify his far-ranging treatment of religious disinheritance and moral disorder in modern America. Perhaps exhausted by the enormity of this disquieting subject, he had focused in *The Rise of Silas Lapham* on a more limited inquiry into the "truth" about the Gilded Age—the more definable questions of status, wealth, and social justice in new Boston. Yet in trying to define the social "good," he had tapped a deep-seated ambivalence toward the new democracy. The moment had arrived to re-examine his reason for being, to justify his calling as a novelist. Impelled in part by his reading of Tolstoy for the first time, Howells during the next six years filled the columns of the "Editor's Study" with an evolving theory of the modern novel.

He had begun to shape an esthetic for modern American

fiction during his *Atlantic* years. Occasionally, he had
injected bits of it into the dialogue of anti-romanticism
in his early psychological and social novels, as well as in
the passages of *A Modern Instance* and *The Rise of Silas
Lapham* already discussed. But not until this first period
with *Harper's* did he succeed in framing an articulate and
forceful argument for the new novel. In the opening
"Editor's Study," he alerted readers that "a man who
likes or dislikes can never be impartial," and they should
expect to suffer his grudges and prejudices. Throughout
these six years of esthetic controversy, he developed a
persistent theme, the interrelatedness of a writer's vision,
his craft, and his responsibility to humanity. For the most
part during these years, Howells maintained the ardor and
the poise—the "perception at the pitch of passion"—that
James had demanded from the modern critic. Howells
achieved this perception even though he sensed that the
heated literary debate had caught him in various contradictions and dilemmas he could not resolve. These self-
doubts are not heard in the "Editor's Study." One discovers them here and there in letters Howells wrote to his
closest friends. The most sustained and exciting revelation
of this more complex and uncertain Howells appears,
however, in the novel which developed in large part out
of the esthetic controversy in the "Editor's Study." *A
Hazard of New Fortunes*, begun in late 1888, has been
consistently interpreted as an economic or social novel.
It can also be profitably read as a dramatic treatise on
Howells' esthetics. Howells appears to have sensed at the
time that *Hazard* was to be his culminating experiment
in the art and the limits of the novel. To this end, he re-
enlisted the hero of *Their Wedding Journey* (1872), his
first experiment in long fiction, and created the largest
canvas of all his work. It is as though he had heard the
wish Henry James had recently expressed to brother William, that Howells move from his esthetic theorizing in

Harper's and actually write the modern novel which expressed his theory. For he did indeed write that novel in 1889 to climax his fictional achievement in the 1880s. *A Hazard of New Fortunes*, when illuminated by the "Editor's Study" and scattered esthetic views elsewhere, appears to be Howells' most searching expression of his *raison d'être* as an artist. It also embodies the conflicts he sensed in his commitment to what he labeled fictional "realism."[1]

Undeniably, in *Hazard* Howells does treat some of the basic social, economic, and moral problems of capitalism which he had recently examined in *The Rise of Silas Lapham, The Minister's Charge,* and *Annie Kilburn.* But this time he absorbs these questions into the issues of esthetic controversy in the late nineteenth century. The most important moments in the novel are imprinted on the slowly widening sensibility of Basil March, Boston insurance man and, like Howells, an unreconstructed poet who has accepted the editorial assignment for a New York literary journal. Howells also brings to life many other characters who provide a spectrum of esthetic responses current in the period. Most important is Angus Beaton,

---

1 James's letter dated Oct. 1-5, 1887, is in Ralph B. Perry's *The Thought and Character of William James* (Boston: Little Brown, 1935), I, 399-400. Modern interpretations of *Hazard*, all suggestive and valuable, include a reading of the novel as (1) a far-reaching comedy of manners (George Arms); (2) an economic novel underscoring selfishness and moral decay in a commercial civilization (George Bennett); (3) a social tragedy centering on the moral collapse of the newly rich Dryfoos family (Edwin Cady); (4) a study in social dependence with frequent echoes of Christian "myth" (Everett Carter); (5) the alternating estrangement and complicity of the intellectual in the modern world (Richard Foster); and (6) an examination of the new capitalism from the perspective of New England morality (Henry N. Smith).

See Arms, "Howells' New York Novel: Comedy and Belief," *New England Quarterly*, XXI (Sept. 1948), 313-325; Bennett, *William Dean Howells*, pp. 185-199; Cady, *The Realist at War*, pp. 100-133; Carter, *Howells and the Age of Realism*, pp. 201-224; Foster, "The Contemporaneity of Howells," *New England Quarterly*, XXXII (March 1959), 54-78; and Smith, *Mark Twain's Fable of Progress* (New Brunswick, N.J.: Rutgers University Press, 1964), pp. 20-35.

painter and sculptor, an alternate sensibility to March's. Beaton is insensible to the claims of humanity from first to last, and becomes the gauge to measure March's deepening sense that New York life may offer more to the artist than merely "picturesque" and romantic surfaces. Howells, himself deeply dissatisfied with American capitalism by then, was clearly tracing some of his own recognitions in the portrait of Beaton and the growing sympathies of March. But after this knowledge, how did the literary man bring his art to the service of his humane vision and thereby help to alter the conditions of his society? March at the end envisions no writing career for himself and no change in the editorial stance of his *Every Other Week*; and by the same token, Howells at the end of *Hazard* sets forth no dynamic role for literature and the arts in promoting social change. Why? Some of the reasons lie explicitly within the fabric of *Hazard*, as I hope to suggest in a new and fairly close paraphrase of the novel. Others become apparent when one relates the esthetic dilemma of Basil March to certain difficulties in Howells' current theory and practice of the novel. Finally, Howells could not prescribe a forceful role for art in an urban democracy because, as he revealed inadvertently in *Hazard*, and more frankly to closest friends, he could not cultivate an unequivocal alliance with the races and classes who populated the new democracy in America.

I

Hazard opens as Basil March is being persuaded by a brisk promoter, Fulkerson, to abandon the circumscribed world of Boston insurance in favor of a less certain fate as editor of a New York literary journal. In the months ahead, March will try to establish esthetic order out of his New York hazard of new fortunes. Within this sprawling new urban America, almost as complex and unfamiliar to Howells as to his literary hero, a fictional world of art and humanity gradually forms, and, as Howells recalled years later, the drama unfolded "as nearly without my conscious agency as I ever allow myself to think such things happen."[2] He experienced part of this organic flow of composition by building on recent events he could verify: his own househunting in New York; seeing a natural gas boom in the Midwest of the type which would turn his fictional Dryfoos into a millionaire; observing a wealthy young Conrad Dryfoos at a New York socialist meeting; and experiencing a New York streetcar strike early in 1889. Second, he could frame his materials at once within the esthetic issues he was currently articulating as literary editor of a New York journal. Finally, the doubts which lay for Howells within these issues could become the esthetic uncertainties of Basil March, his "literary adventurer" (p. xiii) whom he already knew intimately from several previous portraits.

In *Hazard*, March comes to life in a stroke: "After many years' experiment of a moustache and whiskers, he now wore his grizzled beard full, but cropped close; it gave him a certain grimness, corrected by the gentleness of his eyes" (pp. 1-2). His predominant trait is uncertainty, combined with a humane but skeptical openness to possibilities. Talking with Fulkerson about the New York magazine, March begins to feel a stirring of the dull roots of his earlier literary talent and says, " 'I gave up smoking and the Muse together. I suppose I could still manage a cigar, but I don't believe I could—' " (p. 2). Since the magazine will enlist painters, he will be inept: " 'I don't know anything about art' " (p. 7). Fulkerson is content, however, that March has the esthetic gifts which will supply a broad editorial approach for an American journal

2 My text is the New York Bantam Books edition by Van Wyck Brooks, 1960, selected here because it includes the highly revealing preface which Howells wrote in 1909 for the Library Edition of *Hazard*. The present quote, taken from this preface, is on p. xiv. All subsequent page numbers will appear in the text.

of the arts. To him, March is without " 'prejudice,' " a man of " 'taste,' " " 'conscience,' " and " 'horse sense' " (pp. 2, 3). Given his residence in both West and East, March will be able to " 'make this thing go, from ocean to ocean' " (p. 4). And he can impose his vision from the metropolitan hub of the country: " 'There's only one city that belongs to the whole country, and that's New York!' " (p. 6)

March is like the other husbands in Howells who turn to their wives for moral strength. Isabel March must supply the nerve and decisiveness which finally uproot them from their safe, uncommitted life in Boston and propel them onto the train southward and into the search for a new home in a strange city. They settle in a quiet New York hotel, where they had stayed on previous visits, and feel safely insulated from care, change, and the advancing future of the city. The Negro porters "never seemed to get older," the service recalls to them "the experience of an Arabian Nights hero" (p. 30), and they are willing to default on all worldly duties. But the present, in the form of the energetic Fulkerson, bursts in on them and sends them forth, supplied with immediate leads to New York flats for rent.

In their househunting, the Marches discover a broad range of life in the New York neighborhoods, from the well-to-do society of the comfortable flats to the disorder and poverty of the tenement areas. Most important, the colors and shadings and sounds of New York life begin to register on March's imagination, while the practical common sense of his wife serves as foil to her husband's poetic musings. But as success in their hunt recedes, he shares her urge to retreat from this new involvement within a burgeoning metropolis so changed from the New York of their earlier years. Still, March has an imagination in conflict with itself, for he is attracted to the present "gayety" and "picturesque" qualities of the heterogeneous city. And further, he is aware, but only dimly aware, that his "esthetic" yearnings lack any significant moral dimension. Emerging from breakfast on the second morning, the Marches, who are not Catholic, retreat from the noise of the streets into a matin service at the cathedral. When they come out into the "dazzle and bustle of the street," March defines their present motive as a non-religious effort to wall out the present by an esthetic pilgrimage into the past:

"No matter how consecrated we feel now," he said, "we mustn't forget that we went into the church for precisely the same reason that we went to the Vienna Cafe for breakfast—to gratify an aesthetic sense, to renew the faded pleasure of travel for a moment, to get back into the Europe of our youth. It was a purely Pagan impulse, Isabel, and we'd better own it" (p. 42).

They venture once more into the variegated city and regard "with equal esteem" the respectable old mansions on the north of Washington Square and the new "picturesque raggedness" on the south (p. 43).

Several times, March senses that wholesale misery dwells behind the "picturesque" spectacle of human life which they accidentally stumble onto in their wanderings. He expresses his conflicting feelings, however, not in moral anger but instead with protective irony. Riding in a "coupé" through a tenement district (the abode of "a poverty as hopeless as any in the world," says Howells), March comments: " 'I must say they don't seem to mind it. I haven't seen a jollier crowd anywhere in New York. . . . The only way for them is to keep an unbroken intimacy with the wolf; then they can manage somehow. I don't know how, and I'm afraid I don't want to' " (pp. 51, 52). His wife rebukes March for projecting, however ironically, his inexperienced responses onto the unfamiliar scene. " 'I don't believe there's any *real* suffering— not real *suffering*—among these people,' " she explains;

" 'that is, it would be suffering from our point of view, but they've been used to it all their lives, and they don't feel their discomfort so much' " (p. 54) . Then she proposes that they "go to the theatre"—to retreat once more from actuality. But at this moment, New York life suddenly impinges forcefully and she decides, on the spot, to go home to Boston and leave to her poetic husband the momentous choice of selecting their New York home. She has just witnessed an apparently starving man, an immigrant "with the hard hands and broken nails of a workman" (p. 55) , hunting for food in the gutter and among garbage heaps. Riding in the evening on the "Elevated" to the depot, however, revives her spirit and she enjoys, at a safe remove, "the fleeing intimacy you formed with people in second and third floor interiors" (p. 61) . March concurs, seemingly without irony, that it is "better than the theatre, of which it reminded him. . . . What suggestion! what drama! what infinite interest!" (p. 61) . Life in New York, briefly once more, has become magically picturesque for them, an exciting and glittering spectacle out of the *Arabian Nights.*

Several days later, after a bit of half-hearted searching, March, with his "absent-minded, dreamy inefficiency" (p. 62) and "the native lawlessness of his temperament" (p. 63) , makes what might be termed a decision. Egged on by Fulkerson, he decides to rent the apartment of Mrs. Green, an esthetic hodgepodge in interior decoration which reflects the formless and vulgar taste of the raw new city. Meanwhile, he dines with Fulkerson at Maroni's Italian restaurant and is brought even closer to the human mixture that is New York City. Equally important, Fulkerson acquaints March with some of the characters who will form his entourage in the future. He learns that his "angel" is Dryfoos, a newly rich oil millionaire-farmer from March's native Indiana and, like March, now transplanted to New York. Dryfoos hopes to gain respectability in New

York, says Fulkerson, in order to " 'get his daughters into the old Knickerbocker society' " (p. 73) and to dissuade his son from the ministry and into the business world of literary journalism. As they leave the restaurant, March meets the man who will provide him with the crisis of his esthetic career. Lindau, his old German literary teacher from Indianapolis, has, like Dryfoos, become an alien figure in New York. After losing his hand in the Civil War, Lindau has been living in urban poverty during the postwar years. He has lost, in addition, his faith in the American dream. After listening to the radical Lindau, and also to Fulkerson's casual dismissal of this " 'soured old German,' " March is "half-consciously tormented" (p. 78) by the mysterious ill-fortune which has overtaken his old teacher. The first part of *Hazard* closes here, with March on the outer edges of his first great commitment. As editor of a literary magazine in New York, he has been thrust not only into the hub of American esthetic life, but has faintly sensed the encircling implications of social and economic disorder within this life. Unaware of trouble ahead, however, except in doubts about the "art leg" of the journal, March eagerly plunges into his new career:

In giving rein to ambitions long forborne he seemed to get back to the youth when he had indulged them first; and after half a lifetime passed in pursuits alien to his nature, he was feeling the serene happiness of being mated through his work to his early love (p. 83) .

In Part First of *Hazard*, Howells describes the reawakening of March's poetic attitudes toward life and art. Howells does not employ the key terms of his critical warfare—"realism" versus "romanticism"—but these opposing concepts are obviously at the heart of March's initiation. For Howells, too, the tug of the past and old-world esthetic associations of order and tradition jarred against his conviction that the writer should treat the homely variety of commonplace life in modern America. March's impulse, shared by his wife, to escape the unpleasant encounter with a starving man and instead attend the theatre, or to blink the moral degradation of tenement life by responding to its "picturesqueness"—these were social and moral issues at the heart of Howells' own esthetic dilemma.

Regarding the theatre, for example, Howells had currently been asking in the "Editor's Study" for a new drama on the American stage which would treat modern life as honestly as the current fiction he was championing. When he praised a current *Mark Rutherford* novel by W. H. White as a work that would appeal to the mind rather than provide escape through mere amusement, Howells added testily, "Or rather it will do this with readers who can think and feel; and the other sort had better go to the theatre and see a modern play."[3] Just as the older fiction of "romanticism" had done, the modern theatre produced sensational effects to shock and amuse. Howells borrowed a term from the contemporary Spanish master of fiction, Valdés, to condemn "the *effectists* who delight genteel people of all the theatres, and in most of the romances." Like most of the fiction of the past, Howells wrote, "we believe the stage play to be still almost wholly injurious, through its falsehood, its folly, its wantonness, its aimlessness."[4] Yet these tirades against the current theatre may have derived part of their heat from Howells' own inconsistency. He was currently writing farces which, though pointedly anti-sentimental, were mainly designed to delight genteel people with harmless folly. In April 1889, he collected for popular amusement his "The Garroters" (1885), "The Mouse-Trap" (1886), "Five O'Clock Tea" (1887), and "A Likely Story" (1888). And for the reader who craved more of the same, Howells supplied a second volume the next month: "The Parlor-Car" (1876), "The

<hr>

[3] See "Editor's Study," *Harper's Monthly*, LXXII (Feb. 1886), 485. These columns are shortened hereafter to "Study." Howells appears to have written most of them three or four months before they were printed.

[4] "Study," LXXIX (Nov. 1889), 965, and LXXIV (April 1887), 825.

Sleeping-Car" (1882), "The Register" (1883), and "The Elevator" (1884).[5]

The theatre is not March's only "romantic" peccadillo. He prettifies the facts of New York life by observing effects of the "picturesque." In the "Editor's Study" from 1886 to 1889, one can trace the term often enough to establish Howells' immediate implication in *Hazard*. Reviewing books on New York life, he commented on H. C. Bunner's *Midge*: ". . . in the characters generally the author abandons himself in regrettable degree to queerness and quaintness and picturesqueness." Cable's *Bonaventure* was a "romance" with "picturesque material"; his *Grandissimes* had been a "novel" with "powerful realities." J. K. Hosmer's *Life of Young Sir Henry Vane* was "simple, familiar, personal, without being undignified. . . . It is a very different sort of thing from the romantic picturesqueness attempted formerly in minor historical narrations. . . ."[6] But Howells, like his hero March, felt the pull of "romantic picturesqueness" as he responded to life in New York, as earlier he had experienced Venice, through the eye of the poet and painter. He wrote to James at the outset of *Hazard*, "At the bottom of our wicked hearts we all like New York," and then suggested the reaction which March will experience in the "gay ugliness, the shapeless, graceful, reckless picturesqueness" of New York City. As Howells told James in October 1888: "I hope to use some of its vast, gay, shapeless life in my fiction."[7]

---

[5] Louis J. Budd, "W. D. Howells' Defense of the Romance," *PMLA*, LXVII (March 1952), agrees that Howells temperamentally was far more inclined toward the "romance" than is commonly believed, that "Howells throughout his life published poetry, drama, and fiction which was improbable and farfetched and which hoped for little more than to amuse or bemuse the reader (and to assure the author's livelihood)" (p. 39).

[6] "Study," LXXIV (April 1887), 828; LXXVII (Oct. 1888), 801; LXXVIII (March 1889), 660-661.

[7] *Letters*, I, 417.

II

After establishing March's incipient romanticist-realist conflict in Part First, Howells proceeds in Part Second to place his hero within the community of art in New York. Through an ample gallery of characters, Howells portrays the many facets of esthetic life in the American city. Alma Leighton blends her deceased father's cheerful ministerial temperament with an artistic nature inclined to be "not systematic; she had inspiration but not discipline" (p. 87), and as a woman trying to enter a field dominated by men, she lacks firm direction in her projected career in the city. Her fellow students in Mr. Wetmore's class also fail to relate art meaningfully to life: " 'There isn't one of us really knows what she's doing it for . . .' " (p. 91). She describes her teacher as primarily a technician who believes that inspiration suffers if the painter can verbalize his intentions. Colonel Woodburn, the professional Southerner who is writing a critique of postwar carpetbagging, asserts that in America " 'the law of commercialism is on everything. . . . The final reward of art is money, and not the pleasure of creating' " (p. 147). Happily verifying much of the Colonel's indictment is the journal's literary huckster Fulkerson, a first-generation Babbitt in both his hustle and his hearty American slang, who is alert to the female reader's " 'tastes and their sensibilities and their sex-piety' " (p. 119). Colonel Woodburn's daughter gayly hopes to become a painter merely by taking lessons. (Consistent with his current championing of native speech for the American novel, Howells records her older Southern accents with the same relish as Fulkerson's new slang and, in fact, weds them at the end of the novel.) Angus Beaton is a dabbler in literature and sculpture, but a painter of some talent who has half-heartedly agreed to serve as art editor of March's journal. March's old tutor Lindau poses for Beaton's Biblical portraits, and also is a model at the studio of Mr. Wetmore. The Dryfoos family represents the newly rich patrons of the arts in the late nineteenth century. They have taken an expensive box at the Met, have hired Mrs. Mandel to put a cultivated finish on daughters Christine and Mela, and are financing *Every Other Week*—" 'a tie between the Arts and Dollars,' " Beaton cynically but accurately terms it (p. 150). In contrast to the Dryfooses are Beaton's friend Mrs. Horn, the established dowager-patron of New York artists, and her cultivated niece Margaret Vance, who is "proud to know literary and artistic fashions as well as society fashions" (p. 149).

Within this diverse world of art, Howells orders his drama chiefly through the developing sensibility of Basil March. The new editor is a compound of minor uncertainties and major confusions. He believes that contributions to an American journal of literature and art criticism must be lively, varied, and, above all, brief. He feels that painted illustrations, though popular and necessary, distract from the pure literary interest of a story. He abhors abusive criticism. (Howells in the "Editor's Study" was ambiguous on the wedding of fiction and illustration, but emphatic on the mischief created by bad-tempered critics.) On the larger problems of art in its relation to social forces and the broader problems of humanity, however, March has, at best, only the certainty that he understands very little. In this innocence and doubt, he is challenged and provoked by confrontations with the ministerial Conrad Dryfoos and with the embittered Lindau. Discussing with Conrad the aims of *Every Other Week* on their first meeting, March is brought up short by his young publisher's assertion that they can " 'do some good' " with the art magazine.

March asked rather absently, "some good?" Then he added: "Oh yes; I think we can. What do you mean by good? Improve

156

the public taste? Elevate the standard of literature? Give young authors and artists a chance?" (pp. 123-124) .

Howells was willing to risk the bad art of intrusive comment to underscore this crucial early moment in March's education: "This was the only good that had ever been in March's mind, except the good that was to come in a material way from his success, to himself and to his family" (p. 124) .

After Conrad explains that in writing literary sketches of New York life March can help to acquaint the well-to-do with the plight of the poor, March agrees "from the surface only" that " 'those phases of low life are immensely picturesque' " (p. 124) . But to his credit, March senses that the role of art in producing social change is more difficult and more subtle than Conrad may realize. The poor need to be educated as well as the rich; and overt morality can drain the life out of art. March says later to his wife, " 'I confess I was a little ashamed before him afterward for having looked at the matter so entirely from the aesthetic point of view. But of course, you know, if I went to work at those things with an ethical intention explicitly in mind, I should spoil them' " (p. 125) .

Some days later, Fulkerson urges March to prepare a sketch of New York life for the first issue of the magazine. The previous talk with Conrad has clearly left its mark. March realizes that he must aim at more than the picturesque, but he is not sure how he will manage the larger treatment: " 'I want to philosophize the material, and I'm too new to it all yet. I don't want to do merely superficial sketches' " (p. 152) . His indoctrination in the New York scene presently deepens with an errand across town to ask Lindau to interpret contemporary foreign literature for the journal. Riding the Elevated to Chatham Square, March observes the West Side residents on the car— "American" husbands and wives, with the "picturesque admixture" of "American Hebrews" with their "well-clad

comfort and citizen self-satisfaction" (p. 154)—and decides that he prefers the East Side part of the journey.
There he observes the more "entertaining" variety and
"interesting shape of shabby adversity" (p. 154) of the
immigrant poor—Russians, Poles, Czechs, Chinese, Italians, Germans, and Scandinavians. His painter's eye is
"amused" by the "strident forms and colors," by the "gay
ugliness—the shapeless, graceful, reckless picturesqueness
of the Bowery" (p. 155). But the claims of humanity are
also beginning to reach him, however faintly, and in his
"waking dreams" he muses on "what these poor people
were thinking, hoping, fearing, enjoying, suffering; just
where and how they lived; who and what they individually
were . . ." (p. 155). But the "frantic panorama" (p. 155)
leaves him with a confused sense of Darwinian struggle.
As an artist, he cannot frame the larger scene which he
suspects is there:

> The whole at moments seemed to him lawless, godless; the ab-
> sence of intelligent, comprehensive purpose in the huge dis-
> order, and the violent struggle to subordinate the result to the
> greater good, penetrated with its dumb appeal the conscious-
> ness of a man who had always been too self-enwrapped to
> perceive the chaos to which the individual selfishness must
> always lead (p. 156).

These stirrings of social conscience bring sharp but only
momentary discomfort, and he descends the steps at
Chatham Square "with a sense of the neglected oppor-
tunities of painters in that locality" (p. 156).

Proceeding on foot to Lindau's squalid quarters on the
East Side, March has one human confrontation—with a
"shabby-genteel ballad-seller" of folk art—and briefly is
entertained by the spectacle of a local prostitute being
arrested near the Catholic Church on Mott Street. In
Lindau's room, however, March observes human poverty
at close range. Yet he receives from Lindau no real perspective on its causes, for Lindau has become so violently

opposed to American capitalist society that he no longer has any rational perspective to communicate. Though he will translate some modern Dostoevsky for the first issue of *Every Other Week,* Lindau is a throwback to the 1848 Revolution. He still quotes from Heine and is "a romanticist of the Victor Hugo sort" (p. 166) in his art and politics. Lindau does suggest to March the necessary human experience which will integrate the moral and social elements in his literary sketches of New York: " 'You must zee [poverty] all the dtime—zee it, hear it, smell it, dtaste it—or you forget it. That is what I gome here for. I was begoming a ploated aristograt. I thought I was nodt like these beoble down here . . .' " (p. 161). But March is put off by the violence of Lindau's tirade and misses the truth which lies beneath the "Ruskinian" flow of Lindau's rhetoric. "In his own life of comfortable reverie," Howells notes, March has never before spoken with a social anarchist, and does not understand the inequities of American life which have deranged "the cheery, poetic, hopeful idealist" of prewar days (p. 164).

Howells explored the relation of art to New York life in Part Second of *Hazard* with an amplitude which he had gained only after years of private doubts that he could manage a large American scene in his novels. In the 1870s, he had debated with Charles Dudley Warner the relative merits of the novel of extended scope and the shorter or, as Howells saw it, the "dramatic" novel with a "strong motive" and three or four central characters. Howells cited Turgenev for support, as well as a private preference for "people" rather than "society."[8] Not until the end of 1885, after *Silas Lapham,* did Howells read his second great Russian author, this time Tolstoy, to discover an esthetic justification for the big novel and extended gallery of characters. In the "Editor's Study" columns of 1886, he extolled the art and complex humanity of the

[8] To Warner, Sept. 4, 1875, and April 1, 1877, *Letters,* I, 210, 232, 233.

widely ranging Tolstoian novel. Yet Howells himself did not feel capable of emulating this larger form. In 1887, he argued that the American novel was necessarily limited in scope due to our more provincial relationships, though within these narrow limits the American novelist could achieve a microcosmic fullness.[9] The forces were at work, however, which would create in *Hazard* the first extended treatment of New York art and society in the American novel. Howells continued to read Tolstoy and to acquaint readers of *Harper's* with the Russian's Christian socialism; in November 1887, he laid bare his widening concern over social injustice by making a public plea for clemency on behalf of the Haymarket anarchists; he moved to New York City; and he felt the pressure of age bearing down on his fifty-first birthday to remind him that the big novel must be written soon if at all. In the spring of 1888, he was clearly beginning to discover the New York materials which would become Part Second of *Hazard*. He wrote to T. S. Perry:

. . . I have been trying to catch on to the bigger life of the place. It's immensely interesting, but I don't know whether I shall manage it; I'm fifty-one, you know. There are lots of interesting young painting and writing fellows, and the place is lordly free, with foreign touches of all kinds all through its abounding Americanism: Boston seems of another planet.[10]

Even by autumn of 1888, Howells reflected his self-doubts over the work now germinating. "There are few places, few occasions among us," he wrote in the "Study," "in which a novelist can get a large number of polite people together, or at least keep them together." Specifically, the problem was the absence of a literary model. No novelist had successfully assembled and explored the "too transitory, too intangible" life of the American city.[11]

[9] "Study," LXXV (Sept. 1887) , 640.
[10] April 14, 1888, *Letters*, I, 413.
[11] "Study," LXXVII (Nov. 1888) , 964.

This esthetic problem, for Howells, extended also to moral and emotional obstacles. At the outset of *Hazard*, he was perhaps voicing the admitted limits of his own social empathy when he sounded Mrs. March's fear that she could not make her sympathies go around to so many New Yorkers. And Basil speaks for Howells when he warns Conrad, in effect, not to oversimplify the shared moral obligations of rich *and* poor. Howells had earlier printed J. B. Harrison's essays in the *Atlantic* "to show the rich what excellent types of character exist among workingmen and their wives"; but Harrison had also a larger design, "to teach the poor how a capitalist may be necessarily their friend. . . ." During the clamor stirred up by sympathizers of American labor when John Hay's anonymous *The Breadwinners* appeared several years later, Howells wrote a letter of support to Hay. Howells praised the novel because "it courageously expressed a fact not hitherto attempted: the fact that the workingmen *as* workingmen are no better or wiser than the rich *as* the rich, and are quite as likely to be false and foolish." When he repeated this defense in a review, Howells stressed that Hay's range and balance had "done the cause of labor and the cause of art both a service."[12] In *Hazard*, Howells moved with his hero into the New York scene and deepened his involvement with the vast materials which the city offered the novelist. The alliance of his heart and pen seems to have accompanied the creative process as he traced the growth of his fictional hero. New York materials are at first intractable for March, too transitory and intangible, because he cannot organize them emotionally, cannot discover moral purpose within this urban chaos. In his first esthetic confrontation in Part Second, he is predictably unsettled when young Dryfoos proposes that March, in his New York sketches, try to do some social and moral

12 *At.Mo.*, XLV (June 1880), 849; letter to Hay, Jan. 7, 1884, *Letters*, I, 357; letter to *Century* signed "W," XXVIII (May 1884), 153.

"good." The suggestion surprises and goads March, for his slowly evolving esthetic has not accounted for the "good" within the beautiful. This question of estheticism and morality, which permeates Part Second, had a long foreground in the esthetic controversy of the period, and Howells had placed himself squarely in the center of the debate.

Though he complained that his monthly column for *Harper's* became a burden, Howells must have been gratified that here lay the opportunity to clarify his theory of art. The most pervasive note in the "Study," as I have said, became the relation between art and morality. "The finest effect of the 'beautiful' will be ethical," he wrote, "and not aesthetic merely. Morality penetrates all things, it is the soul of all things." He praised the fiction of Sidney Luska (Henry Harland) because "nothing that is good is sacrificed to any mere literary end in his work." Luska's work illustrated Howells' esthetic credo: "The finest work of our day teaches that to be morally false is to be aesthetically false."[13]

Part of Howells' comments were aimed at the late nineteenth-century *l'art pour l'art* advocates whose anti-sentimentalism he, of course, shared. But the artist had a higher calling than merely unwavering dedication to craft. Reviewing Christmas literature of 1888, Howells wrote: "The old heathenish axiom of art for art's sake is as dead as great Pan himself, and the best art now tends to be art

---

[13] "Study," LXXIII (Nov. 1886) , 963, and LXXVIII (May 1889) , 987. Howells had complained during the early months of Harper's contract that he was forced to "switch off" his current fiction to "do a 'Study,'" and added, "What a fool I was to undertake that!" (To Twain, May 23, 1886, in *Letters*, I, 384.) The novel was *April Hopes* (1888) . Appearing after *The Minister's Charge* and before *Annie Kilburn*, this was his first novel written concurrently with, and actually benefitted by, the "Study." While he dramatized less of his realist credo here than in *Hazard*, Howells showed in *April Hopes* a new awareness of his art. An interviewer reported ten years later that Howells remembered *April Hopes* to be "the first he wrote with the distinct consciousness that he was writing as a realist. . . ." See Marrion Wilcox, "Works of William Dean Howells," *Harper's Weekly*, XL (July 4, 1896) , 655.

for humanity's sake."[14] This was plainly the rhetoric of combat, for estheticism was very much alive. Charles Eliot Norton in the same year had told a public audience:

It is the creed of a powerful school of artists, perhaps the predominant school at the present day, that art and morality are absolutely independent, that the relation between the Beautiful and the Good is purely external, and that it is an impertinence to ask for anything in a work of art more than that it should be well executed.[15]

Clearly the enemy was not dead. But Howells still announced that serious artists, critics, and public audience alike held no brief for the doctrine of art for art. Indeed, all criticism was moving toward the moral criterion in judging "any work of the imagination," said Howells, and he proceeded in the didactic vein:

We must ask ourselves before we ask anything else, Is it true?— true to the motives, the impulses, the principles that shape the life of actual men and women? This truth, which necessarily includes the highest morality and the highest artistry—this truth given, the book *cannot* be wicked and cannot be weak; and without it all graces of style and feats of invention and cunning of construction are so many superfluities of naughtiness.[16]

Before March can go to work on his literary sketches of New York, he must first achieve this vision of the ideal within the real. That he has a considerable distance yet to go becomes apparent in Howells' description of the first issue of *Every Other Week*. The contents are a mishmash of light essays, poetry, and fiction, together with a "dramatic trifle" and some "dashing criticism" of the arts (p. 166). The issue mirrors in large degree March's esthetic confusion. Nor has Lindau helped March to achieve a clearer esthetic purpose. In the first issue appears "a bit

[14] "Study," LXXVIII (Dec. 1888), 159.
[15] In an address at Norwich, Mass., 1888 (Harvard).
[16] "Study," LXXIV (April 1887), 826.

of vivid Russian realism" which Lindau has selected to translate from among the foreign literature March had brought him. The translation, significantly is from Dostoevsky. One recalls that Howells cited Dostoevsky three years before in one of his most famous assertions in the "Study," that it would be "false and mistaken" to view American life with the tragic vision of the Russian. "The smiling aspects of life are the more American," Howells had announced, and then added an economic judgment which Lindau could hardly share: "in a land where journeymen carpenters and plumbers strike for four dollars a day . . . and the wrong from class to class is almost inappreciable," an American Dostoevsky would sound a false note.[17] Howells later added to this statement in *Criticism and Fiction* (1891): "though all this is changing for the worse." Yet he reaffirmed that the peculiarly American conditions could not be understood with the vision of a Dostoevsky. In brief, Lindau, who also poses as Judas for Beaton and ultimately is involved in the death of the Christlike Conrad Dryfoos, betrays in his literary preference the impairment of his social outlook. He is not, as Van Wyck Brooks has implied, a bearer of the Tolstoian message in *Hazard* (p. xi), but is in fact an alternative to that vision.

III

Part Third of *Hazard* introduces March to life at the top (or the high middle) in New York, among both the newly rich and the older established society. He meets Dryfoos, pathetically isolated from all New York life (save Wall Street) and aware that the pastoral dream of going home to Indiana has been obliterated. The new millionaire has grown tough on Wall Street, however, and sniffs at the meager profit of the magazine. He shows no interest whatsoever in the esthetic aims of *Every Other Week*,

[17] "Study," LXXIII (Sept. 1886), 641.

though he wants, of course, to attach its respectability to his new fortune. At an evening musicale at Mrs. Horn's salon, Howells exposes this parvenu crudity of the Dryfoos family in the persons of Christine and Mela, the unmannerly and unmusical Dryfoos sisters (they prefer the banjo to the piano). By contrast, the reader senses the refinement and cultivation of the hostess and her niece Margaret Vance, who, incidentally, like Conrad Dryfoos, works among the poor in New York. March again arrives in the midst of it all to absorb the experience in his growing impressions of art and humanity in the American city, this time in the life of well-to-do New Yorkers, both the established and the "upwardly mobile," as we now term them. The relation between the arts and the dollars extends, for him, also into Part Fourth. Fulkerson has arranged a dinner party at the Dryfoos home to advertise the magazine and flatter the owner: " 'The natural-gas man in literature is a new thing, and the combination of your picturesque past and your esthetic present is something that will knock out the sympathies of the American public in the first round' " (p. 241). On the fateful evening, March listens helplessly as the talk moves from harmless but revealing literary chatter to a subject Dryfoos can discuss. Fulkerson explains how Dryfoos had routed laborers who tried to introduce collective bargaining in the oil fields in Indiana, but an enraged Lindau steps in to bring the evening to a violent close. March, his career now in jeopardy, discovers the error of his earlier notion that working for a literary magazine " 'involves tastes and not convictions' " (p. 191). Taken together, Parts Third and Fourth are rich in moments which deepen for March the artist's "sense of complicity" (p. 261) among the poor, the established wealthy, and the newly rich. These varied experiences prepare him for the crisis of his career in Part Fifth. Their meaning enlarges, also, when one refers, once again, to the esthetic criteria in the "Editor's Study." The

Dryfoos dinner party, to cite only the climactic scene among these actions, can be read as an expanded dramatization of various columns in *Harper's,* particularly the "Study" of May 1889. The parallels reveal how intimately Howells was linking his literary criticism to the creative art of *Hazard.*

The dinner, as earlier in *Silas Lapham,* enabled Howells to compress into a miniature drama the central issues of the novel. It commences amiably enough as Howells creates light literary talk to identify both the tastes and convictions of the guests. For Col. Woodburn, Scott and Addison are "the only authors fit to form the minds of gentlemen" (p. 285). Kendricks is too agreeable a dilettante to contradict, but proposes to add the stylist Flaubert: " 'Style, you know, is the man' " (p. 285). Beaton's masters are, predictably, the French estheticists Baudelaire and Maupassant. Lindau argues for the German Romantics, Hugo and Schiller. March adds Heine (Howells' boyhood passion whom he later had "sweated" out of his system), though patently less out of conviction than to relax Lindau with nostalgic memories of their prewar reading at Indianapolis. Fulkerson, preeminently the businessman, knows that this literary talk cannot lead up to the business aspects of *Every Other Week,* and that old Dryfoos has nothing literary to say. By shifting the conversation to the personal basis of Western reminiscence, Fulkerson senses that Dryfoos now can talk. Moving out of literature into life, however, becomes perilous. Before long, Fulkerson has explained how Dryfoos hired Pinkerton detectives to defeat a workers' attempt to unionize his oil fields. Kendricks praises the drama of Dryfoos's move, seeing it "purely from an aesthetic point of view" (p. 293); Beaton regrets that the Pinkertons failed to shed a little blood of the uppity laborers; Fulkerson flatly opposes unionism and strikes; Col. Woodburn observes that unions and management are both commercially self-interested, and reiterates the need for a feudalistic *noblesse oblige* to reconstruct America. Lindau, whom March can no longer pacify, counters with the proposal of a workers' State. " 'You are talking paternalism, sir,' " answers Woodburn to the romantic old revolutionary. " 'And *you* are dalking feutalism!' " Lindau replies to the Southern admirer of Scott (p. 295). Fulkerson tries to save the evening by directing the stormy argument back to their mutual art enterprise. Who would trouble to read *Every Other Week* if men lived under any one of these ideal arrangements in political economy? But the effort fails, and the evening ends a dismal failure.

Howells was passionate in his literary preferences and did not idly sound the names of Flaubert, Scott, Hugo, or Maupassant. In the May 1889 "Study," he wrote that "Flaubert's *Madame Bovary* is one impassioned cry of the austerest morality, far above the conception of the art of Scott's time. . . ." Presumably, then, Kendricks ranks above Col. Woodburn, until one recalls that Kendricks chiefly admires Flaubert for the wrong reason, as a stylist rather than austere moralist. Assigning Scott to Woodburn's literary pantheon is clearly no compliment. Lindau labels the predisposition of the Colonel " 'feutal,' " and Howells would have the reader concur. In the same "Study," he contrasted Scott unfavorably to Tolstoy: "Beside that most Christian of the moralists, Scott is the spirit of the world incarnate, and of the feudal world at that; and beside that conscientious and perfect artist he is a prentice artificer."[18] On the other hand, Lindau is no Tolstoian. Indeed, Howells refused to invoke Tolstoy's name anywhere in *Hazard*. (Conrad Dryfoos would be the obvious character to have read Tolstoy.) Lindau, instead, is a disciple of Victor Hugo, and here one has a clue to the ambivalent treatment of Lindau in the novel. Though Howells ranked Hugo above Scott, and presumably, then, Lindau over Col. Woodburn, Hugo was also for Howells a "romanticist" of the highest "flamboyant" order. Howells

[18] "Study," LXXVIII (May 1889), 983.

doubted that the narrowly personal orientation of "the Victor Hugoish martyr," such as Dickens' Sydney Carton, embodied the spirit necessary to create a world of love and brotherhood. "It is not in such romantic wise that men really die for men," he wrote.[19] In Part Fifth of *Hazard*, Conrad's martyrdom—achieved out of his concern for mankind—will contrast with Lindau's death, incurred during his theatrical denunciation of a specific enemy. On the other hand, Lindau, living close to the suffering of the East Side poor, has (like Hugo) his democratic virtues. Howells allowed that the revolutionary Hugo possessed a "generous sympathy and noble faith," and in December of 1888, when the outlines of Lindau's character were perhaps in Howells' mind, one reads again the uncertain and mixed praise: "The romantic spirit worshipped genius, worshipped heroism, but at its best, in such a man as Victor Hugo, this spirit recognized the supreme claim of the lowest humanity."[20]

Finally on Maupassant (and Beaton), Howells reveals the ardor with which he could repudiate a literary passion when technique clearly did not serve a moral vision—the case with Beaton. Howells praised Maupassant's avoiding the American "vice of over-explanatory fullness" which our misled writers had inherited from the English, "who seem to address their fiction to the aesthetically idiotic." Perhaps the motive here was to praise technique in the French author in order to continue paying insults to the school of Scott, Thackeray, and Dickens. For the next year, Howells cited the fiction of his genuine heroes—Tolstoy, Björnson, and Valdés—by contrast to assail the "loathesome experience" of reading Maupassant's *Notre Coeur*: "The Frenchman grovels into mere romanticism, and is false even to the fashionable filth he studies."[21]

---

19 "Study," *ibid.*; LXXII (May 1886), 973; *ibid.* (Jan. 1886), 322.
20 "Study," *ibid.* (May 1886), 973, and LXXVIII (Dec. 1888), 159.
21 "Study," LXXX (Feb. 1890), 482, and LXXXII (Feb. 1891), 483.

IV

In Part Fifth, Howells centers his concluding action on a streetcar strike in New York. By describing the effects of the strike on the various people related to *Every Other Week*, he brings to a close his fable on art and humanity. That he was not chiefly propounding a sociological message in this final section stands revealed in his later comment on the violent moments of the strike:

> They offered me the material of tragedy and pathos in my story. In my quality of artist I could not regret these, and I gratefully realize that they offered me the opportunity of a more strenuous action, a more impressive catastrophe than I could have achieved without them. They tended to give the whole fable dignity and doubtless made for its success as a book (p. xvi).

The violence and tragedy of the strike jolt March for the first time into a clear recognition of where his new career has carried him. Resuming an esthetic life has meant not retreat into the past, nor escape to the New York theatre, nor the solitary indulging of his painter's eye in the "picturesque gayety" of the city. Instead he has been thrust into the violent actualities of modern urban democracy. Almost in spite of himself, he has made his private sympathies go around to sixteen other people, and has probed below the surface of the lives of the urban rich, middle, and poor.

In the last section of the novel, Howells indicates the breadth of March's experience by allowing the main narrative focus to alternate between March and Angus Beaton. The responses of the selfish and irresponsible artist frame the strike chapters and dominate five of the final six chapters. Yet Beaton will remain unmoved by the human tragedy created by the strike. Though his father is a poor workingman, Beaton decides not to send his father money but instead to buy himself an overcoat. He then visits Alma

Leighton, but she tells him he merely looks "picturesque" in his overcoat (p. 330) and rejects him as a self-centered poseur. He next tries his romantic talents on Margaret Vance, but she wants to talk about "social questions"; and the artist, "son of the working-people as he was, . . . had never cared anything about such matters." He decides that she is "becoming a little too exacting for comfort in her idealism," and he leaves (pp. 342, 343). Next, he visits Christine Dryfoos, but old Dryfoos has given Mrs. Mandel orders to determine if Beaton is trifling with Christine's affections. She decides that a trifler he is, and sends him away. " 'By heavens! this is piling it up,' " Beaton exclaims (p. 349). But he continues undaunted. Waiting for a surface-car, he learns from a policeman that the streetcar workers are on strike. " 'If you'd take out eight or ten of those fellows, and set them up against a wall and shoot them, you'd save a great deal of bother,' " he advances in solution to the labor crisis (p. 350). After the death of Conrad in the strike, we see Beaton again as the grieving elder Dryfoos comes to ask the artist to make a memorial sketch from a photograph of the dead son. Beaton suspects no higher motive than an attempt by the old man to regain, even purchase, a suitor for his daughter, and so refuses the request.

Beaton's hunch is, of course, partly right. Though bound up tight in self-concern, he has an artist's ability to gather impressions. He correctly assumes that Dryfoos is sacrificing pride to help Christine win back her bachelor artist. Dryfoos' trip to Beaton's studio touches on but it also goes beyond paternal guilt over Christine's thwarted romance or Conrad's sacrificial death. More or less consciously, the old father is trying, through the artist Beaton, to reconstruct the identity of the Dryfoos family. The effort deepens the reader's sense that here is only the latest of many unhappy business journeys this Western millionaire has ventured upon since an urban-industrial economy has left him both wealthy and homeless. Dryfoos has been living an increasingly shattered existence since the sale of his Indiana farm. The loss of his identity has culminated now in the death of his only male heir. He senses that Beaton, as an artist, may interpret and bring back from photographic detail the gentle humanity of the lost son. But Dryfoos also links Beaton the artist to Conrad the impractical "preacher," and within his "quiescent dislike" for Beaton the old man feels, at the same time, a paternal closeness to this impractical son of a workingman (pp. 396, 399). Perhaps more obscurely, he has been drawn to his daughter's suitor as Boynton had felt strangely mixed reactions to Ford, or Squire Gaylord to Bartley. Just as Egeria and Marcia had received rings from their overly protective fathers, so an emotionally thwarted Christine Dryfoos wears the ring her father has given her, only to hurl it back at him when he drives her suitor Beaton away. Dryfoos then wears the ring and with it strikes Conrad shortly before his death. With this brief, effective symbolism, Howells hinted at a wide spectrum of guilt, alienation, family discord, and loss of identity within the tragedy-laden house of Dryfoos.[22] Whatever multiple and confused motives have directed Dryfoos on his pathetic mission to the studio of Beaton, arriving there he fails to receive human solace from the esthete. When old Dryfoos collapses from grief, Beaton thinks only of sketching him on the "aesthetic couch covered with a tiger-skin" or, even more unfeelingly, of sometime sketching Christine there as a Cleopatra. "In his life of selfish immunity from grief," Howells pointedly explains, "Beaton could not understand this experience that poignant sorrow brings" (p. 401). Fearing the old man may die on his hands, Beaton ushers Dryfoos out.

[22] For a fuller and slightly different treatment of Howells' ring symbolism, see Everett Carter, *Howells and the Age of Realism*, pp. 165, 214-215. George Bennett (*William Dean Howells*, pp. 195-199) challenges Carter's interpretation.

Once again, Beaton tries to restore his ego through romantic errands, but Margaret Vance (also grieving over the death of Conrad) has renounced the fine arts as " 'barren amusement' " (p. 403) , and Beaton echoes Mrs. Horn's earlier fears, that Margaret is "altogether too far gone in good works for the fine arts to reach her . . ." (p. 406) . He tries Alma Leighton once again, but she prefers to devote her life solely to art: "More and more she saw him selfish and mean, weak-willed, narrow-minded, and hard-hearted; and aimless, with all his talent" (p. 412) . Finally, Beaton visits Christine Dryfoos, his proper match in that "she had no idea, except such as related intimately to herself . . ." (p. 424) . By now she has become a caged tigress, however, repressed by her social suspicions and their counterpart in her sexual frustration. "As he talked on she felt all her passion for him revive, and the conflict of desires, the desire to hate, the desire to love, made a dizzying whirl in her brain" (p. 424) . But Mela blurts that they are " 'goun' to Europe,' " and Beaton senses failure once again (wrongly this time) . To his astonishment, when he puts out his hand in farewell, the rejected Christine claws at his face. Returned to his studio, the gravestone-cutter's son finally contemplates the tragedy of human life and death—his own. He stares into the muzzle of a pistol "which he had kept loaded to fire at a cat in the area" (p. 425) . The suicide weapon slips through his fingers, fires a shot from the floor, and misses the esthetic non-hero. Beaton will live to paint again for the indulgent and forgiving Fulkerson and March, new co-owners of *Every Other Week*.

In the frustrated and self-seeking excursions of Beaton, Howells made a satirical and pervasive comment on the bankruptcy of the artist who severs himself from the immediate claims of humanity. To encompass and prove the human meanings of the strike, Howells returns, once again, to the sensibility of March. Before the tragedy occurs, March "with his temperance in everything" (p. 356) tries to understand the total picture and maintain the roles of "philosophical observer" (p. 357) and prudent family man by judging impassively the rival claims of labor and management. Fulkerson urges him to go to the strike scene with Beaton " 'and take down its aesthetic aspects. . . . With your descriptions and Beaton's sketches —well, it would just be the greatest card!' " (p. 355) . But March can no longer entertain the New York scene as a mere instance of the picturesque: "He was very curious about some aspects of the strike, whose importance, as a great social convulsion, he felt people did not recognize . . ." (p. 356) . Pondering a larger literary treatment of the strike, March rides past his car stop and, in spite of his resolves to stay his distance from the violence, is carried into the heart of it. Present there also are Lindau, who is taunting the police as they protect the newly hired car-operators against the strikers; and Conrad Dryfoos, who had just arrived to fulfill the wish of Margaret Vance a few moments before, that someone intervene as peacemaker. March arrives in time to hear the gun report which kills Conrad as he tries to protect Lindau from a policeman's club, and to see Lindau fall to the ground mortally wounded. The part of March which prefers to meditate on New York life from the remove of an Elevated car and heed the voice of prudence (his wife's) tells him to run from the scene. But another part of him, "something stronger than his will drew him to the spot, and there he saw Conrad dead beside the old man" (p. 366) . This personal experience with social revolution and tragedy completes the present education of March. The brief scene becomes, as later in Joyce, a composed and luminous image that recalls a sequence of earlier scenes anticipating this climactic moment. In the aftermath of grief which draws all of the characters together in shared human sympathy (Beaton and Christine

Dryfoos excepted), March tries to locate the "truth" at the heart of his total experience in New York.

In his wanderings throughout New York, March has been an urban Ishmael in quest of the abiding truth which might create meaning and order out of his maze of new fortunes. With his Melvillean counterpart, he has encountered several versions of good and "evil," this time in the sprawling city: the safely picturesque surfaces of the happy observer; the subliminal violence and suffering in the maimed and monomaniacal Lindau; the gentler moral world of the pious and good-hearted Conrad Dryfoos; and the meaningless, blank disorder which March has confronted with mild, inarticulate terror. To a degree, the breadth of his search itself has implied the answer to its own question—the universal answer on Queequeg's coffin. If truth resides anywhere, it is everywhere, among the rich as among the poor, amid squalor and opulence. By Part Fourth, March had begun to frequent the churches on Sunday, not to satisfy his esthetic fondness for traditional ritual and Gothic form, as before, but to hear Christianity presented "as a system of economics as well as a religion" (p. 261). Religion, that is, should relate eternal truth to the present needs of humanity. The truth that he had begun to perceive was implicitly Emersonian also, the relatedness of all living things. Howells had plainly acknowledged his debt to Emerson the year before: "In humanity, as in his theories of what literature should be to us, Emerson is still the foremost of all our seers, and will be so a hundred years hence."[23]

One of Emerson's relevant "theories of what literature should be to us"—an esthetic criterion of transcendental truth—resides implicitly and pervasively in the language of *Hazard*. Emerson held that literary vitality and truth grew out of a nation's fresh and original everyday speech, and Howells concurred. In his first "Editor's Study,"

23 "Study," LXXVI (Feb. 1888), 478.

Howells had maintained that American democracy, reflected on a heterogeneous literary scene, ruled out any predominant regional center, be it Boston or New York. Literary decentralization in America, moreover, allowed for the vigor and freshness of a "local flavor of diction" which had already appeared within the regional ferment in American literature. Howells then had quoted Daudet's envy of Turgenev's " 'great big untrodden barbaric language to wade into.' "[24] In February 1889, Howells again took the occasion in the "Study" to discourse on native speech. He praised Björnson for the vigor of his language, "refreshed . . . from the never-failing springs of the common speech" of Norway. In similar manner, American humorists and " 'dialect' story-tellers" were following the example of Björnson in creating a native literature out of the common speech of America.[25] In New York, Howells now heard, as Whitman had, the varied sounds and speech of urban America. The "truth" of the American megalopolis, for Howells, was inseparable from his characters' dialectal uniqueness within a shared language. The drawl of the Southern Woodburns, the immigrant dialect of Lindau, the Midwest vernacular of Mrs. Dryfoos, and the losing battle with grammar waged by her younger daughter Mela, all contrast sharply and colorfully with the plain and sometimes flat style of the narration. One can only guess at the pleasure which Mark Twain and even Lowell must have derived, in addition, from the slangy accents of Fulkerson, the forerunner of Dreiser's breezy salesman Drouet and, even more closely, of Lewis's Babbitt. Fulkerson cajoles a desultory Beaton:

"Well, have you come round to go to work? Just hang up your coat on the floor anywhere" (p. 114).

Or again to Beaton:

24 "Study," LXXII (Jan. 1886), 324.
25 "Study," LXXVIII (Feb. 1889), 492.

"Take these along, Michelangelo Da Vinci, my friend, and put your multitudinous mind on them for about an hour . . ." (p. 120) .

Meeting the Marches and others, present or fabricated, at the Dryfooses:

"Ah! Hello! Hello! Regular gathering of the clans. How are you, Mrs. Dryfoos? How do you do, Mrs. Mandel, Miss Christine, Mela, Aunt Hitty, and all the folks? How you wuz?" (p. 136) .

Giving advice to March as editor:

"This thing isn't going to have any sort of get up and howl about it, unless you have a paper in the first number going for Bevans's novels" (p. 150) .

Warning March not to count unhatched profits of the magazine:

"Why, old man, you're coming in on the divvy" (p. 170) .

Later in the novel, March pauses to discover that he has begun to talk like Fulkerson (p. 414) .

Hearing this variety of American speech, and sensing within it the connectedness of the separate lives touched by *Every Other Week*, March has felt a "complicity" unknown to him in his Boston career. He comes home to New York. The American past—the agrarian West of March, Lindau, Fulkerson, and the Dryfooses—cannot be returned to. Still a Christian ideal from the past remains viable and accessible in the present to bind these transplanted New Yorkers together. March did not fully recognize this answer until he discovered a key to the life of Conrad Dryfoos. In his charity, suffering, and death, Conrad had moved beyond theoretical to practical brotherhood. To March, Conrad had re-enacted the Christian "law of love on earth" (p. 390) . And Margaret Vance, at the end of the novel, seems to be continuing Conrad's charity work in the same spirit of selfless love of others.

By contrast, Lindau had pursued the same social good among the poor, but his had been the "romantic" spirit of violence, revolution, and disorder.

In March's moral discovery, Howells was expressing, at the same time, a truth which was the cornerstone of his "realism." One difference between the "realist" and "romanticist," he had explained in the "Editor's Study," was that "in life [the realist] finds nothing insignificant; all tells for destiny and character; nothing that God made is contemptible."[26] Conrad had told March that "sometimes it seems to me that the only trouble is that we don't know one another well enough" (p. 124). Howells had written earlier of the novelist's moral duty: "Let us make [men] know one another better, that they may be all humbled and strengthened with a sense of their fraternity." This knowledge of the good and the true was the deepest revelation of the serious arts, for "except as they somehow, clearly or obscurely, tend to make the race better or kinder, are [the arts] to be regarded as serious interests."[27] At the end of *Hazard*, Conrad in his sacrificial death had expressed for March the universal law of love; the year before, Howells had quoted from the heart of Valdés' *Maximina*:

Love is the law that rules the universe; the sublime law that unites your heart to mine is the same law that unites all the beings of the universe, and keeps them at the same time distinct.[28]

By creating in *Hazard* a multitude of characters, united yet distinct, Howells was describing this law of love. He had also tried to follow the example and meaning of Tolstoy. In *Anna Karenina*, Howells had praised "the multitude of figures [which] pass before us recognizably real, never caricatured or grotesqued, or in any wise un-

26 "Study," LXXII (May 1886), 973.
27 "Study," LXXV (Sept. 1887), 639.
28 "Study," LXXVI (Jan. 1888), 319.

duly accented, but simple and actual in their evil or their good." And in depicting Conrad's Christian altruism and "suffering for the sins of others" (p. 391), Howells was embodying the truth in Tolstoy's conviction that "there is no such thing as personal happiness, no bliss but forgetting ourselves and remembering others, no life but in its loss for goodness' sake."[29]

March ends his quest with this awakening of his altruism and human fraternity, to realize that Americans live in a hateful " 'economic chance-world' " (p. 378) which has made them insecure, greedy, and fiercely competitive. This lesson in humanity the artist Beaton never learns. For all his moral fatuity, however, Beaton possesses artistic talent; and March, feeling the vibrations of humanity which permeate the American city, appears to lack the necessary talent to clarify his vision of connectedness, love, and non-violent melioration, and to enter it in the service of humanity, either as writer or editor. In the final chapter, Mrs. March hopes that he will rid *Every Other Week* of " 'that detestable Mr. Beaton . . . in the reforms you're going to carry out' " (pp. 426-427). But it turns out that these "reforms" are not esthetic or humanitarian at all. At best, they are narrowly economic. Though March dispenses with the literary services of Kendricks, this is not a gesture toward anti-estheticism, for Beaton remains (and we are told in *An Open-Eyed Conspiracy* [1897] that Kendricks has remained a frequent contributor to *Every Other Week*). March cuts back on illustrated articles, not because illustrations interfere with literary seriousness, but to save money; and he will employ the original profit-sharing plan, though the writers and artists may be the losers. The journal previously "had got to paying rather lavishly for material without reference to the sales" (p. 427). So the new owners March and Fulkerson, though no longer trembling before the personal whims of a status-

---

29 "Study," LXXII (April 1886), 809, and LXXIX (Aug. 1889), 479.

seeking patron, must tremble now before the impersonal laws of supply and demand which control the arts in a business civilization.

V

Nowhere in his novels does Howells seem more inconclusive than in the ultimate meaning of *Hazard*. In its vagueness, however, the ending poses questions that lead one to the most significant parts of Howells' theory and practice of realism. Was he evasive on the relation between art and social reform at the end of *Hazard* because of his esthetic stricture against the doctrinaire novel? Or is the ending vague because Howells was unsure of his own conclusions about "realism" and social reform?

He had regarded overt explanation to be bad art early in his career when he was discovering Turgenev and Björnson for readers of the *Atlantic* and lecturing his contemporaries on the art of the dramatic novel. Even James received warning in those pages for his "tendency to expatiate upon his characters too much, and not to trust his reader's perceptions enough."[30] In the "Editor's Study," Howells repeated his warnings against narrator intrusion and pointed moralizing. The novel should reveal transcendent truth through objective and even "scientific" focus upon things as they are. The heart of the doctrine appears in March's early response to Conrad Dryfoos's urging him to "do some good" through his literary sketches: "If I went to work at those things with an ethical intention explicitly in mind, I should spoil them." As his editorial experience grows, March understands the basic confusion in certain of the new writers hoping to publish in the journal who "called themselves realists" while others termed themselves "romanticists." He muses that "none of them seemed to know what realism was, or what romanticism: they apparently supposed the difference

[30] *At.Mo.*, xxxv (April 1875), 494.

a difference of material" (p. 262). The difference, of
course, was in attitude and technique. In the "Study"
Howells attacked the partisan crudeness of novelists who
expose their message: "If any one would see plainly the
difference between the novelist's work and the partisan's
work," he wrote, "let him compare [James's] *The Princess
Cassamassima* and Mr. W. H. Mallock's last tract . . .
which also deals with socialism."[31] Though Howells' treatment of socialism in *Annie Kilburn* and, later, in *A Traveler from Altruria* would come close to the esthetic error
of Mallock—creating "stalking horses for his opinions"—
he would discover for *Hazard* a closer model in James's
novel. Exegesis and speech-making occur in *Hazard*, to be
sure, but Howells seems purposely to have made such
moments as brief as possible.

Howells must have found it far more difficult to adhere
to his and James's ideal of esthetic distance when he
learned more profoundly than before, through Tolstoy,
that the novel could awaken and instruct mankind in
social evolution and brotherhood. But Howells the critic
stood firm: "We suspect that fiction, like the other arts,
can only do good . . . indirectly; when it becomes horta-
tory, it is in danger of becoming dull, that is to say, sui-
cidal." Howells continued into 1889 to instruct native
writers on the dramatic art of the well-made novel. This
was also the year when he stepped up his attack on the
English school of fiction. Scott was "tediously analytical
where the modern novelist is dramatic, and . . . he trusted
his readers' intuitions so little that he was apt to rub in
his appeals to them." George Eliot was "first ethical and
then artistic" and therefore fell below Jane Austen, who
was, for Howells, the first novelist to master "the form and
method most essential to art." One of the worst to violate
the dramatic illusion was Trollope, who was

[31] "Study," LXXIV (April 1887), 829.

so warped from a wholesome ideal as to wish at times to be like the caricaturist Thackeray, and to stand about in his scene, talking it over with his hands in his pockets, interrupting the action, and spoiling *the illusion in which alone the truth of art resides.*[32]

The voice from the "Editor's Study" sounded confident and secure as Howells propounded the esthetic of the realist of commonplace life who could reveal transcendent goodness and human complicity through a technique which preserved the dramatic "illusion in which alone the truth of art resides." Beneath this apparent confidence and ease, however, resided conflicts which prevented his ever again writing another *Hazard*. The massive upheavals in turn-of-the-century American life demanded expression from an American Tolstoy. Yet Howells could not model his later work after Tolstoy, despite his continued admiration for the Russian. The reasons rest within an esthetic dilemma which Howells could not resolve.

In 1886 and the years after, Howells immersed himself deeply in vital questions of social justice in America, and in particular the increasing struggle of labor in the economic "chance world." This is a story which has been told ten times over. Less familiar are the frustrations which Howells experienced in trying to bring his theory of literary realism to terms with his emerging socialist ideology. He could do nothing effective, he came to feel after his unsuccessful citizen's plea for the Haymarket anarchists, except perhaps in his capacity as an artist. Yet he had developed a theory of dramatic, objective fiction which would not lend itself to the direct advancing of social causes. The dissatisfaction can be heard especially well in a letter to E. E. Hale on August 30, 1888, shortly after Howells had completed *Annie Kilburn*. He had hoped to suggest in his recent novel the relevance of

---

[32] "Study," LXXVI (March 1888), 642; LXXVIII (May 1889), 983; LXXIX (Nov. 1889), 966-967, italics mine.

Christian ethics for a capitalist society, but he admitted that "I solve nothing":

> The most that I can do is perhaps to set a few people thinking; for as yet I haven't got to *doing* anything, myself. But at present it seems to me that our competitive civilization is a state of warfare and a game of chance, in which each man fights and bets against fearful odds.

What more could he do? As a writer, he planned to take up residence in New York during the winter in order to "get intimately at that vast mass of life."[33] Writing again to Hale on October 28, in the midst of "harassing cares" over the health of daughter Winny (she would die five months later, as he was writing the early chapters of *Hazard*), Howells repeated his unhappiness with life in America, together with his frustration as a novelist committed to an art which presents "mere actuality" without advancing causes. How could he convert words into deeds? "With me they only breed more words. At present they are running into another novel, in which I'm going to deal with some mere actualities; but on new grounds—New York namely; though I take some characters on from Boston with me." He then hinted at private guilt in his desire to improve the present conditions of American life. With admirable frankness and insight, Howells detected the uncertainty and ambivalence of his own socialist thought:

> I am neither an example nor an incentive, meanwhile, in my own way of living; I am a creature of the past; only I do believe that I see the light of the future, and that it is this which shows me my ugliness and fatuity and feebleness.[34]

The admission makes his effort in *Hazard* the more remarkable. But his getting intimately at that vast mass of life in New York appeared, as with his previous fiction, to solve nothing. Soon afterward, he wrote to James Par-

[33] *Letters*, I, 416.   [34] *Ibid.*, p. 419.

ton, longing again for escape from people and the city:
"I look forward to an old age occupied with poultry and
English violets, perhaps varied with a pig or two." Then
he sounded the recurring note of tension in his social
sympathies. Living once more in Boston, he wrote, "I
should try this winter to interest myself in some of the
charity work here; but while I see the necessity of it, I
see the futility so clearly that I have not much heart for
it. If it were possible to write and read sixteen hours and
sleep eight it would be very simple."[35] The last sentence
also hints, once more, at his doubt that as a novelist he
was achieving any good, was working any revolution in
the hearts and minds of men. His writing, he appears to
say, has no relation to the effects of charity work, and
even such non-literary efforts at doing good for humanity
are at present futile.

He had conceded before that the fine arts achieved no
"good," that they were decorative and provided mere
amusement. But he had insisted that the novel was
different. He had quoted approvingly Tolstoy's declaration: " 'I can no longer pursue amusements which are oil
to the fire of amorous sensuality, the reading of romances
and the most of poetry, listening to music, attendance at
balls and theatres.' "[36] The statement suggests that in
Hazard narrator sympathy accompanies Mrs. Dryfoos, of
good and simple Dunkard origins, when she scores the
sensuality of painting and ballet in New York (p. 135);
and again when Margaret Vance gives up painting ("barren amusement . . . like enjoying an opera, or a ball") in
favor of charity work (p. 405). Unique among the arts,
however, was the novel. With *Hazard* perhaps under way
in late 1888, Howells was writing in the "Study" on the
persisting view that literature was, after all, like the other
arts, decorative, escapist, amusing. "This may be inevi-

---

[35] Jan. 3, 1890 (Harvard).
[36] "Study," LXXII (April 1886), 809.

table, and forever inevitable; literature is an art like the rest; we do not ask people to be vitally concerned about a picture, a statue, an opera, a building," he wrote. He made this concession, however, that he might suggest more emphatically the unique opportunity that awaited the literature of "real life": "but it sometimes seems as if it ought to be unlike the other arts, since if it would it could speak so frankly, so brotherly, so helpfully, to the mass of men."[37]

Yet what had *Hazard* spoken to the mass of men that could help to reform the ills of capitalism? The reader had participated in March's recognitions: his intimation that the law of love might transform a society whose economy thrives on the psychology of competition, envy, hate, and fear; his criticism of Lindau's more direct social action; and in a phrase, his belief that we can legislate peaceful reform—with the monumental provision " 'if we're honest, and don't buy and sell one another's votes' " (p. 391). Further comment on social reform by the narrator, or by March, presumably would have violated the esthetic of the dramatic and non-prescriptive novel. That Howells must have been dissatisfied with the end of *Hazard*, however, would appear evident when one recalls that he had criticized the very similar vagueness in socialist Laurence Gronlund's vision of a cooperative commonwealth the year before. Howells had hailed Gronlund's wisely recognizing that production and distribution in the United States were clearly moving toward a system of collectivism. He approved Gronlund's urging "the peaceful solution of the problems before us." But Gronlund failed to set forth a program of peaceful evolution from free enterprise to a socialist state: "He does not point out the measures to be actually taken by a people accustomed to express their purpose in suffrage and legislation; and here is the point at which the interest of the average American

[37] "Study," LXXVII (Nov. 1888), 963.

reader must falter."[38] *Hazard* failed more excusably, Howells could feel, because the novelist's hands were tied esthetically. But one can rightly doubt that Howells felt ready to project a clear vision of either the franchise or *Every Other Week* as formative instruments in the creating of a humane socialism. He was already searching for a political third party; he was questioning more strongly than before the wisdom of a mass electorate; and in 1892, after a few months' effort as editor of *The Cosmopolitan*, he gave up this opportunity, with his own *Every Other Week*, "to do something for humanity as well as the humanities."[39] When he returned to clarify the issues of *Hazard* in *A Traveler from Altruria*, he labeled the effort a "romance," and for all the searing wit and sarcasm in this new critique of capitalism, Howells had retreated from the alternating involvement and detachment which exhausted the novelist when treating the stubborn facts of American life. Instead of the dramatic novel, he invented a thinly dramatized symposium of generalized American social types. Behind the curtain loomed Howells the social critic, wearing the robes of puppet master and ventriloquist.

The dubious enlightenment possible through the novel and the declining chances for an "honest" vote in urban politics were not the only discouragements which almost certainly prevented Howells from clarifying the ending of *Hazard*. Within his esthetic of realism, he was caught in a quandary both religious and social which collided with his hope for social reform. Did a transcendent spirit reside, after all, amid the commonplace or within the larger Darwinian struggle in New York which outwardly appeared to March "lawless, godless" (p. 156)? Similarly, was there in capitalists like Dryfoos a "Holy Spirit indwelling" (p. 420) waiting to be quickened by personal

---

38 "Study," LXXVI (April 1888), 803.
39 To Norton, Dec. 12, 1891, *Letters*, II, 19.

tragedy? Or were public and private morality strictly matters of external conditioning? "Conditions *make* character" March also asserts (p. 379). His guarded statements on "conditions" and the forming, or re-forming, of "character" reflect his author's own attempt to clarify a basic philosophical confusion. Howells had written, in a now-famous passage of the "Editor's Study," that he cherished the "natural" over the man-made "artificial" grasshopper for his esthetic model. But while he shared with Emerson this "passion for the common," Howells was not so certain that the natural individual was superior to the artificial, or formed, representative of an ordered society.[40] This uncertainty may explain why Howells at the end of *Hazard* was necessarily vague on ways to reform the character and structure of American society at large.

The inconclusive and uncommitted ending of *Hazard* hints, then, at a basic disharmony in Howells' esthetic of realism. Earlier, in *The Rise of Silas Lapham* and *The Undiscovered Country*, he had fashioned a pastoral resolution at the end to restore the claims of the natural in an increasingly civilized, urbanized America. Except for the power of feeling and love to transform life in a new age of the streetcar and the police club, the elements of the pastoral compromise no longer seemed viable in *A Hazard of New Fortunes*. Yet even the new formula of "complicity" and brotherhood appears to reach the mind of Basil March more profoundly than it reorders his heart. Howells, too, was currently impressed by the distance which separated his own theoretical and practical complicity. March envisions the law of love but knows that he has gained only the germ of an ideology, the hint of an explanation. He cannot become a Conrad Dryfoos. Neither could Howells embrace the complex humanity of New York, from the ghetto's striving immigrants to Wall Street's hard-driving

[40] "Study," LXXVI (Dec. 1887), 155; and "Recollections of an Atlantic Editorship," *At.Mo.*, C (Nov. 1907), 600.

new millionaires. For the most part, he preferred Boston to New York, the Old Gold to the New Gold, the establishment to the rampant, even demonic, individualism of a rising plutocracy. Margaret Vance, from wealthy established New York society, receives at least a share of narrator sympathy as she moves through the arts into a wider humanity. But the newly rich Dryfoos sisters remain untouched by the arts, and are crude and perhaps altogether too "natural" in their uncontrolled behavior both in New York and at Saratoga. Predisposed like his Marches to respond to New York with the Anglo-Saxon values of an older and more orderly Boston, Howells could not unburden himself of prejudices toward the new plutocracy or toward the new races in the cities who were complicating the already confused social and economic picture in the late decades of the century. I have already traced these conflicts to their origin in the preceding chapter. They reappear in *Hazard*, and because they enter the novel obliquely, they are the more revealing of a hidden malignancy within Howells' Christian socialism. Three random examples will serve.

After the Dryfoos dinner-party fiasco it is probable that March will lose his job if he does not obey Dryfoos and fire Lindau. March's daughter Bella hopes that if they return to Boston, they will live on the Back Bay, because "it's awfully Micky at the South End" (p. 311). A very brief comment from an exceedingly minor character, to be sure. Yet the point is that the opinion stands with no preceding motivation, no clear intention of narrative irony in the childish bigotry, no rebuke from her father. This comment, taken together with what seems an insistent notation that the Irish are the inferior servant class in New York, plus Howells' own confessed dread of the growing influence of Irish in American politics, allows one at least to question his intention here. Indeed, he inserts as narrative comment elsewhere in *Hazard* that

"New York is still popularly supposed to be in the control of the Irish" (p. 154). The hallmark of Howells' narrative method is supple mastery unless he happens to be fencing with ideological uncertainty. The reader is prepared, next, for the reason why Irish control of New York is an erroneous popular notion. The new immigrant races—"the people of Germanic, of Slavonic, of Pelasgic, of Mongolian stock"—now outnumber the Irish. Has control of New York, then, passed into the hands of these newcomers? Not exactly. The "prepotent Celts" still "outvote" all other groups (p. 155). That is to say, after all this mild sophistry and confusion, that the Irish maintain their control of New York. Howells may have wished it otherwise, but a New York electorate had recently chosen, for a second time, a mayor from the servant class of prepotent Celts.

Curious also is that, in *Hazard*, among the "foreign touches" in New York March never identifies any of the new immigrants on the East Side as Jews. But he pointedly discovers the wealthy "American Hebrew" at the center of the otherwise "purely American" neighborhood of the vulgar newly rich, amid "the culture that furnishes showily, that decorates and that tells; the culture, say, of plays and operas, rather than books" (p. 258). Anti-Semitism in the Gilded Age formed precisely from this facile and one-sided portrait of the opulent Jew in America. One can acknowledge that Howells gave generous support to the individual Jewish writer—a Sidney Luska or an Abraham Cahan—and wonder all the more at the complexity of feeling which issued in his reinforcing the stereotype of a race. Nor are the racial overtones in *Hazard* explained away by his reactions the next summer at fashionable Saratoga. To Charles Eliot Norton, who would understand, Howells complained of the numbers and crass manners of Jewish guests: "There are no end of Hebrews and Hebrés; the ladies all go about bare headed at night." And he would express the identical sentiment some years later to Mark Twain. Chief among the sights which made resort society at Carlsbad, Austria, "duller than the ditchwater one drinks" were the new "troops of yellow Jews with corkscrew curls before their ears. . . ."[41]

Finally, Howells hints at his conflict over complicity and the new democracy in the portrait of Angus Beaton. When the self-centered esthete, who is also a practical aristocrat, has a brief moment of conscience over the welfare of another (his father), he decides "in an anguish of self-reproach" to spend his money instead for "a fur-lined overcoat" (p. 330). Several months before, Howells had written to James of "the audacity of my social ideas" and admitted his anguish over the directions American capitalist society was taking. He dreaded the eventual results unless the nation could reform itself "on a real equality." He then admitted with customary frankness, "Meantime, I wear a fur-lined overcoat, and live in all the luxury my money can buy."[42]

To the degree that Howells was unable to sort out and resolve these conflicting attitudes toward the urban rich and poor, or the Irish and the Jews, he reflects the ongoing malaise of the proper white America. Eighty years after *A Hazard of New Fortunes*, we learn that this same failure to locate and forcefully confront the sources of urban poverty and racism has chiefly advanced the now-explosive civil disorder of the American city. But also among Howells' heirs today are the rebellious if impractical young men and women termed the "flower children." These young idealists currently urge the return of feeling and the power of love as redeeming counterforces in our own age of the police club and enslavement to the machine. And another segment of the same generation pursues the ends of human

[41] To Norton, Aug. 21, 1890 (Harvard), and to Twain, Aug. 25, 1909, *Twain-Howells Letters*, II, 847.

[42] Oct. 10, 1888, *Letters*, I, 417. In 1958, Edwin Cady estimated Howells' income in the years after *Hazard* at a modern equivalent of $100,000 a year (*The Realist at War*, p. 192).

decency and freedom through Howells' peaceful recipe of political activism. In short, Howells posed the question in *Hazard* which has grown ever more crucial in modern American life: Will the violence of a Lindau or the love of a Conrad Dryfoos or "the vote" of Basil March recover the sanctity of human life in an urban civilization? Most important, Howells addressed the question to the hearts and minds of a metropolitan audience by extending as never before his resources and power in the art of fiction.

For all his social ambivalence, Howells continued for thirty more years to press for reform of America's economic chance-world. He encouraged younger writers like Crane, Norris, and Garland, and he continued to practice the craft of fiction, though he came to feel his influence and achievement in the novel grown more limited. A number of his later novels are distinguished enough to deserve close and extended reappraisal. Never again, however, would he move so close as in *Hazard* to a creative expression of his critical realism—the esthetic which embraced both the claims of art and his hoped-for gains in the brotherhood of man. The single effort was enough to chart a new course for the modern novel. Having no literary model at hand, Howells had explored the esthetic world of New York to create the first major city novel in our literature. He had also armed himself with a comic spirit to create a new protagonist for our fiction, the man of sensibility as a non-hero in the modern world. James pronounced the result "simply prodigious"—the epithet he had reserved for Tolstoy—and soon would produce Lambert Strether as a lineal descendant of Basil March. Howells had probed the limits of individual compassion and responsibility in the American city to open the way, diversely, for *Maggie, Sister Carrie, Babbitt, Manhattan Transfer, Miss Lonelyhearts, Invisible Man,* and other city novels of the next century. When he paused twenty years afterward to look back on *A Hazard of New Fortunes,* Howells ranked it "the most vital of my fictions." He fully deserved the modest satisfaction of reliving some of the creative moments he had conceived "in the prime, such as it was, of my powers" (p. xiv).

SUMMARY AND AFTERMATH

SINCE his death in 1920, William Dean Howells has served a long term as our favorite literary scapegoat. For fifty years, his influence as a writer and editor had been so formidable that, by the 1920s, Howells seemed the literary figure answerable for the lingering Victorian gentility in modern American life and letters. In my chapters on *The Undiscovered Country* and *A Modern Instance*, I hope to have corrected, at least to some degree, this simplistic view of Howells. A second judgment, sounded in the 1930s, was that Howells' alleged apathy in the face of imminent social and economic revolution was directly related to our failure to curb the later excesses of capitalism. I have indicated my reservations on this judgment in the chapter on *The Rise of Silas Lapham*. By the 1940s, a third charge was levelled against Howells, and I have spoken to it in my reading of *A Hazard of New Fortunes*. Howells had failed in his novels to probe the psychological and social disorders of modern American life, this new argument had it, because ultimately he lacked an impassioned dedication to the craft of fiction and the revelation of art. This conclusion seemed obvious if one merely set Howells' apparently placid esthetic temperament against the ardor of The Master, Henry James. Perhaps through some paradox of human personality which defied clear analysis, Howells the novelist, playwright, poet, editor, critic, friend of artists, sponsor of young novelists and poets, and friend or mentor to older writers seemed a figure somehow uncoordinated and passionless in his commitment to the life of art. Granted of course, the recurring note one heard in his published letters and later reminiscences was the perennial discovery of a new "literary passion" more profound, or excited, than the last. From his boyhood heroes—Poe, Moore, Campbell, Goldsmith, Pope, De-

Quincey, Shakespeare, Heine—he presently advanced to Goldoni, George Eliot, Björnson, Turgenev, Zola, Valdés, and finally to Tolstoy. Both James and Twain, moreover, had given their friendship and respect to Howells and virtually placed their lives as writers in his care. Even so, the world loves a cliché which will smooth over the difficulties we experience in life and art. The milk-toast version of Howells the man and writer has been too useful to abandon.

In the readings of four novels, I have tried to prepare some of the ground for new judgments of Howells. Axiomatic as it should be that one cannot criticize responsibly what he does not understand or has misread, too often in the past the student of the novel has skimmed over Howells' meaning in an apparent hurry to get on with the business of criticism. In this study I have tried to reverse this approach to Howells by attending as closely as possible to his vision and major techniques as a novelist. My judgments have been relatively brief, though I have made them implicitly and, at times, overtly among the novels studied here. A primary aim throughout has been to reinterpret Howells' meaning through the resources of literary scholarship. To this end, I have used a variety of approaches, intrinsic and extrinsic to the work, which could yield valuable clues to meaning in Howells' fictional world. In the attempt to understand the work by knowing as fully as possible the consciousness and creative impulse of the author, I have presented Howells as a man of passion and complexity and as an artist whose suffering in large part grew out of his concern over the life of his time and a commitment to discover the truth of that life in a new literary "realism." It was Stephen Crane, Howells' most famous young disciple, who wrote shortly after *A Hazard of New Fortunes* that his own *Red Badge of Courage* was "an effort born of pain—despair, almost," and Crane went on to describe the intensity with which the best literature is forged:

> It seems a pity that art should be a child of pain, and yet I think it is. Of course we have fine writers who are prosperous and contented, but in my opinion their work would be greater if this were not so. It lacks the sting it would have if written under the spur of a great need.[1]

Crane may have been thinking of his elderly sponsor as one of the "fine writers who are prosperous and contented." If so, Crane had missed the "sting" and "pain— despair almost" that frequently rested just beneath the surface of Howells' art and life.

From his earliest years, Howells had dedicated his life to literature, and the labor took its toll. He worked all day as a young journalist before turning to literature at night. The result was overwork, nervous prostration, acute headaches, and insomnia. "If I lay awake, noting the wild pulsations of my heart, and listening to the deathwatch in the wall, I was certainly very much scared," he recalled in *My Literary Passions*, "but I was not without the consolation that I was at least a sufferer for literature" (p. 152). The nervous collapse or pressures threatening collapse as he wrote his major fiction of the eighties could have been avoided by a man of lesser commitment to his craft. Outwardly quiet, comfortable, and successful in these turbulent years, Howells was in fact writing, in this decade, out of Crane's "spur of a great need"—a sensitized concern over fragmented values in our postwar religious, social, and esthetic life. In these years, he realized his full powers as a novelist, and they were frequently equal to the intensity of feeling with which he conducted this search for the true, the good, and the beautiful. Like the wayfarer in Crane's poem, Howells learned that the path to his ideal truth was thickly grown with weeds, and

[1] To an editor of *Leslie's Weekly*, c. Nov., 1895, in *Stephen Crane: Letters* (New York: New York University Press, 1960), pp. 78-79.

that each weed was a singular knife. Neither a facile nor complacent novelist described Egeria Boynton's surrealistic journey back to pastoral sanity, Marcia Gaylord's painfully chaotic marriage, her father's joyless agnosticism, Silas Lapham's alienated and emasculated figure on Beacon Street and old Dryfoos' aimless career on Wall Street, or Basil March's struggle to find comprehensive purpose in the huge disorder of New York City. Perhaps we can now see how ironic it is that Howells should be remembered as the American writer who defined "realism" as the simple, painless, "truthful treatment" of our "average" life. I have tried to demonstrate the considerable vitality that remains in his rich and many-sided achievement as a novelist. There has been no pretense here, however, at offering a definitive study even of the works I have chosen to reinterpret in some depth. Hopefully, some of my comments will suggest new paths worth pursuing in Howells studies, including a broader inquiry into Howells' relation to his age and his legacy to the twentieth-century novel. Specifically, I welcome an open and vigorous debate over the validity of the separate readings I have given to the novels.

In addition, I look forward to new and revealing studies of Howells' apprenticeship novels and dramas of the seventies, as well as his other fiction in the 1880s—*Dr. Breen's Practice, A Woman's Reason, Indian Summer, The Minister's Charge, April Hopes*, and *Annie Kilburn*. Nor do the imposed limits of the present study argue that the more than a dozen novels Howells wrote after *A Hazard of New Fortunes* lack substance and artistry. Most of them warrant, in fact, the close reinterpretation given to the four related novels I have considered here. From time to time in these pages, I have glanced ahead to these later years and have hinted at the irresolution of mind and spirit which makes Howells a continuously fascinating subject. He did not cease to explore, in and out of his fiction, the modern crisis of religious faith and doubt, or the dark enigmas of man's psyche which complicate the human quest for identity and "reality." In the conflict between capitalism and altruism, he continued to champion the rights, while he underscored the responsibilities, of labor. And with sometimes failing spirit, he held to the esthetic conviction implicit in *A Hazard of New Fortunes*, that the modern novelist, more than any other artist, might impart the humane vision that could ease all of these concerns of the dawning twentieth century.

In treating the techniques of nuance and drama which Howells brought to these vital themes in his later novels, the literary scholar cannot afford to separate the work from the author's total experience. As in the eighties and earlier, Howells the man provides an indispensable accompaniment to the meaning of his fiction. Even one who holds that the life of the human agent who is moving the pen casts dubious light on his work can still welcome a sense of the personality and soul of Howells the man in these future studies, if only to regain the experience deemed superfluous by many critics and explicators (including those who now specialize in the intricate dissection of "self" in the literary text). I am thinking of the humanistic dimension which has disappeared from too many literary studies. With Howells, one remains fascinated by the puzzle of this durable figure and his achievement. Ironic, mercurial, sensitive, and humane, he continues into his later years brilliantly variable and difficult to characterize both as a man and as a writer.

As before, he was forced to wage a prolonged battle with neuroticism and depression, with dreams and nightmares which were occasionally relieved only by sleeplessness. The effects are evident in his most interesting work. In *A Boy's Town* (1890), written soon after *Hazard*, Howells traced this psychological distress back to his boyhood in Ohio, and much later he returned to it in *Years of My Youth* (1916). Self-analysis and therapy quite clearly were a part of his motive in writing these reminiscences. Perhaps the same motive provided an impulse for the novels which seem, in various ways, to accompany these memoirs. In *The Shadow of a Dream* (1890), *An Imperative Duty* (1892), and *The Leatherwood God* (1916), Howells showed again that he possessed the courage to probe the undersurfaces of sexual guilt in America, and to discover through the texture of the novel obscure psychological forces which underlie modern marriage, racial bigotry, and religious fanaticism in America.

Lurking behind these and other novels from 1890 to 1916, as well as in highly revealing lesser pieces such as "A Difficult Case" (1900) and "A Sleep and a Forgetting" (1907), is the puzzle of Howells the man. Shortly after *Hazard*, he still grieved the loss of his beloved Winny, but felt "consoled a little," he told Twain, after reading Isaac Taylor's *The Physical Theory of Another Life*. A year later, he wrote to Howard Pyle, "I tell you honestly that for the greater part of the time I believe in nothing, though I am afraid of everything." But he was rereading Swedenborg. In 1891, he praised William James's *Psychology* because it did not "snub one's poor humble hopes of a hereafter." In his birthday greeting to Stedman in 1893, Howells argued the "nonsense of pretending to stop living, merely because we began living, here." After the death of Susy Clemens in 1896, Howells consoled Twain with the reassurance that she was "somewhere in conscious blessedness that knows and feels your love." In 1902, however, he described his indifference to religion. "I find that I care with difficulty for the answer to the Great Conundrum of all, 'If a man die shall he live again?' " he wrote to Aldrich. Then came a resurgence of his old hope in doubt. Thanks this time to science, he wrote in a review of Alfred R. Wallace's *Man's Place in the Universe*, one could feel a quickening of "the hope, the longing, which has been eloquent or inarticulate in every human heart

197

since the beginning. If a man die, shall he live again?"
After the deaths of his wife and Mark Twain in 1910,
Howells wrote to his brother Joseph, "I feel that we are
in the power of an awful force," and then echoed the
closing words of *The Undiscovered Country*—"I submit,
and we must all submit." Yet the day before, he had
written to William James, "I wish I could believe in a
meeting with her, but she believed in none, and how can
I?" In 1914, he returned to the "imagination" if not the
"revelation" of Swedenborg's *Heaven and Hell*, and could
not "help wondering at the realistic circumstantiality of
his account of the spirit after its arrival in the other
world. . . ." Near the end of the year, however, life for
him had become "like a dream." But in 1916, he began to
attend church and "to follow the sermon with much
greater, or more unbroken, attention than I once
could. . . ."[2]

Equally elusive is the Howells who continued to criticize a money-oriented America in *The Quality of Mercy*
(1892), *The World of Chance* (1893), *A Traveler from
Altruria* (1894), and in later novels and sketches. One
can easily make a case for Howells the outspoken critic of
capitalism in these works, and also in the private discontent with social, economic, and political democracy
which he expressed during this later phase of his career.
After *Hazard*, he had returned in 1889 to live in Boston.
For two years, he associated with the Christian Socialists
of Boston—Bliss, Bellamy, Ely, Garland, and others—
though he did not become an activist within the group.
To Twain, Howells described his discontent with America, no longer a republic "but an aristocracy-loving oli-

2 See letter to Twain, July 17, 1889, in *Twain-Howells Letters*, II, 606;
to Pyle, Dec. 22, 1890, and Jan. 30, 1891, in *Letters*, II, 10, 14; to Stedman,
Oct. 13, 1893, in Butler Library, Columbia University; to Twain, Sept. 13,
1896, in *Twain-Howells Letters*, II, 662; to Aldrich, Jan. 19, 1902 (Harvard) ; "Easy Chair," *Harper's Monthly*, CVIII (March 1904) , 644; to
Joseph Howells, June 9, 1910, in *Letters*, II, 285; to William James, June 8,
1910, *ibid.*; to Mrs. J. G. Mitchell, Feb. 9, 1914, *ibid.*, p. 332; to W. B. Dean,
Nov. 29, 1914, *ibid.*, p. 339; and *Years of My Youth*, p. 161.

garchy." In 1892, living once more in New York, he confronted again the massive reaches of poverty existing in a land of plenty. Howells wrote to Norton in 1892, "I lay yesterday wondering of the great mass of human suffering. . . . What a hideous spectacle life is from that point of view." In this year, Howells must have taken note that the New York *World* uncovered 3,045 millionaires in America, while the *Tribune* counted 4,047. John D. Rockefeller reportedly had amassed by this year a fortune of nearly a billion dollars, and Carnegie's empire would net seven and one-half million dollars profit annually from 1889 to 1899. Reading Henry D. Lloyd's *Wealth Against Commonwealth* in 1894, he informed Lloyd that this account of wealth and corruption in America was "so astounding, so infuriating, that I have to stop from chapter to chapter, and take breath." Through Stephen Crane, Howells gained at the same time immediate reports of the squalor in New York's slums; and he recorded his own direct impressions and experiences of that life after touring on foot the West Side tenements and East Side ghetto. Just before the declaration of war in Cuba, Howells foresaw the only outcome to be "an era of blood-bought prosperity, and the chains of capitalism will be welded on the nation more firmly than ever." To fulfill Howells' prophecy, Carnegie obligingly netted forty million dollars profit in 1900. What could be done to promote a more equitable life for the poor? "One is so limp and helpless in the presence of the injustice which underlies society," Howells wrote to Twain in 1903, "and I am getting so old."[3]

Through the nineties, he had looked for a third party

[3] Letter to Twain, Dec. 29, 1889, *Twain-Howells Letters*, II, 627; to Norton, March 20, 1892 (Harvard); to Lloyd, Nov. 2, 1894, *Letters*, II, 54; "New York Streets" and "An East-Side Ramble," in *Impressions and Experiences* (1896); to Aurelia Howells, April 3, 1898, *Letters*, II, 90; to Twain, May 1, 1903, *Twain-Howells Letters*, II, 769. Statistics are taken from John Tipple, "The Robber Baron in the Gilded Age," *The Gilded Age: A Reappraisal*, ed. H. Wayne Morgan (Syracuse: Syracuse University Press, 1963), p. 17.

to rescue the nation from the greed and corruption issuing from plutocracy and Tammany politics. He turned to Hamlin Garland for information on a new farmers' party, and in the 1892 campaign supported the Populist's General Weaver. In 1896, though he had never voted for a Democrat before, he supported Bryan for president. Later he cheered Roosevelt's efforts to bring back the income and inheritance taxes. (The income tax had been abandoned in 1872, the inheritance tax in 1870.) These moments of hope were few, however, as were also the signs that the working classes were gaining political wisdom. He sympathized with the workers during their numerous and sometimes bloody strikes of the nineties, but echoed Basil March's sentiment in *A Hazard of New Fortunes*: why did the laborers employ the violent weapon of the strike when they could vote into law their share of the profits of industry? But by 1898, in a letter to Sylvester Baxter, Howells was ready, at last, to admit the probable impotence of the popular ballot to solve the problems of the new industrial order.[4] Returning to *Harper's* in 1900, he tried, from his monthly "Easy Chair," to reach once again an audience who might be receptive to his quiet version of a socialist rebellion in America. In 1906, he contributed to the congressional campaign fund of the Socialist candidate on New York's lower East Side, and the next year returned to the adventures of his Altrurian, Aristides Homos. *Through the Eye of the Needle* was "my own dream of Utopia," he wrote Norton, "which I fancy your not liking, unless for its confessions of imperfections even in Utopia." The more profound pessimism over the democratic experiment in America, however, belonged not to Norton, but to Howells himself. This Howells presently recognized, somewhat to his surprise, after reading the posthumous edition of Norton's letters.

[4] Letter dated May 11, 1898, in Huntington Library, San Marino, Calif.

"I suppose most people would not call him an optimist or me a pessimist," Howells wrote in a review, "but I believe that he liked more of the recent things than I did. . . ."[5]

Committed to a vision of America peacefully transformed into a benign socialism, and discouraged to see the prospect become progressively more bleak, Howells felt, on the other hand, the ongoing shame of a "practical aristocrat." I have touched on it previously in my discussion of *The Rise of Silas Lapham* and *A Hazard of New Fortunes*. In the final thirty years, he celebrated equality, social justice, and the poetry of the commonplace at the same time that he betrayed a fondness for the satisfactions and privileges that money can buy, and the high culture which a stratified society can enjoy. He admired the Tolstoian reflexes of a Stephen Crane, but when Howells went on his own walks into the open sores of the New York ghetto, he admitted an incapacity to absorb the punishment into his psyche. "I become hardened, for the moment," he wrote of these scenes. "I feel their picturesqueness, with a callous indifference to that ruin, or that defect, which must so largely constitute the charm of the picturesque. . . ." He preferred to take his socialism in Central Park where the day-to-day messiness of urban democracy appeared only in the quietly "ragged and dirty" citizens who ventured into his own more comfortable green neighborhood. At the same time that he urged that dollars damn America, he made uneasy revisions to soften his Altrurian's satire against the plutocracy. And why

[5] See Louis J. Budd, "Howells, the *Atlantic Monthly*, and Republicanism," *American Literature*, XXIV (May 1952), 151; letter to Norton, May 11, 1898, in Huntington Library; Morris Hillquit, *Loose Leaves from a Busy Life* (New York: Rand School Press, 1934), pp. 115-116; letter to Norton, April 15, 1907, *Letters*, II, 242; "Charles Eliot Norton: A Reminiscence," *North American Review*, CXCVIII (Dec. 1913), 843. See also my "Howells and Norton: Some Frustrations of the Biographer," *New England Quarterly*, XXXVII (March 1964), 84-89.

not? Charles Fairchild and Company was managing his stock investments in 1897 when Howells tallied his net worth at $93,000. His "longing for the cleanly respectabilities" began in Ohio and continued to his final years. "I still cannot think that a bad thing," he wrote near the end, "or if experience cannot have more than the goodly outside in life, that this is not worth having."[6]

Precisely here one feels at a loss to manage these widely ranging contradictions in Howells. The temptation is either to simplify the evidence by ignoring parts of it, or to simplify the conclusion by charging Howells with feeble commitment if not double-dealing. Yet Howells was not very different from his elder contemporaries, sensitive Westerners and Easterners alike, who shared these apprehensions of a prewar generation. Howells had watched closely and participated in America's growth into a mass-industrial civilization, a change for which his boyhood had scarcely prepared him. Given his Western origins, his intelligence and taste and "morbid nerves," Howells travelled a long way to the streets of New York City. The range of his concerns, and in somewhat lesser degree his sympathies, is what constantly startles. Nor should it be less than predictable, then, in his New York career after 1890, with old age slowly advancing, that he should periodically yearn for the simpler, the less strident and more orderly America which had been a part of his earlier experience. So it was that amid the subsequent hurry and press of a metropolitan life in these later years, he came to grace our literature with his reminiscences of a budding career that flowered in Cambridge and Boston and, before that blessed fulfillment, had strangely come into being on the Ohio frontier. The biographer of this earlier life moves gingerly among these memoirs, mindful

[6] See "New York Streets," in *Impressions and Experiences* (New York: Harper and Bros., 1896), pp. 250-251; to his father, Oct. 22, 1892, *Letters*, II, 28; Clara Kirk, *W. D. Howells, Traveler from Altruria* (New Brunswick, N.J.: Rutgers University Press, 1962), pp. 118-135; Edwin Cady, *The Realist at War*, p. 192; and *Years of My Youth*, p. 142.

of Howells' own warning to beware "those pleasing illusions of memory which men in later life are subject to."[7] For his later life, however, these reminiscences provide the afterglow to a famous and varied career which had become, at the same time, perhaps the most productive and influential in our literature. Nor were his services to the modern American novel yet over.

Between his reminiscences of people, places, and older literary passions, Howells formed new enthusiasms. Familiar now are the encouragement and sympathy with which he greeted a younger generation of writers: Garland, Crane, Norris, Fuller, Cahan, Whitlock, and countless others. Equally important, and far more dramatic, is the story of Howells the writer. After 1890, he felt his old zest for the novel constantly undermined by both fatigue and the fear of a dead talent. He confided to Norton in 1892, "I ask myself very serious questions about my power and fitness to go on in the line I have kept so long." And to the same friend in 1894: "I don't work much. . . . I am terribly sick of literature, at times, and would be better content if there were some other honest way of earning a living." Within months, however, he was planning to write another novel. "It is strange how the love of doing it survives," he wrote to James. And so it went. In 1899, he told Twain that "the old zest is gone." Six months later, to Stedman, he repeated, "I am very, very tired of writing." But before the end of the year, he wrote, "As usual, I am full of schemes of all sorts, and am by no means looking forward to quitting work."[8]

---

[7] *My Literary Passions*, p. 70. If Howells at times idealized the West in his later years, as Benjamin A. Sokoloff argues, the cause was not impairment of his memory for details. After Howells had visited Hamilton, Ohio, in 1905, his old schoolmate George Earhart claimed that Howells had recalled all of the houses and stores which were standing since the 1840s, and who had occupied them; and he also remembered where others, since torn down, had once stood. See Sokoloff, "William Dean Howells and the Ohio Village: A Study in Environment and Art," *American Quarterly*, XI (Spring 1959), 58-75; and "A Day in Howells's 'Boy's Town,'" *New England Magazine*, XXXVI (May 1907), 289-297.

[8] Letter to Norton, Oct. 16, 1892, *Letters*, II, 28, and March 11, 1894 (Har-

To maintain a steady income at the turn of the century, he accepted the assignment of monthly critic in *Harper's* "Easy Chair," though he resented the burden of supplying literary criticism on schedule; "to write fiction, on the other hand, is a delight," he told Aldrich. *The Kentons* (1902), *The Son of Royal Langbrith* (1904), and *Miss Bellard's Inspiration* (1905) came forth with remarkable energy for a writer approaching seventy. But the fountain apparently had begun to run dry, and he was also disheartened by the success of better-publicized young writers of a brand of fiction more sensational than his own. After several more efforts, he was convinced that it was "past the time for me to write fiction." He confessed to Henry B. Fuller "a kind of sickness of the job. . . . I should once never have believed that I could feel so." It was time to enjoy an old man's satisfaction in the harvest of a lifetime. In 1909, while preparing the prefaces for the "Library Edition" of his works, he paused to reassess his career. To his brother Joseph, Howells summed up what now seemed his final legacy as a writer:

In going over my books I find that 18 or 20 volumes have been written since I came to Harpers in 1886, and 10 or 12 before that. Of course, my meat went into the earlier ones, and yet there are three or four of the later novels which are as good as any. I hope I shall get my "wind" again, but just now I am fagged, there's no denying it. I can look back, and see the like has happened before, but I wasn't then 72 years old. I can't get hold of a subject that interests me.[9]

But there would be more. A few years earlier, he had mentioned a story he hoped to develop into "my last great novel." The title would be *The Leatherwood God* and

<hr/>

vard); to James, Dec. 13, 1894, *Letters*, II, 56; to Twain, March 5, 1899, *Twain-Howells Letters*, II, 688; to Stedman, Sept. 13, 1899, Butler Library, Columbia University; and to Aurelia Howells, Dec. 24, 1899, *Letters*, II, 117.

[9] Letter to Aldrich, May 21, 1901, in *Letters*, II, 144; to Fuller, March 14, 1909, *ibid.*, p. 264; and to Joseph Howells, July 4, 1909, *ibid.*, p. 268.

the subject revivalism in early Ohio. As he approached his eightieth birthday, having seen nearly two hundred volumes through the press, Howells defied once again the pattern of truncated achievement familiar in the career of the modern American writer. *The Leatherwood God,* like the major novels of the eighties, was an effort born of pain. The most eminent figure in American letters, who had championed younger writers ever since his years as assistant editor of the *Atlantic,* Howells was now at the mercy of a more callous breed of young assistant editors. "I could not 'serialize' a story of mine now in any American magazine, thousands of them as they are," he wrote gloomily to James in 1915. "I am comparatively a dead cult with my statues cut down and the grass growing over them in the pale moonlight." But *The Leatherwood God* still would come forth during the year. A forerunner of Sinclair Lewis's *Elmer Gantry,* it is a remarkable achievement, but Howells felt less than elated afterwards. The novel was "hard to do and I did it badly in great part," he wrote. Moreover, *Harper's* itself had been unconditionally rejecting his fiction (Century publishers had taken *The Leatherwood God*) . And so now it was all over with Howells. "I am nearly eighty years old," he wrote Fuller, "and tired, tired. It is a strange experience. I used only to need the chance to work; now the chance dismays me." Yet the end had not yet come. Like Goethe and Verdi, octogenarians before him, Howells continued to tap the hidden springs of his creative energy. Three years later, he was exulting to Hamlin Garland, "Never since I came to eighty have I been so well. I work as of old, or of young, and if the stuff is not so good as before, still it is stuff, and I don't complain."[10]

[10] Letter to Joseph Howells, Feb. 24, 1907, *Letters*, II, 235; to James, June 29, 1915, *ibid.*, pp. 349, 350; to Mrs. Anne Howells Fréchette, Dec. 31, 1916, *ibid.*, p. 367; to F. A. Duneka, Nov. 19, 1916, *ibid.*, p. 365; to Fuller, Oct., 1916, *ibid.*, p. 364; to Garland, June 29, 1919, *ibid.*, p. 384.

These glimpses into Howells' ongoing religious, social, and esthetic interests after *A Hazard of New Fortunes* suggest some of the materials for a new and widely ranging study of the later novels. But this is not that book, and here I must cease.

To ATTEMPT a full-scale bibliography for this study of Howells would be unfeasible and, to an extent, redundant labor. William M. Gibson and George Arms's *A Bibliography of William Dean Howells* (New York: The New York Public Library, 1948), though inevitably not quite complete, stands as the finest reference of its kind, and is the starting point for my own and other studies which have come forth in the past twenty years. Additional "finds" by various Howells scholars have been added from time to time to the Gibson-Arms bibliography. In my Index, I list the writings of Howells which have received mention in this book.

Howells' correspondence has been edited in Mildred Howells' *Life in Letters of William Dean Howells* (1928, 2 vols.) and in *Mark Twain–Howells Letters*, ed. Henry N. Smith and William M. Gibson (1960, 2 vols.). For the convenience of the reader, I have cited these two works even when I had read some of this correspondence first in manuscript collections. The reader should be warned that some of Miss Howells' notes are not accurate. A fuller collection of Howells' letters is currently under preparation by George Arms and others. Helpful for the scholar working with unpublished Howells materials are John K. Reeves, "The Literary Manuscripts of W. D. Howells: A Descriptive Finding List," *BNYPL*, LXII (1958), 267-278, 350-363; and *American Literary Manuscripts*, compiled by Joseph Jones and others (Austin: University of Texas Press, 1960).

Separate volumes of Howells' fiction and collections of his criticism have been reprinted, often in paperback editions, during the past two decades. The most significant effort to make Howells available in accurate text is currently under way with the preparation of a 35-volume "Selected Edition," under the general editorship of Edwin H. Cady, to be published by Indiana University Press.

Selected critical writings on Howells, from his early career to the present, are variously reprinted, listed, or discussed in the following: Gibson and Arms *Bibliography*, pp. 158-170; *Howells: A Century of Criticism*, ed. Kenneth E. Eble (Dallas: University of Texas Press, 1961); *The War of the Critics Over William Dean Howells*, eds. Edwin H. Cady and David L. Frazier (Evanston: Row, Peterson and Co., 1962); and James Woodress, "The Dean's Comeback: Four Decades of Howells Scholarship," *Texas Studies in Literature and Language*, II (Spring 1960), 115-123. The "Howells Center" at Indiana University has issued to the co-editors of the "Selected Edition" a 49-page mimeographed list of 845 books, articles, and reviews on Howells. This convenient listing speeded considerably my search through the scholarship and criticism on Howells.

I have not indicated fully in the footnotes, nor can I here, the extent of my debts to intellectual historians who have provided background scholarship for this study, particularly in later nineteenth-century science, religion, nativism, labor history, political debate, and social Darwinism. Following is a partial listing of discussions by literary scholars and critics who have stimulated my own work on Howells. The first monograph to appear amid the resurgence of interest in Howells was James Woodress' *Howells and Italy* (Durham, N.C.: Duke University Press, 1952). Mr. Woodress' study of the Italian phase has been basic to an understanding of Howells' early growth as a "realist." Since 1952, we have witnessed a steady flow of explication, criticism, and biography of Howells, some of it fully cited in the footnotes. Everett Carter's *Howells and the Age of Realism* (1954) defined Howells' "critical realism" and placed it in literary context within the period. Edwin Cady's two-volume biography appeared in 1956 (*The Road to Realism*) and 1958 (*The Realist at War*). One has only to duplicate a part of Mr. Cady's journey through Howells manuscripts and other sources to appreciate the breadth and accuracy of this superb biography. Olov Fryckstedt's *In Quest of America* (1958) and George Bennett's *William Dean Howells* (1959) traced Howells' development as a novelist, Mr. Fryckstedt exploring international influences to good advantage up to *A Modern Instance* and Mr. Bennett combining esthetic with biographical interpretations of the works from 1866 through *A Hazard of New Fortunes*. Robert Hough's *The Quiet Rebel* (Lincoln: University of Nebraska Press, 1959) remains useful in the chapters on Howells' reform thought during the 1890s and after. A more specialized treatment of the same topic is Clara M. Kirk's *W. D. Howells, Traveler From Altruria: 1889-1894* (1962), indispensable in its tracing the genesis and development of the Altrurian cycle. Mrs. Kirk's

W. D. Howells and Art in His Time (New Brunswick: Rutgers University Press, 1965) will become the standard reference work on Howells and painting.

Two recent books have contributed to our growing knowledge of Howells. In his *The Immense Complex Drama: The World and Art of the Howells Novel* (1965), George Carrington offers a lively, provocative analysis of the alienated artist who devised a fictional technique which could express his satiric vision of the world. William McMurray in *The Literary Realism of William Dean Howells* (Carbondale: Southern Illinois University Press, 1967) postulates that William James's pragmatism explains the quest for truth in the Howells novel. Mr. McMurray then provides abbreviated readings which argue that a pragmatic debate unifies twelve of the novels. His book would have profited had Mr. McMurray set forth the relationship between Howells and William James, and touched on relevant Howells studies since 1960.

Augmenting earlier literary period-studies by Everett Carter and Alfred Kazin have been recent books by Warner Berthoff, Robert Falk, Donald Pizer, William Wasserstrom, and Larzer Ziff. To this list can be added Ernest Samuels' three-volume biography of Henry Adams, valuable both for the portrait of Adams and his circle and for the historical studies which Mr. Samuels has cited liberally in his pages.

Following are a few suggested readings for each of the novels treated in the present study.

CHAPTER ONE:
The Undiscovered Country

See the footnotes to this chapter for readings of the novel by Bennett, Cady, and Fryckstedt. McMurray, *The Literary Realism of William Dean Howells*, devotes Chapter 3 (pp. 27-34) to a paraphrase of *The Undiscovered Country* as a study on the necessary limits of human existence. Still useful on Howells and science is Hannah G. Belcher, "Howells's Opinions on the Religious Conflicts of His Age as Exhibited in Magazine Articles," *American Literature*, XV (Nov. 1943), 262-278; and also Harry H. Clark, "The Role of Science in the Thought of W. D. Howells," *Transactions of the Wisconsin Academy of Science, Arts, and Letters*, XLII (Madison, 1953), 263-303.

CHAPTER TWO:
A Modern Instance

This novel has attracted more critical attention than *The Undiscovered Country.* Beyond the debate indicated in Chapter Two, the reader will be interested in Edwin Cady's suggestion that Swedenborgian ideas and imagery inform Bartley Hubbard's "sinful self-destruction" (*The Road to Realism*, pp. 212-216). George Bennett insists, too, that Howells argued on behalf of moral responsibility in the novel and, further, that his intention was not to write tragedy (*William Dean Howells*, pp. 113-123, 211-212). Olov Fryckstedt speculates on the moral influence of George Eliot and *Romola*, and he compares the degeneration of her Tito to Howells' Bartley (*In Quest of America*, pp. 242-247). For a discussion of science and religion in the period just before *A Modern Instance*, see Ernest Samuels' treatment of Henry Adams's *Esther* (1884) in a chapter entitled "The Warfare Between Science and Religion" (*Henry Adams: The Middle Years*, Cambridge: Harvard University Press, 1958, pp. 227-235, 461-463). With admirable brevity, Mr. Samuels touches on the work of Comte, Darwin, Spencer, Mill, Lewis, Stephen, Draper, Ingersoll, Fiske, Gray, Holmes, William James, and others.

CHAPTER THREE:
The Rise of Silas Lapham

My chief debts for background materials are included in the footnotes, with one exception. *Recollections of Life in Ohio*, by William Cooper Howells, intro. by Edwin H. Cady (Gainesville, Florida: Scholars' Facsimiles & Reprints, 1963) reveals the early conditions in Ohio that influenced the remarkable man who would merit the respect of his novelist son over a period of nearly fifty years.

Silas Lapham itself has been the most discussed and admired of all Howells' works through the years. Recent studies, including the introductory essays to several reprintings of the novel, carry moral interpretations, however, which are not essentially different from each other or from earlier readings. I have already acknowledged my debt to Edwin Cady's biographical revelations which led to the political emphasis in my reinterpretation. We differ somewhat in reading the nature and extent of Howells' "disengagement" from the Cambridge and

Boston scene. Louis J. Budd, "Howells, the *Atlantic Monthly*, and Republicanism," *American Literature*, XXIV (May 1952), 139-156, reveals that during Howells' editorship, the politics of the magazine was essentially conservative. Two helpful studies of unity in the novel are Donald Pizer, "The Ethical Unity of *The Rise of Silas Lapham*," *American Literature*, XXXII (Nov. 1960), 322-327; and G. Thomas Tanselle, "The Architecture of *The Rise of Silas Lapham*," *ibid.*, XXXVII (Jan. 1966), 430-457. On "Daisy Millerism," David Hirsch argues that Howells was ambivalent toward James's heroine and that he portrayed Silas's wife sympathetically as a more responsible model for American womanhood. See "William Dean Howells and Daisy Miller," *English Language Notes*, I (Dec. 1963), 123-128. Two sketches of the Howells-James relationship in these years are by Edwin Cady, *The Realist at War* (pp. 40-48), and Oscar Cargill, "Henry James's 'Moral Policeman': William Dean Howells," *American Literature*, XXIX (Jan. 1958), 371-398.

CHAPTER FOUR:
A Hazard of New Fortunes

To the previous readings by Bennett, Cady, Carter, Foster, and Smith, cited in the footnotes, can be added Carrington's analysis of Howells' satiric elements and strategies in *Hazard* (*The Immense Complex Drama*, pp. 82-100, 206-218). Clara Kirk has reviewed the appearance of the Marches in eight works. See "Reality and Actuality in the March Family Narratives of W. D. Howells," *PMLA*, LXXIV (March 1959), 137-152. The possible influence of Marx on Howells' social thought at this time is argued among Jacob W. Getzels, "William Dean Howells and Socialism," *Science and Society*, II (Summer 1938), 376-386; Conrad Wright, "The Sources of Mr. Howells's Socialism," *ibid.*, II (Fall 1938), 514-517; and George Arms, "Further Inquiry into Howells's Socialism," *ibid.*, III (Spring 1939), 245-248. Louis J. Budd, "William Dean Howells' Debt to Tolstoy," *American Slavic and East European Review*, IX (Dec. 1950), 292-301, explains that opposition to selfishness, violence, and public charity were among the social attitudes Howells endorsed in Tolstoy. Clare R. Goldfarb, "From Complicity to Altruria," *University Review*, XXXII (Summer 1966), 311-317, qualifies the Tolstoyan influence. Howells did not endorse Tolstoy's withdrawal from society, nor did he embrace the Russian's mystic approval of the peasantry. Max Westbrook's "The Critical Implications of Howells' Realism," *University of Texas Studies in English*, XXXVI (1957), 71-79, describes Howells' attempt to balance the tensions between the natural (individual) and the formed (society), in four novels, not including *Hazard*.

More studies treating esthetic controversy in this period are badly needed. Howells' role in the debate, as critic in the "Editor's Study," is summarized in Leonard Lutwack, "William Dean Howells and the 'Editor's Study,' " *American Literature*, XXIV (March 1952), 195-207; and in Edwin Cady, *The Realist at War*, pp. 10-27. Everett Carter compares these columns to Howells' later cut-and-paste editing of them for *Criticism and Fiction* (*Howells and the Age of Realism*, pp. 185-194). Edd W. Parks' "Howells and the Gentle Reader," *South Atlantic Quarterly*, L (April 1951), 239-247, shows the disparity between Howells' critical dictum against narrative intrusion and his fictional violations of this dramatic principle. Mr. Parks does not discuss *Hazard*. Roger Stein's recent *John Ruskin and Aesthetic Thought in America, 1840-1900* (Cambridge, Mass.: Harvard University Press, 1967) helps to close one gap in nineteenth-century art history. Hopefully, this volume will suggest further studies in esthetic theory, influence, and controversy in America.

CONCLUSION:
Summary and Aftermath

For invidious comparisons of Howells to James, see Alfred Kazin, *On Native Grounds* (New York: Reynal and Hitchcock, 1942), pp. 46-50; Lionel Trilling, "W. D. Howells and the Roots of Modern Taste," *Partisan Review*, XVIII (Sept.-Oct. 1951), 523-524; Everett Carter, *Howells and the Age of Realism*, pp. 249-263; and Richard Chase, *The American Novel and Its Tradition* (New York: Doubleday, 1957), p. 177.

On turn-of-the-century religion and science, see Hannah G. Belcher, previously cited, pp. 267-270. On the same topic, with interesting evidence from *Heroines of Fiction* (1901), see Harry H. Clark, previously cited, pp. 263-303.

The fullest treatment of Howells and social reform through these later years is Robert L. Hough's *The Quiet Rebel*, pp. 40-118. For Howells as a literary figure in the final thirty years, see Edwin Cady, *The Realist at War*, pp. 181-272. George Carrington, *The Immense Complex Drama*, offers several interesting glimpses into *The Kentons* (1902) and *The Son of Royal Langbrith* (1904). William McMurray's chapter on *The Landlord at Lion's Head* (1897) is his best (*The Literary Realism of William Dean Howells*, pp. 90-100). *The Leatherwood God* (1916) has been the subject of more than one genetic study in recent years. And *The Vacation of the Kelwyns* (1920) receives a short, provocative reading by Richard Chase in *The American Novel and Its Tradition*, pp. 177-184. One last encouraging bit of evidence that attention is being paid the later Howells can be found in George Arms's "Howells' English Travel Books: Problems in Technique," *PMLA*, LXXXII (March 1967), 104-116. Mr. Arms provides extensive analyses of *London Films* (1906), *Certain Delightful English Towns* (1906), and *Seven English Cities* (1909). Among his discoveries are the departures which Howells made from the realistic novel. In addresses to the reader, moralizing passages, imagery of haze, and so on, Howells allowed his travel sketches to act as a safety valve. They permitted him to indulge his poetic and "romantic" self without committing esthetic heresy against the principles of his fiction.

NOTE: Under HOWELLS, WILLIAM DEAN, WORKS, the writings discussed or cited in the preceding pages are listed in chronological order.

INDEX

197; *Heaven and Hell*, 198; in *MI*, 86, 210
Swiss Anabaptists, 54

Taine, Hippolyte, *Art in Greece* and *Notes on England*, 83
Tammany Hall, 200
Tanselle, G. Thomas, 211
Taylor, Bayard, 52, 110, 130
Taylor, Isaac, *The Physical Theory of Another Life*, 197
Tennyson, Alfred Lord, 55n
Thackeray, William Makepeace, 129, 168, 181
theatre, Howells writes for, 104, 153-54, 154n; in *HNF*, 151, 169
Thoreau, Henry D., 41, 45, 90, 91
Tilden, Samuel, in *MI*, 80
Tipple, John, 199n
Tolstoy, Leo, 142, 143, 144, 159, 160, 164, 167, 168, 178, 180, 181, 183, 190, 193, 201, 211; *Anna Karenina*, 177
Trilling, Lionel, 212
Trollope, Anthony, 129, 180
Turgenev, Ivan, 12, 159, 175, 179, 193
Twain, Mark, friendship with Howells, 72n, 99, 109, 110, 197; and Jews, 125, 189; literary connection with Howells, 10, 48, 49, 103, 104, 135n-36n, 162n, 175, 193, 203; Mugwumps, 140; shares Howells' ambivalence toward socialism, 115, 142, 143, 198-99
Tweed, William M. ("Boss"), 113. *See also* Tammany Hall
"The Undiscovered Country," manuscript version, 13, 29n, 33, 36, 47n, 49

Unitarian Church, in *MI*, 60

Valdes, Armando, 153, 168, 193; *Maximina*, 177
Vance, Margaret, in *HNF*, 156, 165, 170, 172, 173, 176, 183, 187
vegetarianism, 20
Venice, *see* HOWELLS, WILLIAM DEAN, wartime consul in Venice; and "picturesque"
Verdi, Giuseppi, 205

Victorian morality, 27, 65, 192
village, American, Howells' ambivalence toward, 32, 42, 109; in *MI*, 50, 61, 88, 89, 92, 93; in *RSL*, 137; in *UC*, 15, 24, 41, 43, 46
Virgil, in *MI*, 91

Wallace, Alfred R., *The Malay Archipelago*, 17; *Man's Place in the Universe*, 197
Walsh, Thomas F., 75n
Warner, Charles Dudley, 12, 124n, 130, 159
Washington, D.C., 199; in *April Hopes*, 140
Wasserstrom, William, 209
Waters, The Reverend Mr., in *Indian Summer*, 141
wealth, Howells' attitude toward established, 7, 126, 187; Howells' attitude toward new, 99, 108, 116-26, 186-88, 199; Howells' own, 104-105, 109, 142, 189n, 201-202; established, in *HNF*, 150, 164, 165, 169, 174, 187; established, in *RSL*, 96-143 *passim*; new, in *HNF*, 157-58, 164, 165, 169, 174, 187, 188, 195; new, in *RSL*, 96-143 *passim*; new, in *UC*, 46
Weaver, Gen. James B., 200
Welsh, and Howells' ancestry, 107
Wendell, Barrett, 117
West, American, Howells' feelings toward, 108, 141, 203n; in politics, 124n-25n; postwar migration, 42; in *HNF*, 148, 149, 151, 164, 166, 176; in *Indian Summer*, 142; in *MI*, 49, 51, 61, 72, 88, 90-91, 93, 95; in *RSL*, 124; in *UC*, 41, 43
West, Nathanael, *Miss Lonelyhearts*, 190
Westbrook, Max, 211-12
Westover, in *The Landlord at Lion's Head*, 48
Wetmore, Mr., in *HNF*, 155, 156
White, William H., 153
Whitlock, Brand, 203
Whitman, Walt, 175; *Democratic Vistas*, 92
Whittier Dinner (1877), 103, 135n-36n
Wilcox, Marrion, 96, 162n